HITCHHIKERS

HITCHHIKERS

One man's amazing journey from a homeless and hopeless childhood to a life of conversion and faith

BERNARD PODUSKA

Covenant Communications, Inc.

Cover image: *Boy (6–8) sitting on steps next to backpack with head resting on knees* © Getty Images

Cover design copyright © 2013 by Covenant Communications, Inc.

Published by Covenant Communications, Inc.
American Fork, Utah

Printed in the United States of America
First Printing: March 2013

19 18 17 16 15 14 13   10 9 8 7 6 5 4 3 2 1

ISBN: 978-1-62108-341-2

Prologue

As an associate professor at Brigham Young University, I was occasionally asked what it was like to grow up poor and homeless. And, when it seemed appropriate, I'd openly share bits and pieces of still vivid memories. But more than just relate the events, I tried to convey a deeper understanding of how it felt to be hungry and tired with neither kitchen nor bed. What it was like to be treated like a stray by people who feared that you might not go away if they fed you. What it meant to have traveled everywhere and yet belong nowhere.

What it meant to be homeless.

It has been a long journey from being a semi-literate vagrant to becoming a university professor. However, for me, the greater journey has been one of redemption: the transformation from a life as an atheist to having a firm testimony of Jesus Christ.

Hitchhikers is a compilation of childhood memories. It is a true story of struggle and perseverance. It is a story about the incredible tenacity of the human spirit. But it is also the story of God's love for each and every one of us. Even though some of us may give up on Him, He never gives up on us.

Chapter 1

Spring 1997

Provo, Utah, to Bakersfield, California

I HAD JUST RETURNED FROM teaching a class at Brigham Young University when my office phone began to ring.

"Hello, Dr. Poduska here," I responded habitually.

"Well, hello yourself, stranger," the caller replied.

I wavered a moment and then hesitantly asked, "Carolyn?"

"Guess you weren't expecting a call from your long-lost sister."

I was completely caught off guard. It had been several years since either of us had contacted the other. In an unspoken childhood agreement, we had realized that we would need to go our separate ways, and as a consequence, five to ten years would often pass between encounters. Even as children, we had intuitively known that if either of us was ever going to "make it in life," we would have to do it on our own.

"Hey, this is a surprise," I acknowledged and then quickly added, "but nevertheless, a pleasant surprise."

"I'm afraid the reason I called isn't a very pleasant one."

"Has something happened?" I cautiously asked, already feeling apprehensive.

"Mom's had a heart attack."

"How bad is it?"

"It looks pretty bad," she answered, a slight quiver in her voice. "You'd better come right away."

"Where is she?" I asked while struggling to put on my sports jacket.

"She's in the Heart Hospital, here in Bakersfield."

"I'll get someone to cover the rest of my classes, and I'll leave as soon as possible," I assured her. "I'll probably have to fly into LA and then drive up to Bakersfield, but I can get there in just a few hours."

"Hurry," she pleaded, "Mom's ninety years old, so she may not have much time."

Fortunately, I was able to get space on an afternoon flight to Los Angeles and arrive in Bakersfield just after dark. Carolyn was waiting for me in the lobby.

"How's Mom?" I called out as I came through the doors.

"She's still alive," Carolyn answered with a worried look.

We gave each other a brief hug and then hurried toward the elevator.

"I was with her when it happened," Carolyn explained. "She got up for her hair appointment. She called me around noon, not feeling well, and asked if I'd take her to the hospital."

We stepped onto the elevator, but it seemed to take forever to reach the second floor. While we obediently stared at the glowing numbers informing us of our progress, Carolyn continued to fill me in on the details.

"Mom and I had barely sat down in the emergency room when she gasped and grabbed her chest. I called one of the nurses, she called a doctor, and they took Mom away. I haven't gone up to see Mom yet. I wanted to wait until you arrived so we could go up together."

As soon as the elevator doors opened, we rushed down the hall to the nurses' station.

"We'd like to see our mom," I blurted out.

One of the nurses looked up. "Does she have a name? I mean besides 'Mom'?" the nurse inquired with a tired sigh.

"Gladys Poduska," Carolyn and I answered simultaneously.

The nurse glanced down at her chart and informed us, "Mrs. Poduska is in room 217. You can see her, but only for a few minutes. She needs her rest."

We quietly slipped into her room and stood on opposite sides of her bed. Mom's eyes were closed. She looked small and frail. I found it hard to believe that someone who now looked so weak and fragile was the same lady who could walk fifteen or twenty miles through a desert without complaint.

I cautiously reached out and touched her hand. "How ya doin', Mom?" I said softly.

Her eyes fluttered open, and an inquisitive look came across her face as she studied the two of us, and then she smiled.

"Carolyn . . . Buddy," she said in a weak, raspy voice. Then she closed her eyes and slowly began rocking her head back and forth. "I'm afraid I've really made a mess of things this time," she sighed.

"Now, Mom," Carolyn objected, "this isn't your fault."

"Besides," I added, "we've been in some pretty bad messes before, and we've always managed to pull ourselves out."

"Don't try to humor an old nurse," Mom chided, staring unfocused at the ceiling. Then, turning her head to look up at me, she patted my hand and asked, "And what about you?"

"What about me?"

"It's been a few years since we've seen each other. What have you been doing with your life?"

I wasn't exactly sure what she was looking for and hesitated. Apparently she became annoyed with the delay and persisted with an impatient, "Well?"

"Sorry, I wasn't quite sure what you were asking."

"Do you still go to that church?" she prompted.

"Do you mean am I still a Mormon?"

"Doesn't matter. Only the first baptism counts," she admonished. "As far as I'm concerned, you're still Catholic."

"Whatever you say, Mom."

"Well, I do say," she snorted with a slight jerk of her head.

"Are you still teaching at that university?" she continued.

"Yes. They haven't fired me yet."

Mom shook her head and smiled. "Your father never could hold a job."

"I guess I didn't turn out to be 'just like him' after all."

"Thank God," she sighed.

"I do every day," I replied, as much to myself as to Mom.

Mom wrinkled her brow and added, "I worried about you."

"Worried about me?"

"Yes, I didn't know whether you'd be tough enough."

"Tough enough?" I echoed.

"Tough enough to take life's lumps and keep on going like Carolyn," Mom said as she turned her head in Carolyn's direction.

"You're the one who taught me how to be tough," Carolyn reminded our mother and stepped closer. "I remember you working double shifts as a waitress just so Buddy and I would have something to eat."

"I know you're tough, Carolyn," Mom continued, "but are you happy?"

"I am now," Carolyn insisted.

"You say you're happy now," Mom said with sigh, "but I know you've had a rough life, rougher than most."

Carolyn scoffed, "Ha! You think my life's been rough. Compared to yours, my life's been a cakewalk."

Mom rolled her head from side to side and sighed again. "I've got so many regrets. I should have never made you two grow up homeless, sleeping under cardboard or newspapers, hitchhiking around the country like we did. That's no life for a child."

"We survived," I assured her.

"I should have left your father long before I did," Mom continued. "So many regrets . . . Looking back, I don't think my life amounted to much."

"Now, Mom," Carolyn interjected. "Stories about your life, and our childhood, are probably going to be told and retold for generations to come."

I took Mom's hand in mine and added, "Mom, the sacrifices you made for us have been an inspiration to me. One of the reasons I've worked so hard to make something of my life is so all of the suffering we went through wouldn't have been in vain."

While I was still refuting Mom's assessment of her life, she closed her eyes, appearing to be asleep. Carolyn looked at me and put her index finger to her lips, then motioned for me to follow her out of the room.

Once the two of us had stepped out into the hall, Carolyn dabbed at her eyes with a tissue, and I leaned back on the wall, completely exhausted.

A nurse came down the hall and went into Mom's room. I sighed and pushed myself to a standing position. Carolyn blew her nose, and then we slowly walked down to a little waiting room next to the elevators.

The two of us sat in silence for a while, and then I asked, "Are you okay?"

"I'm hangin' in there," she replied as her eyes looked up at the ceiling and her head began to slowly rock back and forth. "How about you?"

"I'm hangin' in there, too," I acknowledged. "But my belief that I will be able to be with Mom again, no matter what happens, makes it a little easier." Then with slight shrug, I added, "But it's still tough."

"Mom being in the hospital like this reminds me of the time we had to take her to the hospital in Reno," Carolyn reminisced. Then, shaking her head, she added. "It's hard to believe that was almost fifty years ago."

"Has it really been that long?" I wondered aloud.

"Remember when we were evicted from that run-down duplex in Albuquerque?" she continued.

"Do I ever!" I exclaimed. "That's when we first became homeless."

Carolyn looked up. "I was only eleven!"

"Heck, I was only eight," I recounted, shaking my head.

Then, in a deep voice, Carolyn mimicked, "Pay up by tomorrow morning or you'll have to vacate the premises."

I grinned and added. "I remember Mom arguing with him because we didn't have enough money to pay the rent."

"Because Dad had been fired again for drinking on the job," Carolyn interjected.

"As Mom said, keeping a job was never one of Dad's strong points," I pointed out. Dad usually took a job as a meat cutter in a local butcher shop or as a fry cook in some cheap café. His dark hair and grey eyes easily captivated most people and, coupled with a strong, muscular build, made it fairly easy for him to talk himself into a job. But Dad was an alcoholic, and like most alcoholics, he was more talk than action. His smooth talking also allowed him to stay on a job even after repeated warnings about his drinking. But inevitably, his addiction would prevail.

I continued, "His typical reaction to losing a job was to find the nearest bar, order a shot of whiskey with a beer chaser, and tell the bartender how he had 'planned on quitting that stupid job anyway.' When he didn't come home, Mom would send me to the bars looking for him. Once I found him, I'd down cold bottles of soda and beg nickels for the jukebox while Dad drank his boilermakers. I'd watch him drain one glass after another until the money was gone."

"Then there was nothing left for living expenses," Carolyn finished, "including the bare essentials like food and rent."

"At the age of eight, poverty wasn't something new," I said, "and understandably, I had not yet set my aim on achieving anything in particular, let alone begun tackling the task of forging my own destiny; feelings of despair were common, and I was pretty much convinced that there was no one I could really count on."

"Not even God?" Carolyn probed impishly.

I grinned awkwardly and replied, "Now it's hard to imagine that there was a time in my life when I didn't believe I could count on God. But the truth is, while we were living on the road, everything seemed so hopeless; there were times that I questioned whether or not God even existed."

"I remember that feeling of hopelessness," Carolyn admitted. "And some days I still feel that way. Drifting from town to town meant being on our own, constantly on the move, staying in trailers and hotel rooms that we rented on a daily, weekly, or if times were good, monthly basis. Although we never owned a home, I always thought being able to pay the rent helped create at least some sense of belonging."

"But feelings of belonging were always fleeting," I remembered. "Places that were just beginning to feel familiar would quickly be replaced with unexplored neighborhoods—invisible boundaries, obnoxious bullies, and unlikely friendships. Having to cope with the bullies was tough enough, but it was even harder to leave friends."

With a tired sigh, Carolyn continued. "When Mom and Dad ran out of money, we merely packed up in the middle of the night and skipped town. However, that was *not* what happened when we were evicted from the duplex."

"Yeah, it was still dark out when the landlord and sheriff began pounding on the front door."

"They handed Dad an eviction notice and told us we had fifteen minutes to get out," Carolyn recalled.

"The really cruel thing was how little we were allowed to take with us."

With a tone reflecting a long preserved resentment, Carolyn recounted, "The landlord was able to confiscate almost all of our things 'in lieu of nonpayment of rent.'"

"All we were allowed to pack was one suitcase and one box of kitchen goods," I added, shaking my head. "We weren't even allowed to take any blankets with us."

We were both quiet for a moment, lost in our own memories of that day. "Do you remember the four of us standing on that street corner?" I asked, somewhat rhetorically. "We had no idea which way to go or what to do."

"That is one scene that has been permanently engraved in my scrapbook of childhood memories," Carolyn lamented. "I remember Mom turning her head away; she was taking short, jerky breaths, so I knew she was crying."

"I noticed that too, and I was about to say something to her when I saw you shake your head. So, I turned to Dad, hoping to get some idea of what we were going to do next. I remember him looking up and down the street a few times, and then with a shrug of his shoulders, he picked up the suitcase and motioned me to take the box from Mom. 'Might as well make yourself useful,' he said."

The unspoken implications of those words had caused me to shiver. Dad had repeatedly told us, "Anything that isn't useful gets left behind." So using my private logic, I made a point of making myself useful in order not to get left behind.

"In the rush of the eviction," she began, staring at the waiting room wall, "Mom had put on her light blue waitress uniform with her 'GLADYS' nametag still clipped to the pocket."

She looked old and frail now, but back when we were hitchhiking, Mom could make herself really look pretty, especially when she was wearing a uniform. Even Dad would occasionally comment, "For a woman in her forties, she's still got one great looking figure." With her dark hair and brown eyes, she could have been in the movies, so she seldom had trouble getting a job as a waitress and earning above-average tips, which prompted Dad to frequently remind her that customers could look but not touch.

"The thing I remember about standing on that corner is when Mom noticed me staring up at her. She smiled, reached over and ruffled my hair, and then made a comment that really caught me off guard."

"What was that?" Carolyn asked.

"She said, 'Don't worry, Buddy. As long as we stay together, we'll manage somehow.' I wondered, 'Why wouldn't we be able to stay together?' I worried a lot about us not being able to stay together."

"Man, I didn't pick up on that at all." Carolyn shook her head. "It's a wonder you didn't worry yourself sick. My main concern was the fact that we were broke."

"Dad took care of that problem when he conned that Catholic priest out of enough money to buy us bus tickets—lying to him about having a job waiting in Phoenix."

"Which was pretty typical of the way Dad treated just about everyone," Carolyn added.

I silently mulled over what I had been told about Dad's childhood and how it helped explain, but did not justify, Dad's lack of character. Dad had been born and raised on a small farm in Minnesota. Although his real name was Bernard, his older brother began calling him Bernie when he was still a toddler.

As the story went, there was a death in his extended family when Dad was in his late teens. His parents asked him to stay home and tend to the chores while they, along with his two brothers and his sister, attended the funeral in a town some distance from their farm. However, the day after they left, Dad told the neighbors that his parents had decided to stay in the other town and had instructed him to auction off all of the household furnishings and farm equipment as preparation for selling the farm. So Dad held the auction, absconded with all of the money, and with no more than a ninth-grade education, struck out on his own.

Upon their return, his parents and siblings were shocked to find that most of their belongings had been sold. Fortunately, some of the neighbors returned the items on the condition that they were repaid for what they'd spent at the auction—a financial burden that I understand took years to resolve. Needless to say, Dad was no longer welcome, and to my knowledge, he never attempted to go back.

Seeming not to notice my lack of attention, Carolyn continued, "Fortunately for us, with his lack of conscience and his ability to manipulate, he was able to get us enough money for bus fare to Phoenix."

"That was fifty years ago," I sighed, "and yet my memories of those days have remained as vivid and dynamic as ever."

***

Early spring 1947

Phoenix, Arizona

The bus ride from Albuquerque to Phoenix was monotonous and mind numbing, the boredom only occasionally interrupted by brief stops at unremarkable service stations in the middle of nowhere. We finally pulled into the Phoenix bus terminal just as the sun was dropping behind the orange clouds on the horizon.

"Phoenix!" the bus driver called out. Then steering the bus in a wide arc, he neatly wedged it between two other buses. The air brakes let out a loud, tired sigh, and the door swung open.

Carolyn's head came up and she rubbed her eyes. The driver glanced at the passengers in the big mirror above his head and announced, "End of the line. Everyone has to get off the bus."

"I'm glad we've finally stopped," Carolyn said, sounding a little exasperated. "I need a potty break and my hair's a mess."

Carolyn's hair was a beautiful reddish-brown that fell all the way down to the small of her back. It had always been her treasure, the one thing that kept her from outright hating herself. When she ran, those light strands of hair would stream out behind her like a horse's tail, unintentionally providing me with something that was easy to grab when I was chasing her.

Before we got tossed out of the duplex, she had taken great pride in caring for her hair. Each night, she would sit crossed-legged, tilt her head to one side, and brush the long strands fifty times. This seemed like a waste of time to me. Pushing my dark brown hair off my forehead was enough grooming for me. Nevertheless, Carolyn would sometimes stop me and comb a part on the left side of my head. That seemed like a long time ago, and now, her hair didn't seem quite as red as it used to be, and she was right—it looked a mess, having been badly tangled by the wind.

Dad reached up into the overhead storage, pulled down our cardboard box, and handed it to Mom. "You and the kids wait for me inside while I get the suitcase," he said.

Mom answered with a tired nod, nudging Carolyn and me toward the front of the bus. Carolyn shoved me in the back to hurry me along.

"Cut it out!" I said.

"Make me."

Mom intervened. "Behave yourselves. We've got enough trouble without you two squabbling."

I stepped off the bus and watched Carolyn walk toward the terminal. She looked smaller than usual. At four feet, she stood a head taller than me and could easily pin me in a wrestling match. For that matter, she could pin most any kid her size and some who were bigger. Being somewhat shy and introverted, I tended to avoid contests of strength. Carolyn was the assertive one, a mother hen who seemed old for her age and who had taken upon herself much of the responsibility of taking care of me.

I followed them to the terminal entrance, too hot to care who had won the short skirmish. The terminal was larger than most I'd seen, and its high ceiling was lined with large, round metal tubes with square air vents that protruded downward. White ribbons fluttered erratically in front of them. As the cool air swept over me, I let out a quiet sigh of relief.

Boisterous children were weaving their way through the lines of people waiting to buy tickets, while harried agents scurried back and forth behind the ticket counter. An odd assortment of suitcases was being stacked in the baggage claim area, and several travel-weary passengers were flipping baggage tags over on the handles of suitcases, searching for a match-up with their claim tickets.

Mom and Carolyn had just sat down on a wooden bench in the middle of the lobby when Dad walked up with our suitcase. "Come on, let's go," he said impatiently.

"Why be in a rush to go nowhere?" Mom said, and then with a look of resignation, she turned to her children. "Better use the bathroom now. I don't know when we'll find another one."

I would soon discover that having no access to a bathroom was one of the pervasive challenges of the homeless. A related one was that whoever wasn't using the bathroom was expected to stand guard over our meager belongings.

As I stood sentry for the first time, I wondered, *What on earth are we doing in Phoenix?* No immediate answer came to mind, so I sat down on the suitcase and rested my elbows on my knees. "At least we're still together," I mumbled to myself.

We stepped outside the bus terminal and waited for Dad to decide which way we were going to go. Carolyn nudged me with her elbow, and then, holding her hands close to her stomach so the others couldn't see what she was doing, she pointed her index finger to her right. Getting her meaning, I partially covered my right hand and pointed to the left. Dad decided to go right. I lost the bet and got punched in the shoulder for my trouble.

Like stray cats making their rounds, we began roaming the streets of downtown Phoenix. "Getting familiar with our surroundings," Dad called it. "Wandering aimlessly," was what I called it.

I finally asked him where we were going.

"No place in particular," he replied. "But it looks better if we're on the move."

Puzzled by his comment, I asked him what he meant.

"As long as we're moving it looks as if we're going somewhere. But if we're just sitting, it looks like we're going nowhere."

"We may be moving," I mumbled to myself, "but it still feels like we're going nowhere."

Mom heard me, rolled her eyes, and said with a sigh, "You think too much, Buddy."

Eventually, our wanderings around Phoenix led to a Salvation Army soup kitchen. Facing the street was a large plate-glass window with the faded words, "All Sales Final" and "Everything Reduced," barely visible beneath the freshly painted "Wayfarer's Mission" sign.

As soon as I stepped inside, the smell of food made my mouth water. When I wiped my mouth with my sleeve, Mom gave me a look that said I should know better.

Four rows of wooden picnic tables filled the middle of the room. Each row consisted of three tables butted end to end with long wooden benches bracketing each table. About twenty-five or thirty men were scattered around the tables; a polite, non-intrusive spacing seemed to have been intuitively agreed upon because none of the men were sitting right next to another.

The four of us stood patiently inside the entrance until an overweight lady wearing a fishnet over her hair came through the swinging double door in the back and motioned for us to sit down. Carolyn and I obediently climbed over one of the wooden benches, and Mom and Dad did the same directly across from us.

While awaiting further instructions, I prodded Carolyn with my elbow, and while rolling my eyes, I held my nose and pointed over my shoulder. She glanced at the man sitting behind me and giggled.

Suddenly, the man turned and looked right at us. We instantly redirected our attention to the salt and pepper shakers sitting in the center of our table, but hard as we tried, neither one of us could control our snickering.

The odor coming from the man wasn't the pungent, sweet odor emitted by the sweat of hard labor. It was the musty stench of decay. It was as if he and all the other solitary men in the room were decomposing. I shuddered at the thought and wondered if I could possibly end up like them someday—old, dirty, alone, and smelling like a dung heap?

Gratefully, the arrival of the lady with the fishnet carrying four plates of spaghetti smothered in tomato sauce instantly refocused my attention. I was beyond hungry, and without so much as a "thank you," I grabbed my fork and began shoveling the contents of my plate into my mouth. Carolyn was matching me fork-full for fork-full.

"Will you two stop acting like a couple of farm animals at a pig trough?" Mom scolded under her breath, glancing around the room to see if anyone was watching. "Now wipe your mouths off, hold your forks properly, and behave yourselves."

Carolyn began wiping her mouth with her fingers.

"For heaven's sake, child!" Mom exclaimed. "Use a napkin." She then began peeling paper napkins out of the stainless steel container sitting at the far end of the table. "Whatever's to become of this family?"

After eating my fill, I began stuffing my pockets with packages of saltine crackers, not knowing where or when we'd get our next meal. I heard Dad asking the fishnet lady if she knew of some place that might take us in for the night. She gave him some directions, but I paid little attention to which way or how far. We had a place to stay, and that's all that mattered.

It was getting dark fast, and Mom asked Dad if he was sure he knew where we were going. Dad answered gruffly, "Can't get lost . . . just like the lady at the mission said, the streets were named after the presidents."

"I know," I moaned, "Carolyn's been reading their names out loud at every corner."

"And there's supposed to be a hotel near the railroad tracks," Dad continued, sounding tired and irritated as his eyes scanned the buildings in front of us.

"I don't want to end up in some alley, sleeping under newspapers," Mom chided.

Her comment surprised me, and while readjusting the cardboard box I was carrying, I looked over at Carolyn. She nonchalantly said, "If we do end up sleeping under newspaper, I've got dibs on the comics section."

"No one's going to end up sleeping under newspapers," Mom countered. "Sooner or later, we're bound to find the hotel."

"I *said* I'd find it, so get off my back."

The two of them were still bickering when we reached the vicinity of the railroad tracks and spotted the Imperial Hotel.

The Imperial Hotel wasn't anything to brag about, an all-but-forgotten building in the sleazier part of town—where the elephants come to die. The white paint was peeling, revealing a dull, faded gray. Tongue-and-groove boards ran horizontally down the side of the two-story structure, and several of the narrow slats had fallen out, leaving dark, gaping wounds in the wall. The wooden structure sagged in the middle, making it look more like a grounded whaling ship than a cheap hotel. The *I* in *Imperial* no longer lit up, and the small marquee over the entrance was slowly pulling its support rods out of the wall. I told Mom and Dad that it could fall on someone someday, but they didn't seem to care.

When I asked how we were going to pay for a room, Dad explained that the Imperial Hotel was a temporary shelter for transients and was operated by "a bunch of do-gooders."

The two rooms we moved into were located on the second floor near the sag. They were small, with a transom over the hall door. They had high ceilings, taller than they were wide, and the wallpaper was peeling. There wasn't much in the way of bedroom furniture: a dilapidated chest of drawers with three of the knobs missing and two tall nightstands on either side of an old-fashioned metal bed. A string ran from the metal headboard to a bare lightbulb hanging from the ceiling. A yellowish-gray sheet partially covered a torn and stained mattress. The pillows had no cases on them, and the black-and-blue stripes had long ago faded into light and dark gray. One of the nightstands had a pea-green ceramic lamp with a torn shade. Like the hotel, the bedsprings sagged. They squeaked with the slightest movement, like the floors.

The living room/kitchen wasn't much bigger than the bedroom but felt even smaller because much of the space was taken up by the sink, two-burner stove, and icebox. The cracked linoleum in front of these fixtures had well-worn traffic patterns. Mom used an old towel for a throw rug to cover one section that had been worn all the way through to the floorboards. Occasionally, she'd wipe the floor with a wet rag, but no matter how hard she scrubbed, it still felt sticky to walk on with bare feet.

A wooden table sat in the middle of the room, surrounded by a mismatched assortment of wooden chairs. A badly stained brown couch sat against one wall, its stuffing protruding from several holes. The couch was mostly Dad's territory, which was fine with me since it smelled like a cat had peed on it. I preferred to sit on the windowsill. The rooms had tall, double-hung windows that, due to the stifling heat, were usually open as wide as they would go. I could sit on the sill and watch the comings and goings in the alley and around the rear door of the hotel.

That door had a broken window and was so badly warped it wouldn't shut all the way. The decrepit stairwell just inside always stank of urine, since the winos that slept in the alley used it for a bathroom. That was the main reason Carolyn and I almost always used the front entrance, but the flies were another. "Great plagues of Moses," Mom would say whenever she took out the garbage. She hated the flies.

"How long do we have to stay here?" I asked her one day.

"This is only temporary."

"However long that'll be," I grunted.

"We can only stay here for a little while," she sighed. "It isn't much, but at least we're off the streets."

I wholeheartedly agreed.

Chapter 2

THE NURSE CAME OUT OF Mom's room, and both Carolyn and I watched her closely, looking for some indication of Mom's condition, but none was offered. The nurse merely returned to her desk and began writing.

Carolyn sat down in the chair next to mine and leaned toward me before she began to share her thoughts. "At the age of eleven, poverty wasn't new to me, but homelessness was. I was already exhausted from trying to cope with the problems that come from just being poor, but after we became homeless, the struggles got even worse, and they just kept coming. Life seemed so meaningless. One of us could have gotten sick, or hurt, or even died, and it wouldn't have mattered. It's still depressing to even think about it."

"I used to get depressed a lot," I interjected, "but not anymore. I used to think that because we were poor and wandered around like gypsies that I had missed out on the things that normal kids with normal childhoods would have experienced. But I no longer believe that. I now realize that I had actually been given a unique opportunity to learn valuable lessons about enduring hardships and accomplishing the impossible."

"And just what kind of lessons do you think you've learned?" Carolyn countered, drawing back a little.

"That I have the ability to make choices, for one," I answered. "I've learned that what happens to me in life isn't nearly as important as what I *do* with what happens to me, and that is up to me; it's my choice—I have agency."

"Ha," Carolyn scoffed. "What kind of choices did we have as a couple of homeless vagrants? We couldn't count on Dad, and Mom was too busy trying to survive, so we were on our own. The life we were living was just the way life was; complaining wouldn't change things, pleading wouldn't help, and as far as I knew, there was no one who even cared—not even God."

I nodded with an understanding that only comes from having a common experience, and I confessed, "I used to feel that way."

"And you don't feel that way anymore?" she guessed.

"Not anymore. I now know that there *is* someone who cares, someone who cares a great deal about each and every one of His children. I now know that my Heavenly Father looks down on me and my earthly struggles with the same compassion and love as when he witnessed the suffering of His son, Jesus Christ."

"This Heavenly Father of yours seems to be big on having people suffer," Carolyn noted.

"He isn't the one who causes us to suffer; God wants us to have joy. We bring on most of the suffering ourselves. In many situations, including our childhoods, I find examples of what I call self-perpetuating misery. How we choose to interpret the events in life can make a heaven of hell or a hell of heaven. We want to blame God for our misfortunes, but in most cases, we do it to ourselves."

"What about floods and tornadoes?" Carolyn chided. "What about the suffering caused by those acts of God?"

"I think disasters like those could more accurately be called acts of nature rather than acts of God. God established the laws of nature when he created the universe. The very existence of the universe testifies to the existence of a Creator. But not only does the universe exist; its existence is intelligently organized by the laws of nature, physics, chemistry, and biology. Without these laws, there would be chaos. Sometimes when we ask God to perform miracles, we're asking Him to interfere with these laws. If we were to ask Him to cancel the laws of physics every time we're about to have a car accident, the world would become unpredictable—chaos."

"Maybe you're right, Buddy, but the way we moved around, I'm not sure God would have even known, let alone cared, where we were. Granted, sometimes we would stay in one place for several months, but most of our stays were shorter—many times, no longer than overnight. We didn't *belong* anywhere, and we were never in one place long enough to call it home. Occasionally, people would take us in for a day or two, but most of the time we'd merely get a meal at a nearby soup kitchen and rent a room in some skid-row hotel."

***

Spring 1947

Phoenix, Arizona

Mom said we were fortunate to have two rooms and both a sink and a stove. But neither of the rooms had a toilet, so I didn't feel quite as fortunate as she did.

She was right about the sink and stove, though. I sometimes think we might have starved to death if we hadn't been able to cook our own food. Even after Mom got a job as a waitress and sometimes snuck food home from the café where she worked, it soon became clear that if we were going to eat, Carolyn and I would have to feed ourselves.

I gradually began to expect less and less from the others. I still relied on Carolyn's help occasionally, but even then I knew the day was coming when it would be everyone for themselves. Although we never talked openly about it, I sensed from some of Carolyn's remarks that she had come to the same conclusion, maybe even before I did.

Mom seemed too busy working as a waitress to notice the change, but Dad sometimes commented on how both Carolyn and I were becoming too independent for our own good. And it was true; I was gradually rescinding whatever power I had previously given to others, including my parents, so conflicts with Dad were far more frequent.

A landmark confrontation occurred on an especially hot afternoon shortly after Carolyn and I had returned from school. Dad asked me to do something for him, and although I no longer remember exactly what it was, I do recall that it seemed unreasonable. So I refused.

"Why should I do anything for you?" I dared, hands on my hips.

"Because I'm your father, that's why."

"You're too drunk to be a real father." Once I'd said it, I didn't know whether to stand my ground or make a break for the hall door.

Dad slowly set his beer down on the table and wiped his mouth with the back of his arm. He didn't bother to look at me.

"I'm father enough to kick your skinny little rear end through that door if you don't stop sassing me," he growled.

I was just out of arm's reach. Dad remained seated at the kitchen table, staring straight ahead. Then he slowly and methodically placed the palms of his hands on the edge of the table and leaned forward. My muscles tensed.

"Now are you going to do what I told you to do or not?" he asked in a low, deliberate tone.

"No."

At that, Dad sprang to his feet, sending his chair crashing backward.

I was paralyzed with fear, mouth dry and knees quivering as he started toward me.

In the next instant, Carolyn came out of the bedroom and hurried to my rescue. Her presence gave me some comfort, but I wasn't fool enough to believe I was out of danger.

"We don't have to do everything you tell us to do," she said defiantly. "We're not your slaves."

Dad unbuckled his belt and pulled it through the few remaining loops in his creaseless trousers. His pants sagged with the release, exposing the hair on his stomach. I took a short, quick breath as I watched him slowly double the belt and give it a quick snap. He started toward us.

I frantically tried to interpret the cues. Was he just going to threaten or actually start hitting? But as usual, his lips were poised halfway between a sneer and a smile, and his eyes were like open windows to a dark room—he could see out, but no one could see in.

"Come on. Give it your best shot," Carolyn went on bravely, but her grip on my arm tightened.

I flashed back to the time I had called Dad a wino under my breath. He had grabbed the back of my neck and shaken me like a rag doll. I ended up peeing my pants.

He was within striking distance now, and Carolyn was now holding her arms rigidly by her sides, nervously opening and closing her fists.

I thought I might throw up, but I had to do something. I lunged forward and grabbed the swinging belt with both hands. I yanked on it as hard as I could, but Dad merely sneered down at me. Effortlessly, he jerked me off the floor, and I let go of the belt. He shoved me out of the way and turned his attention back to Carolyn.

His mouth was set in a flat smile. He slowly ran the end of the belt under Carolyn's chin and asked, "Now what was that you said about not having to do what I tell you to?"

Carolyn said nothing, her breath coming in gasps. I knew what was coming, and I knew that this whipping was going to be far worse than most.

Dad raised his arm above his head, then hesitated a moment, and I felt my flesh quiver. The belt sliced through the air like a guillotine blade, lashing Carolyn's bare legs just above her knees. Her skin turned a bright red, and a stifled whimper slipped out.

Dad drew his arm back again.

"You can whip me all you want, but you aren't going to make me cry," Carolyn said calmly, and then she squatted down and squeezed her eyes shut. Her thin dress would provide little protection against the next blow.

Dad wouldn't stop until she begged, and the set of Carolyn's jaw told me she had no intention of giving in.

"She didn't mean to sass ya!" I cried out, tears blurring my vision.

"You stay out of this!" Dad shouted as Carolyn cowered at his feet.

I grabbed a half-empty jar of peanut butter and threw it at him. It missed.

Dad turned, pointing the belt at me. "You're going to get yours!"

Quickly, Carolyn started crawling for cover.

But with catlike quickness, he brought the belt down onto her bare arm. Carolyn grimaced, and tears welled up in her eyes.

Someday, you're gonna get yours . . . someday, I vowed silently, watching helplessly.

The next blow struck her legs, which she'd left exposed as she rubbed the welt on her arm.

I grabbed a bottle of whiskey from the kitchen counter and held it precariously over the sink. "If you hit her again," I threatened, "I'm going to pour your whiskey down the drain."

Nothing was more precious to Dad than his booze. He lunged for the bottle, but his beltless trousers fell down around his knees. For a few critical seconds, he was caught in mid-stride.

"Run!" I yelled, then ducked under the kitchen table and bolted for the hall door. Carolyn leapt past the fallen chair, trying to reach the door before Dad recovered. I got there first and yanked the door open. Carolyn was right beside me when Dad grabbed her by the hair, jerking her back.

"Run, Buddy! Run!" she screamed.

So I ran. Down the hall. Down the stairs. Down the alley. I ran from Dad, from Carolyn's screams, from my helplessness.

I ran to a dry pile on the side of the alley and dove behind some boxes, frantically covering myself with scraps of cardboard and smelly rags, pulling my miserable, stinking world down around me. I had learned some time before that garbage could provide a good hiding place, but you had to know your garbage. The trick was to hide in *dry* garbage rather than *wet*. I tried to hold my breath, but I was still winded from running, and my efforts resulted in uncontrollable, jerky sobs. I would have to stay where I was until it was safe to come out.

After what seemed like an eternity, I heard Carolyn's voice coming from somewhere down the alley. "Buddy? You can come out now," she called out softly in a singsong tone. "It's safe to come out now."

"I may be only eight," I muttered as I cautiously pushed one of the boxes far enough away from a garbage can to peer out and make sure Carolyn was alone. "But if there's one thing I've learned, it's that it's never completely safe to come out."

Sometimes Dad would trick us into revealing where the other was hiding, so I wasn't taking any chances. I continued to scan the alley and watch Carolyn for some sign that she was being used as bait.

Finally convinced that it was as safe as it was ever going to be, I began climbing out of my hiding place.

"Sometimes garbage and life can both really stink," I mumbled as I stood up and began brushing off my clothes. Somehow, I had already figured out that I had to be able to be in the garbage without becoming part of it.

Carolyn finally spotted me and began jogging toward me. "I thought you might be in there," she called out.

She waited while I climbed the rest of the way out of the garbage pile. Helping me brush myself off, she accidentally backed into one of the garbage cans.

"Oh, for Pete's sake!" she groaned. "This was my only clean dress, and now I've got muck on it." She spit on her fingers and began rubbing at the smudge, but all she managed to do was to spread it around. "This doesn't look like something that's going to come off." She lifted her dress up for a closer inspection.

"How bad was it?" I asked softly, staring at the horrible red welts on her legs.

"No worse than usual," she said with a shrug. She looked at me for a moment then added, "Thanks for trying to help."

"You still got a licking," I replied sheepishly, feeling more helpless than ever.

Carolyn reached out and picked a small piece of packing straw out of my hair, giving me a cursory inspection. "You're sure getting skinny. You've got to start eating more."

"More what? I just got through breaking the only jar of peanut butter we had left."

"Too bad you didn't hit him with it."

"I wish Mom was around more. She never seems to be around when we need her."

"What difference would her being around make? She can't stand up to Dad any better than we can. Face it, Buddy, we're pretty much on our own."

"She's hardly ever around. She's always off working in the day or drinking with Dad at night. I wish they'd do their drinking during the day and stay home at night."

"Dad says bars aren't the same in the daytime."

"A bar's a bar," I reasoned. "Sometimes I wonder why Mom doesn't just leave him."

"I think Mom's afraid of being alone," Carolyn replied matter-of-factly as we began walking down the alley.

"I heard Dad tell Mom that no one else would put up with her," I confided after a moment, kicking at an empty paint can.

"I think she agrees with him. I guess she figures Dad's better than nothing."

"She's got us," I retorted. "Ain't we something?"

"Grown-ups got grown-up needs."

I didn't fully understand what Carolyn meant by that, so I chucked a rock at an old alley cat that was sitting on top of some discarded tires and tried to change the subject. "Want to roll tires?"

"Nah. We'd end up getting the black all over us."

She paused then pointed across the street. "It's too hot here in the sun. Let's go over to the Eight Ball and see if we can get someone to buy us a soda." We'd been in the Eight Ball lots of times with Mom and Dad.

We waited for a yellow '47 Studebaker to pass and made a run for it. We were barefoot, so we had to run from shady spot to shady spot. "Watch out for glass," I warned. We were constantly on the lookout for glass, almost all of which came from discarded wine bottles.

The Eight Ball, a combination pool hall and bar, was located right across from the Imperial Hotel. Naturally, it had become one of Dad's favorite hangouts.

"We won't get in trouble, will we?" I asked as Carolyn pushed open one of the doors to the pool hall.

"Not if nobody finds out," she replied as the door swung open.

I remember how much I liked those doors. They were made of wood and glass, and they looked old. I liked old things, things that had been in the same place for a long time. The doors were at least ten feet tall; the lower sections were made of solid wood, and the tops had large, frosted panes of beveled glass with floral designs etched into them. A three-inch border of stained glass framed the center panels. Mom told me one time that it was a style used around the turn of the century.

As we stepped inside, I glanced around the room. The pool hall always smelled of sawdust, dirty ashtrays, and stale beer, and a perpetual cloud of cigarette smoke hung over the four pool tables. A long, antique bar with a brass foot rail ran down one side of the long, narrow room, punctuated by a line of tall, four-legged stools that ran down its entire length. Whenever we came over to the pool hall with Mom and Dad, they spent most of their time sitting on those tall stools. And while they were busy drinking up most of Mom's tip money, Carolyn and I would kill time by playing shuffleboard or rolling billiard balls around on one of the pool tables.

But they weren't with us today, and I was getting the feeling that we shouldn't be there. Then Carolyn prodded me with her elbow and gestured toward one of the pool tables. She took off, walking right over to a couple of men who were playing pool.

"Try the four ball in the side pocket," she suggested to a rough-looking character in faded jeans and an army-brown T-shirt. He had a pack of cigarettes rolled up in the shoulder of his T-shirt, and a half-smoked butt hung out of his mouth. He glanced at Carolyn but said nothing. He repositioned himself, though, and took the shot she'd suggested—and made it.

"Got any more suggestions, kid?" he chuckled.

"Hey! Call your own shots," his opponent protested. "Who're these little hustlers, anyway?" He turned toward the bar. "Hey, Sid," he called out. "Are these kids supposed to be in here?"

The bartender was busy washing glasses, but he stopped and looked up. Recognition spread across his face when he saw us. He quickly dried his hands with a towel and walked over to where we were standing.

"Your mom and dad know you're in here?" he asked.

"They told us to meet 'em here," Carolyn lied.

"Well, you're going to have to wait for them outside."

"It's too hot out there," Carolyn whined.

"I'll get you a couple of cold sodas, but you'll have to drink 'em outside." The bartender returned to the bar and reached under the counter for two bottles of grape Nehi.

Wearing a big smile, Carolyn looked down at me and winked.

Mission accomplished.

Finding a clean place outside to sit and enjoy our sodas wasn't all that easy. The winos made a habit of leaning against the buildings to take a leak, letting their urine run down the wall and out across the sidewalk. You could tell where someone had taken a leak by where the dirt had been washed away. So the cleanest place to sit was where it was still dirty.

I finally found a clean spot a few sidewalk squares down the street. A few minutes later, I spotted Mom walking home from work. She was on the shady side of the street, but she crossed over as she neared the hotel. She seemed to be walking slower than usual. Her arms were hanging by her sides, and her purse was dangling so low from her right hand that it was almost dragging on the sidewalk.

My mother was a paradox, willing to sacrifice her life in the service of others if necessary, yet seemingly incapable of the same fortitude on her own behalf. She was born Gladys Ilene O'Conner on a South Dakota farm in 1906, the youngest of three sisters with one younger brother. She was a free-spirited woman, according to what I'd been told, who left the farm for the bright lights of Kansas City, Kansas, to become a nurse after graduating from high school. I've come to believe that she found herself caught up in a social limbo while she was there—a part of her clinging to the strong work ethic of farm life, another part drawn to the excitement and new freedoms of the Roaring Twenties. While vacillating between these two worlds, it's possible that she lost her direction, her self-confidence, and somewhere along the way, her sense of self-worth. She became easy prey for someone like my father, getting caught in a mutually destructive, co-dependent relationship.

"Mom looks tired," I said, thinking out loud.

Carolyn nodded.

"Are you going to tell her what happened with Dad?" I asked.

"Nah. She's never in the mood for kids after she gets off work. Besides, Mom always takes Dad's side anyway." Carolyn scrunched up her face and mimicked Mom's voice. "He's your father, and you have to do what *Bernie* tells you.*"

I grinned with admiration at the imitation, especially the pronunciation of Dad's name with a high-pitched whine.

"And how many times have I told you not to sass?" she continued. "I swear, child, you've been nothing but trouble since the day you were born."

By the time Carolyn finished, I was laughing so hard I snorted grape drink up my nose. She started laughing too, and for a moment I wasn't poor, wasn't sitting on a dirty sidewalk in a run-down neighborhood. For just a moment, it felt the way it had back when we were a *real* family.

"Remember how we used to laugh a lot?" I said as I wiped a tear from my eye.

"No, I don't," Carolyn shot back. "And I don't want to remember 'cause that was then and this is now, and it ain't never gonna be that way again. So you might as well forget it."

I hesitated, caught off guard by the sharpness of her tone. "Well, maybe you can forget it, but I can't. Someday, things will be . . . better."

"Better! Ha!" she grunted. "Dream on, little brother."

Nothing more was said about the past, and for a while, we just sat there drinking our sodas.

Carolyn finished her drink and stood up. "I'm bored," she said.

I was getting bored too and began trying to put the two empty pop bottles over my big toes. One almost got stuck.

"What on earth are you doing?" Carolyn exclaimed, shaking her head. "Honestly, I really wonder about you sometimes." She looked up and down the street and then stepped off the curb. "I'm going to go ask Mom if we can have some of her tip money to go to a movie."

"Don't ask her in front of Dad!" I shouted after her as she started across the street.

"Don't worry. I'll be careful."

Chapter 3

THE CHAIRS IN THE HOSPITAL waiting room were uncomfortable to begin with, and the discomfort only increased with time. I decided to stand up and stretch to get some blood circulating.

Carolyn looked up and asked, "Do you want to walk around for a while?"

"Naw, I'm just getting tired of sitting. How about you?"

"I'm okay. I've sat on worse chairs than these," she assured me, patting the chair next to her. "At least these chairs are in better shape than those in the flophouse hotels we used to stay in."

Carolyn shifted her position in her chair and stared out the window. "Back when we were kids, when things would go from bad to worse, I would sometimes find myself praying to St. Jude, the patron saint of lost causes," she said with a slight smile. "But my prayers seldom got answered. So, along with complaining and pleading, I added praying to my list of things that didn't help."

I leaned against the wall and confided, "When I used to complain about my prayers not being answered, Mom would tell me, 'You've just got to have more faith. God will eventually send you an answer.' My comeback was, 'How can God send me an answer, when He doesn't even know where we are?'"

I paused for a moment before continuing. "Maybe Mom was right, though. Maybe the reason my prayers didn't get answered when I was a kid was because of my lack of faith. Even then, I wanted to believe in God. I wanted to believe in something that would help explain why life had to be so difficult. That was one of my unanswerable questions."

Carolyn turned away from the window and echoed, "Unanswerable questions?"

I chuckled. "I'll give you an example of what I mean: if God is so all powerful, why doesn't He just make everything easy for us? Even though I couldn't come up with any answers at the time, something told me that *someone* had to know the answer."

"And did you ever find anyone who knew the answer?"

"I believe I actually did," I answered with a broad grin of satisfaction. Growing up, my curiosity about such things had been insatiable. I had wanted to learn as much as I could about a God who would allow so much hardship to exist. Sometimes I would ask the Catholic priests about what God was like, but they would usually give me a lecture about sacred mysteries, which didn't make a whole lot of sense to an eight-year-old, so I just stopped asking. "When I was about forty," I continued, "I had an opportunity to talk with a couple of Mormon missionaries."

"Are you trying to tell me that a couple of Mormon missionaries had the answers?" she questioned in disbelief.

"I'll tell you how they explained it to me and see if it doesn't make sense to you, as well," I proposed. "To the question, *if God is all powerful, why doesn't He just make everything easy for us,* one of the missionaries responded by asking me if I had ever known someone who came from a very wealthy family and had been given everything he wanted merely by asking for it. When he wanted a tricycle, his dad gave him one. When he wanted a bike he got it. The same was true when he wanted a car, or boat, or anything else.

"At first this might sound like a pretty good deal, but what kind of personality do you think such a person is likely to develop? What kind of relationships do you think such a person would be capable of developing with others? What kind of value do you think such a person would place on the things he received?

"He told me that much of our character is developed through overcoming difficulties, which also helps us become more self-reliant. The value we place on what we achieve or obtain is often linked to the amount of effort we have to put forth in order to get it. The greater the effort needed to achieve something, the greater the value we place on obtaining it. The greater the challenge we overcome, the bigger the celebration. We value victory more when we have experienced defeat. We value health because of the times when we have been sick. Thus, as part of His plan of salvation, God included opposition in all things. Then the missionary quoted a passage from the Book of Mormon, which I just happen to have here in my

Palm Pilot. 'For it must needs be, that there is an opposition in all things. If not so . . . righteousness could not be brought to pass, neither wickedness, neither holiness nor misery, neither good nor bad.'"

"Then I've certainly been living God's plan," Carolyn interjected, "because I've found opposition to almost everything I've tried to do."

"The inclusion of opposition is not intended solely for the purpose of making our lives difficult, but to enable us to appreciate what we're given. For those who have escaped from tyranny and oppression, being free creates overwhelming feelings of joy, but those who have never known tyranny and oppression tend not to appreciate what they have. Contrast enlightens our understanding."

Carolyn nodded pensively and shrugged. "I'll have to admit that that sounds like a pretty good answer, and it seems to make sense. But when you're poor, things don't always make sense."

***

Spring 1947

Phoenix, Arizona

After we'd stayed at the Imperial Hotel for several weeks, it started to feel like home. We had thoroughly explored the neighborhood, become familiar with the alleys, and located a movie theater. We didn't get to go to the movies very often, though, and most of the time we had to pay our own way by collecting pop bottles and returning them for the deposits.

Finding out that there was a Saturday matinee that included a Roy Rogers western, two cartoons, and a Flash Gordon serial—all for twenty-five cents—was all the motivation Carolyn and I needed to begin collecting pop bottles. Plus, we were able to stay cool for a few hours. However, when we came out of the theater, the Phoenix sun slammed into us.

"Jeez, it's bright!" I said, squinting from the glare.

Once my eyes adjusted, I started pointing my ray-gun finger at passing cars and systematically disintegrating the kids who were climbing onto a city bus.

"Buddy, if you're going to act like an idiot, do it away from me," Carolyn chided.

I ignored her, as usual, and continued zapping people with my imaginary death ray, while making a point of staying as close to her as possible.

Even though the sun was getting lower, it was still hot, making the walk back seem longer. We finally reached the pool hall and crossed over to the hotel. Just outside the entrance, Carolyn spotted the hopscotch game she had outlined in chalk a couple of days ago.

"Come on, let's play," she called out, throwing her coin purse down as a marker.

"It's getting late," I replied. "Let's go on upstairs and get something to eat."

"Oh, all right, but the outline's going to be worn off by tomorrow," she sighed, picking up her coin purse. Following me into the building, she added, "I would've beat you anyway."

She was right. That was one of the reasons I didn't want to play; she always won. She could jump farther and knew all the sissy rules for hopscotch, rules that seemed to change every time we played. But she wasn't better at everything. I could climb trees better than she could, and I could run just as fast.

Inside the hotel lobby, I peered through the hole in the mailbox with our room number on it. "How're we going to get any mail if we don't have our name on the mailbox?" I asked.

"We're not," Carolyn answered knowingly. "People like us don't get mail."

None of what had gone on since we'd left Albuquerque made much sense to me, but it was too hot to ask a lot of questions, and Carolyn was getting way ahead of me. I took the stairs two at a time to catch up with her, but she had already disappeared around the corner at the top of the stairs by the time I was halfway up. I approached the landing cautiously, just in case she was waiting to leap out at me.

The halls were always dark and seemed even darker after just coming in from the bright sunlight. There were plenty of light sockets, just no lightbulbs. People would steal them as fast as they were put in, so the super stopped putting them in. Carolyn paused to eavesdrop at one of the doors, motioning me not to make any noise. Hearing nothing, she continued walking.

We were halfway to our room when Carolyn started to walk faster. I quickly caught up with her and tried to slip past her, but she started running. The race was on. Whoever got to the door first won and got to knock. But like most of our races, we ended up in a tie, so we both started banging on the door at the same time.

Mom's exasperated voice came through the thin door. "For heaven's sakes, stop that noise!" She unlocked the dead bolt and opened the door. "Shush, you two," she whispered. "There's no need to make that kind of racket." She'd tried to sound upset, but I could tell she wasn't really mad. "Now try to be a little quieter. Your dad's still sleeping."

"How come he sleeps so much?" I asked.

"He was just up late last night."

"Up late getting drunk," Carolyn added sarcastically.

"Now that's enough out of you, young lady," Mom scolded.

It never did any good to argue, so I went over and sat on the window ledge and moped.

***

Although I was gradually adjusting to living off other people's charity, learning to live without certain "conveniences"—like a toilet—created some interesting challenges. Dad would always get up before us and use the "can," an empty Folgers coffee can that we kept under the sink. Neither Carolyn nor I liked using it, especially Carolyn, but the only toilet on our floor was way the heck down at the end of the hall. Whenever I'd hear Carolyn get up during the night and use the can, I'd cover my ears with my hands so I couldn't hear her peeing. But this procedure wasn't very effective, since I'd have to pull my hands away and listen every few seconds in order to know when she was through. The worst thing about the can was that each morning someone had to carry it down to the bathroom and empty it.

This particular morning, as soon as I came out of the bedroom, Dad hit me with it. "It's your turn to empty the can."

"It's not either," I protested. "It's Carolyn's turn to dump it. She's the one who used it last."

"It's not either my turn!" Carolyn yelled back. "I took it down yesterday."

"No, you didn't. I dumped it yesterday."

"Give it up, Buddy. Carolyn dumped the can yesterday." Dad's voice was both gruff and muffled as he tried to talk and shave at the same time.

"Aw, Dad . . . I hate dumping the can." No matter how careful I tried to be, some of the pee always managed to spill out. I once dropped the whole thing halfway down the hall. I ran back to our room and shut the door before anyone else came out, so I never did find out who mopped it up.

"You'd complain either way. It's either the can or having to get dressed in the middle of the night," Dad explained for the umpteenth time.

"I know. I just hate doing it," I sighed as I gave in and reached under the sink for the can. "Aw, for criminy sakes," I groaned. "It's almost full."

I carefully lifted it off the floor and slowly stood up. I held the can out in front of me at arm's length, focusing my attention on the brim. I took slow careful steps, trying not to slosh. I finally made it across the room to the door. "Carolyn?" I called out.

"Yeah?"

"Come open the door for me."

"In a minute."

"I ain't got a minute."

"Okay, Mr. Can Man," she said, getting up from the table. After opening the door, she stuck out her finger, threatening to tickle me.

"You wouldn't dare." I glared at her momentarily but quickly refocused on the contents of the can, which had sloshed a little during the distraction.

"Oh, wouldn't I?" she giggled.

"You two stop fooling around," Dad called out. "Carolyn, back off."

I stuck my tongue out at her as I went out. Fortunately, I only spilled a little on the way down the hall, but it took several minutes to get to the bathroom and return. By the time I got back, Carolyn was already dressed.

"Did you remember to wash the can out?" Mom asked as I came through the door.

"Yeah, I washed the can, and I had to wash my hands, too. You guys get it too full."

"It's not our fault," Carolyn pointed out. "Everyone knows you can't stop once you start."

"Such talk," Mom said, pouring milk over a bowl of Malt-o-Meal. "We don't have any sugar," she added with a sigh, "so you'll have to use syrup."

"You kids had better hustle," Dad called out.

He said the same thing almost every morning, trying to get finished shaving and hurry us along at the same time. He shaved over the kitchen sink. The small mirror on the wall made it difficult to see very much at any one time. Sometimes I'd watch him as I ate my cereal and count the number of times he'd scrunch his face up, which meant that he'd nicked himself again.

I quickly finished gulping down my cereal and resumed the task of getting dressed for school. "Has anyone seen my school shirt?"

"It's on the other side of the couch, where you left it." Carolyn always seemed to know where things were. "Hurry up, or we're going to miss the bus," she said from the doorway.

We rode the city bus to St. Bernard's Catholic School. Neither of us liked going to a parochial school but, like most things in our lives, didn't have much of a say in the matter. I thought the nuns were too strict, and our uniforms were dumb: white shirt and dark blue corduroy pants for boys, white blouses with blue plaid, pleated skirts for girls. I thought they made us look kind of weird. Still, the church gave them to us for nothing, along with some bus tokens. Besides, there were only two more weeks left before school let out for Christmas break—I could take looking weird a little longer.

Carolyn didn't want to go to school at all. She had already been held back a grade because of all the moving around we'd done. She should have been in the sixth grade, but she was still in the fifth, which she found both irritating and frustrating. I was in the third grade. Having been pulled out of one school after another hadn't affected me as much, since first and second grade are hard to flunk. But like Dad, Carolyn blamed most her failures either on fate or on others.

"Bye, Mom!" Carolyn and I called out in unison.

"Come straight home from school," Mom reminded us as she did every morning.

I started toward Dad to give him a kiss good-bye, but then I saw that he hadn't finished washing off all of the shaving lather. "Bye Dad," I said. "I think I'll pass on the kiss."

"Hey, break my heart, will ya," he replied.

I couldn't see his mouth because of the lather, but I could see the smile lines around his eyes.

**

The hotel room was usually empty in the afternoon when we got home from school. Mom would be at work, and Dad would be out somewhere "looking for a job," which usually meant swapping lies with other drunks.

We were supposed to change clothes and take off our school shoes, but far too often I'd get involved in something and forget.

Each day ended pretty much the same way: Carolyn would get in an argument with Mom, and Mom would get in a fight with Dad; we would eat something, and then Carolyn and I would be sent to bed as a way of getting us out from under foot.

Next to emptying the can, I disliked having to go to bed the most. I always tried to delay it as long as possible.

"Do I have to go to bed already? It's only eight o'clock," I complained one night.

"Yes, you do. And stop your whining," Mom said firmly.

"Are you and Dad going out?" Carolyn asked Mom as she climbed onto the rollaway bed with me.

I already knew the answer. I had seen the telltale signs: Dad putting on a clean shirt, Mom fussing with her hair. Mom's brown dress with white polka dots had lost its shape, and one of the shoulder pads kept slipping, but I thought she looked pretty anyway.

"We're going out for just a little while," Mom said quietly as she bent over Carolyn.

"Are you going to take all night with those kids?" Dad asked from the doorway. "Let's get a move on it."

"Can we go to sleep in your bed?" Carolyn whispered to Mom as she turned to leave.

Mom stopped at the doorway, turned and nodded, then put the tips of her fingers to her lips and blew us a kiss. "Don't worry, when I leave I'll lock the door behind me so no one will be able to get in. Now you two be good."

I lay there listening for a second or two. As soon as I heard the key turn in the lock, I jumped off the couch, ran to the door, and pressed my ear to it. Their footsteps were growing faint. Once I was sure the coast was clear, I raced over to the radio that the landlady had loaned us on the condition that we promised not to break it. It was almost eight o'clock, which meant that it was almost time for *The Shadow*, my all-time favorite radio program. While Carolyn tuned in the station, I got up and grabbed a box of crackers out of the cupboard then ran back and sat down on the floor beside her.

"These crackers are stale," I complained, struggling to swallow the dry mass of crumbs stuck to the top of my mouth.

At the same time, Carolyn was trying to scrape cracker crumbs from her tongue. "I've got to drink some water." She went over to the kitchen counter and opened one of the cupboards. "How about if I make some cookies!" she exclaimed, holding a box of mix over her head.

"That'd be great!"

After assuring me that she had watched Mom make them many times, Carolyn proceeded to pour out the contents and mix them with what was left of a quart of milk. Minutes later, she had the oven lit and a tray of cookies sliding onto the middle rack.

"Let's listen to *The Shadow* in the dark," she suggested as she closed the oven door. "It'll be twice as scary that way."

I wasn't too sure the idea was all that great, but I didn't want her to think I was chicken, so I jumped up and turned off the lights.

"Hurry, it's starting," she beckoned.

The theme music had already begun as I dropped down on all fours and groped my way toward the glowing radio dial. By the time I reached Carolyn, the Shadow's "Who knows what evil lurks in the hearts of men" had begun to fade into his sinister laugh.

The half-hour program flew by all too quickly, and the echo of his parting laughter soon faded away.

"That was scary," Carolyn commented, turning off the radio.

"Boy, I'll say. And don't you go adding to it," I warned as I followed her into Mom and Dad's bedroom. "Shouldn't we turn on some lights?" I whispered.

"Do you want to be the one who has to go back and shut them off . . . *alone*?" Carolyn asked.

The very idea of groping around in the dark again gave me the willies, so I abandoned the idea and continued to hold onto Carolyn as we made our way to the bedroom. I climbed into bed and pulled the sheet over my head.

"Are you asleep yet?" she whispered.

"Nah, *The Shadow* was too scary. How 'bout you?"

"Oh, sure, you dimwit. Like I'd talk to you in my sleep."

"At least I don't wet the bed," I countered, unable to think of a really good comeback.

"I don't wet the bed anymore. Besides, that was a long time ago, back when Mom and Dad were having their big fights."

"Those fights were scary," I replied. "Remember the time Dad got drunk and was beating up on Mom?"

"Boy, do I!" Carolyn said loudly. "I was hitting him with that broom as hard as I could, and then he yanked it out of my hand and started chasing me. We were all screaming so loud that the neighbors ended up calling the police."

"Boy, was I ever glad when they got there," I sighed. "I wonder what made him start drinking so much?"

"I know what you mean," Carolyn agreed sympathetically. "It ain't much fun . . . not knowing how long we're going to be able to stay in one place."

"And always being hungry," I added, trying to stifle a yawn.

Carolyn reached over and ruffled my hair. "Thanks for talking with me, little brother."

"Even if I'm a dimwit?" I said then turned over and started to drift off.

"I didn't really mean that," she whispered. "You're the only little brother I've got."

I barely heard that last remark as I gave in to sleep. The next thing I knew, I felt someone poking me in the ribs.

"Huh?"

"Buddy, wake up!" Carolyn whispered urgently. "I think I smell smoke!"

She was sitting up in bed, sniffing the air. I bolted upright. "You'd better not be fooling around, Carolyn. It ain't funny."

"I'm not fooling, Buddy. I think I smell smoke."

At first I just sat there in the dark, trying to convince myself that it wasn't smoke I was smelling, but the odor was unmistakable. "I smell it, too. It's smoke all right."

"Turn some—" I began, then began coughing. "Turn some lights on."

When the light came on, I leapt out of bed and ran into the other room.

"The cookies!" Carolyn shouted. "I forgot the cookies in the oven!" She stooped down as low as she could and headed for the stove. But once she opened the oven door, a great billow of smoke poured out and wafted through the open transom.

Seconds later, I heard someone running through the hallway, pounding on doors, yelling, "Fire!"

"We're in trouble," I conceded, choking back a cough.

Someone began pounding on the door, and then there was a loud crash that told us that someone had just smashed open our door. "Is anyone in here?" a man's voice shouted. "Yell out, if anyone's in here."

We both started yelling, and the next thing I knew, we were being rescued. The stranger slung us under his arms and carried us out of the room, down the hall, down the stairs, and out to the street in front of the hotel. Someone rushed over and wrapped us in jackets.

I heard the shrill wail of sirens and looked over at Carolyn. She looked back at me and rolled her eyes. Moments later, fire trucks came careening around the corner.

Mrs. Sheldon, the plump, elderly manager, who lived on the first floor of the hotel, was standing in her bathrobe holding her hands to her face. When she saw us, she clasped her hands together and let out a shout, "Hallelujah! God has spared your innocent little lives!" Then she threw her arms around us and squeezed.

A police officer walked over. "Everyone all right over here?" he asked.

"I just rescued those two kids from that hotel," volunteered the man who'd carried us from our rooms.

"That right?" the officer said kneeling beside us. "You kids okay?"

We both just nodded. We both knew that all of this commotion was because we had forgotten some cookies in the oven, and neither of us dared say a word.

"I'll get one of the firemen to check you out. You're sure you're not hurt?"

When we both nodded again, the policeman turned his attention to Mrs. Sheldon, who was still clinging to us.

"Are these your children, ma'am?"

"Oh my, no! My children are all grown," she replied, and then she looked down at us and frowned. "Do you know where your parents are?"

Carolyn explained, "Mom and Dad are gone bar hopping, so they probably won't be back until late."

Listening to this exchange, the policeman pulled out his notepad. "Is there anyone who can stay with you until we locate your parents? Relatives or a close friend?"

Carolyn shook her head again.

The officer turned his attention to me. "Do you know where your mother is?"

"'Fraid not."

"But she's out with your dad?"

"'Fraid so."

"Do you have any idea when they might return?"

Carolyn answered. "Most of the time, they get home late."

"And Dad's usually drunk," I added.

The policeman was taking notes. "Did your mom ever mention the name of a particular restaurant or bar?"

"They go to the Eight Ball sometimes," I volunteered, pointing across the street.

The officer then asked for their descriptions. "I'll put out an APB on them and get some of our patrols to begin checking a few of the local bars. Don't worry, we'll find 'em."

A fireman arrived about this time, holding a tray of burnt cookies in front of him. We knew we were busted.

"Burnt cookies!" the fireman announced, shaking his head. He turned to Mrs. Sheldon. "There was quite a bit of smoke, but no fire," he explained.

Mrs. Sheldon folded her arms and glared down at us, eyebrows raised high enough to touch the netting over her curlers. "Would either of you happen to know anything about these burnt cookies?" she asked.

Carolyn started to explain about the cookies and *The Shadow*, but the more she explained the more upset the others became: more upset with Mom and Dad than with us.

"Children your age shouldn't be left alone," Mrs. Sheldon said, patting me on the head. "You poor babies," she sighed. "Whatever's going to become of you?"

The policeman put away his notepad and motioned to a police-woman standing nearby.

"Obviously, these kids can't be left here alone," he said, "so we're going to have to make some other arrangements. Take them down to the station for the time being."

"Not much of a place for kids," the policewoman commented.

"I know, but at least it'll get them off the street while we get things sorted out."

The policewoman shrugged then took each of us by the hand. "Beats me how some parents can neglect their kids like this. Come on, you two. Looks like we're going to be spending the night together." With the two of us firmly in tow, she began working her way through the crowd.

We had only gone a little ways, when I saw Mom and Dad pushing their way through the crowd. I tugged on the policewoman's uniform. "That's our parents over there."

"Oh, really," the officer said, with a strong emphasis on the word *really*, and then began to push her way in the direction that I had pointed.

"Are you Mr. and Mrs. Poduska?" the officer asked as they came nearer. With a firm grip on Carolyn, who was holding on to me, the policewoman managed to keep both of us behind her.

For a second or two, Mom didn't respond. "Yes, I'm Mrs. Poduska," she finally replied. "But how did you know my name?" Then her eyes opened wide. "The children!" she screamed. "Something's happened to the children!"

"We thought there had been a fire—" the policewoman started to explain.

"My babies! My babies!"

"Your kids are okay, ma'am," the officer shouted over Mom's screams. "They aren't hurt."

Mom grabbed her arms and studied her face. "Tell me the truth," she said. "My babies?"

"They're both just fine, ma'am," the officer reassured, then gently pulled us forward, and added, "They're right here."

Mom dropped to her knees, threw her arms around both of us, and began sobbing. "Oh, thank God!" she cried. She finally stopped crying enough to wipe the tears and mascara off her face. Suddenly she froze, and a puzzled expression came to her face. "You said something about a fire."

"Well, it wasn't exactly a fire, ma'am," the policewoman explained, "but there was a lot of smoke in your rooms." Then she shook her head and added, "I think it'd be best if we get off the street and finish this inside."

She helped steady Dad while keeping a wary eye on Mom, and we made our way back inside and up the stairs to our rooms. Dad immediately plopped down on one end of the sofa and fixed his eyes on the floor. Mom sat down on the other end.

The policewoman ushered Carolyn and me into the bedroom then went back to speak to Mom and Dad. We sat down on the edge of the bed and waited. She returned a few minutes later.

"You kids can have the bed. Your folks will have to sleep in the other room. But you'd better not do any bouncing on that mattress. It doesn't look like it could take much before you'd be on the floor."

Carolyn and I stood up and took off the jackets the people outside had loaned us. When the officer saw what we wore underneath, Carolyn said quietly, "We don't have any nightclothes."

The policewoman stared at us for a second or two, shook her head, then pulled back the covers and patted the mattress. "Time you guys got some shut-eye."

As soon as she closed the bedroom door, we jumped out of bed and opened the door a crack to see what was going on.

Mom took off her shoes and began rubbing her feet. She tugged on the chenille bedspread that covered the holes in back of the sofa and curled up in a ball. "How are my kids?" she asked, lifting her head a little. "Are they all right?"

"They're not hurt, if that's what you mean."

I pushed the door open a little more.

"I put them to bed in the next room," the officer went on.

"I want to see my kids," Mom slurred as she staggered toward the bedroom door. Carolyn and I quickly dove into bed.

"My poor babies," she sighed after a moment of gazing in on us.

As soon as she was gone, we jumped out of bed and eased the door open again, taking turns peeking through the crack.

"What happened?" Mom was asking.

"Burnt cookies."

"What?"

"That's right. Seems your kids decided to do some baking on their own and could have ended up burning the place down."

"*My* kids?"

"*Your* kids. The ones you left alone."

"I don't know what we're going to do. Bad things just keep happening to us," Mom said. "But it's going to get better. Bernie promised me that things are going to get better."

"Well, there you go then," the officer replied. "Things are going to get better. But not necessarily right away."

Mom looked at her in confusion.

"I must inform you, Mrs. Poduska," the officer said in a formal voice, "in cases like this, I'm required to submit a report to social services."

Mom nodded, then closed her eyes and pulled the edge of the bedspread over her shoulder. Dad was already asleep. Carolyn quietly closed the door, and we climbed back into bed. But sleep didn't come easily. Things were going from bad to worse, and it didn't look as though they'd be improving anytime soon.

Chapter 4

THE LIGHTS IN THE HOSPITAL hallway suddenly went off, leaving only a nurse's call light, the light at the nursing station about halfway down the hall, and one of the lamps in the waiting room, creating a rather subdued atmosphere.

Carolyn was thumbing through a magazine when she suddenly stopped and looked at me with her head cocked to one side. "Wait a minute . . ." She paused for a moment, as if she was organizing her thoughts, and then bluntly stated, "I thought you were an atheist."

"I used to be," I admitted. "I was an atheist for about eighteen years. But I didn't stop at just not believing in God, I actually became anti-Christian, and like Saul, I persecuted Christians whenever I had an opportunity. I never went so far as to physically abuse them, but much to my regret, I seldom passed up a chance to embarrass or humiliate them. In fact, at the college where I was teaching in California, if any of my students said something about having 'found Jesus,' I would find some way to make fun of them. In some convoluted way, I was convinced that it was the Christians who were closed-minded, not we atheists. I even had a large, wooden sign, which read, *Thank God I'm an Atheist,* carved and hung on the wall of my office."

With deep furrows forming on her brow, she again cocked her head and asked, "How does someone become an atheist?"

"No one is born an atheist. Atheism is either taught or individually arrived at as a result of life's experiences. My decision to become an atheist didn't fully emerge until I realized that the hopelessness of youth was not going to fade away merely because I had become an adult. For me, atheism was an intellectual refuge, a philosophical position taken in a desperate attempt to cope with the chaos of life. Atheism was a means by which I could put to rest another one of my seemingly unanswerable questions, *What is the purpose of life?*"

"So, did atheism provide an answer to the purpose of life?" she asked.

"I once thought it did. After I got out of the army and went back to college, I found myself agreeing with the French existentialist, Jean-Paul Sartre, who believed that life had no purpose except for the goals we set for ourselves. He was convinced that God didn't exist; that we are alone, completely abandoned; and that we could count on no one but ourselves. But Sartre was wrong.

"I've since learned that there is a purpose to life, God does exist, and we *can* depend on others—including God," I declared with conviction. "Carolyn, whether you realize it or not, we are all participants in a grand plan that gives each of us an opportunity to come to earth and exercise agency—to choose between good and evil. Sure, we'll occasionally make mistakes and choose not to follow Christ's teachings, like I did, but the beauty of God's plan is that it includes the opportunity to repent, change our ways, and be forgiven."

"That's the only purpose of life?"

"No, but it's one of the biggies," I answered with a smile. "Another purpose is to give us an opportunity to grow personally and spiritually, to overcome our imperfections.

"However, I personally believe one of the most important purposes in life is to learn how to love," I continued. "One of the great commandments that Jesus gave us was to love others. I personally don't think he intended that commandment to be solely for the benefit of others, for Jesus loved everyone, yet many ended up wanting Him to be crucified. I think it's possible that He gave the commandment to love others as He loves us in hope that we could experience what it feels like to love others the way He loves us. Along these lines, if we do manage to get to heaven, I doubt that we will be asked how many people we got to love us. But we might very well be asked how many people we loved."

Carolyn turned to look out the window that was now reflecting the glow of the city lights. She sat in silence for a while before speaking. "While we were children, I tried to believe in God. Though we were raised as Catholics, I never acquired what I could really call a personal knowledge of God. I knew there was something tangible called the Catholic Church, which, along with the Salvation Army, would occasionally provide us with food and clothing, but the existence of God was a little too abstract, and even today, my belief in God is a little shaky. But when I do imagine what God is like, I usually think of that judge we appeared before in Phoenix."

I nodded in agreement. "Judge Malcolm," I recalled.

***

Spring 1947

Phoenix, Arizona

The next morning, I found myself waking to what sounded like someone banging on the hall door. I rolled over, half fell out of bed, stumbled to the bedroom door, and peered through the crack. I saw Dad fumbling around with the lock and then opening the hall door a couple of inches.

"Who are you, and what do you want?" he asked with a definite sharpness in his tone.

"I'm Mrs. Porter. Mrs. Cynthia Porter," the woman in the doorway replied firmly. "I'm with the Arizona Division of Social Services."

"So?"

"I'm here to see Carolyn and Buddy Poduska. Are you their father?"

"That's me, all right," Dad said curtly.

"I don't know about you, Mr. Poduska, but I'd prefer not to conduct business out here in the hall. May I come in?"

"Sorry about that," Dad said and opened the door wide.

Mrs. Porter stepped through the doorway and stopped in the middle of the room, calmly surveying her surroundings. She was tall and slim, wearing a blue two-piece suit. Her blonde hair was cut in a poodle style; the yellow ringlets bounced with each turn of her head.

"So you're a social worker," Dad mumbled as he reached past her to push some of his clothes off the chair and onto the floor. Then, appearing a little flustered, he gathered up the pile and threw it into the closet.

"I assume your wife isn't at home?"

"That obvious, huh?" Dad said, giving a slight smile. "She has the breakfast shift and had to leave early."

"No need to apologize," she replied, a broad smile illuminating her face. I liked the way she smiled.

Dad reached into the paper sack sitting on the floor and pulled out two bottles of Falstaff. While holding them above his head, he asked, "Care for an eye opener?"

"My eyes are already open, thank you."

"Yeah. Of course."

"I *do* need to see the children, Mr. Poduska. For the record."

"They're in the other room. Try not to wake 'em."

I made a beeline back to bed, scrambled under the covers, and closed my eyes. The bedroom door eased open, and several seconds passed before I heard her whisper, "They look like two stray kittens."

I didn't dare open my eyes, but I could smell the sweet aroma of her perfume. A moment later, the bedroom door closed quietly. She was gone, but her fragrance still lingered.

Carolyn, who was awake by now, was just about to say something when we heard someone at the door. I motioned to her, and we both closed our eyes and pretended to be asleep.

The social worker's perfume grew stronger again, and I could hear the rustle of her clothes. Jeez! Is she going to stand there forever? But then the door closed a moment later, and I opened my eyes. Carolyn was staring back at me.

"Who was that?" she whispered.

"Some kind of social worker," I whispered back.

We crept quietly out of bed. Carolyn put her ear to the bedroom door while I bent over to look through the keyhole.

"Can you see anything?" she whispered.

"The lady in a blue suit is sitting on one of the kitchen chairs with a notepad on her lap. Shhh . . . I can barely hear them."

The social worker glanced down at her notes on her clipboard. "One of the officers quoted your daughter as saying, 'Mom and Dad went bar hopping.' Is this a common practice?"

"Jeez, until last night, I hadn't given it much thought."

"Well, Mr. Poduska, perhaps it's time you gave such matters a little more thought. Your parental behavior was not only inappropriate, it's also illegal to leave young children like Carolyn and Buddy unattended. I intend to continue my investigation, and I can assure you that if I do find a pattern of neglect, I'll be forced to take appropriate action."

"Such as?"

"If you and your wife fail to adequately provide for the care and safety of the children, they could become wards of the state and could be placed in a foster home."

I didn't hear much after the words *foster home.* Ending up in a foster home or, worse, being separated and ending up in different foster homes, were two of my greatest fears.

"Did you hear what she said about foster homes?" I asked Carolyn anxiously.

"Only a little."

"I ain't going to no foster home," I whispered defiantly.

I looked through the keyhole again and could see the social worker folding her notebook and pulling the strap of her purse over her shoulder. Apparently, the interview was over.

"It may take me a while to complete my investigation," she informed Dad. "In the meantime, I'll recommend that the children be allowed to remain with you."

"Beats putting them out on the street," Dad said, with a twinge of sarcasm.

"My primary concern is the welfare of the children. The two of you should've considered the possible consequences before you jeopardized the lives of those children. I'm afraid it's out of your hands now."

Three days went by before we saw the social worker again. Carolyn and I were walking home from the bus stop, in no particular hurry to get back to the stifling confines of the small apartment. Even though it was early spring, it was hot and getting hotter. I was pretending to be an airplane, my arms fully extended. Carolyn was entertaining herself by kicking a tin can along in front of her.

As we approached a car that was parked at the curb, a woman climbed out of it.

"Well, hello there," she said in a friendly, cheerful tone.

Carolyn immediately stopped kicking the can and looked up. "Who are you?"

"My name is Mrs. Porter. Cynthia Porter," she answered pleasantly, then shifted her attention to me as I cautiously came up behind my sister. I slowly folded my wings, eying her suspiciously, and then I realized that it was the same lady who'd come to talk to Dad the other morning. She had her hair done up differently, and she was wearing slacks, or I would've recognized her sooner. "You're the social worker!" I blurted without thinking.

At that, Carolyn reached out and took my hand. "Did you come to take us away? We don't want to go to no foster home."

The lady smiled, as if to ease our fears, and then bent down so that we were all more or less on the same level. She spoke in a soothing, caring tone. "No, I'm not here to take you away. I just want to ask you a few questions."

"'Bout what?" Carolyn asked suspiciously, narrowing her eyes. "We're not supposed to talk to strangers."

"Well, I'm not really a stranger. I thought the two of you were asleep during my last visit, but since you recognized me, Buddy, you must have been awake after all."

Pretty smart lady, I thought.

"I stopped by today to see how you're doing."

"We're doing just fine, Mrs. Porter," Carolyn said defensively, pulling me closer.

"I'm sure you are, but I'd still like to know a little more about you." The social worker pulled out her clipboard. "And since we're going to get to know each other, why don't you call me Cindy? Now, let's see . . . Carolyn, it says here you're only in the fifth grade and that you've just turned twelve. Aren't you a little old for the fifth grade?"

"They held her back a year," I volunteered. "They said she couldn't read."

"I can so read," Carolyn countered. "I can read better than you."

"I'm sure you both read very well," Mrs. Porter reassured.

"What else does your little book say about us, *Cindy?*" Carolyn challenged, placing a sarcastic emphasis on the woman's name.

Mrs. Porter didn't react to Carolyn's rudeness. She merely looked down at her clipboard and went on. "And Buddy, I see you're in the third grade. How are you doing in school?"

"Okay, I guess."

"Sometimes it's hard to do well in school if you haven't had enough to eat," she continued in a casual tone. "Tell me, have you ever gone to school hungry?"

"Most of the time we don't have any breakfast," I answered. Carolyn pinched me through the back of my shirt, and I knew I'd said something wrong. I lowered my head and began concentrating on the stick I was rolling under my foot.

"But that isn't our mom's fault," Carolyn interjected. "Mom buys us boxes of Cream of Wheat or Malt-o-Meal, but sometimes the milk goes sour."

"And how about when you come home from school? Do you ever have a snack or, now that it's so hot, something to drink?"

Thinking it would make a funny story, I decided to tell her one of our secrets. "If Dad's asleep when we get home, Carolyn and I sneak a few swigs from the beer bottles he leaves around."

"We only did that once."

"More than once. Remember the time we—"

"That's all right," Mrs. Porter said, letting out a big sigh as she straightened. "I've heard enough for one day."

A subpoena, ordering us to appear before a judge, was served a few weeks later. Mom and Dad argued for hours over whose fault it was. At first they blamed each other, but eventually they concluded that it was the war's fault; nothing had been the same since the war.

The day we were to appear before the judge, Mrs. Porter drove over and picked all of us up in her car. She told Carolyn and me that this was to be "our last interview," which sounded rather ominous. We arrived at the courthouse about twenty minutes before our scheduled meeting with a Judge Malcolm. As we were climbing the courthouse steps, Dad said, "Let's hold up a minute. I want to finish this cigarette."

Carolyn and I sat down on the steps to wait and listen to the adults talk.

Mom's face looked tense and drawn. "Do you think this might be God's way of punishing me?" she asked.

"What's God got to do with anything?" Dad snapped.

"I mean, could God have the kids taken away from me because I haven't been a very good mother?"

Dad's eyes rolled upward. "This may come as a complete shock to you, Gladys, but I don't think *God* gives a rat's rear end one way or another. The only one you've got to worry about is some judge who thinks he's God. He's the one who's going to decide whether we get to keep the kids or not. So if you have to worry about someone, worry about the judge."

"That's just it . . . What if I worry too much and end up saying the wrong thing?"

"Jeez, Gladys, where've you been anyway? In cases like this, the judge has already made up his mind, so it doesn't matter what you say or how you say it. This is already a done deal—we've just been invited to take part in the formalities."

Dad took one last drag on his dwindling butt and then gave it a flip with his index finger. The small missile sailed in an arc over the steps below us and onto the sidewalk, bouncing once in a small shower of sparks before rolling into the gutter.

"Well, we might as well get it over with," Mrs. Porter sighed. "Judge Malcolm doesn't like to be kept waiting."

Mom hooked her hand into the crook of Dad's arm. I think she was trying to conjure up a look of confidence, but she managed only a weak smile that flashed quickly and then disappeared into stress lines.

The five of us pushed our way through the tall glass doors that opened into a large vestibule, a vast openness that made me feel insignificant and vulnerable.

Mrs. Porter stopped at one of the office doors, knocked, and then stepped partway in, motioning for us to follow.

The man standing in the middle of the room was probably in his late fifties, early sixties. He looked exactly like I'd imagined a judge would look—gray hair and bushy eyebrows. A large black robe hung on the wall behind him.

He put an arm around Mrs. Porter's shoulders. "Good morning, Cindy!" he said, almost shouting. "I'm always glad to see a pretty face and a friendly smile."

"And a good morning to you, Your Honor," she replied, with equal enthusiasm, and then turning to us, she added, "I'd like to introduce you to Mr. and Mrs. Poduska and their two children, Carolyn and Buddy."

During the introductions, the judge nodded politely but made no attempt to shake hands, and his smile gradually faded as he escorted us into his chambers.

His next statement explained why the smile had been so brief. "Unfortunately, Cindy, your presence usually means children are being mistreated. So I'm never quite sure just how glad I should be to see you."

Mrs. Porter motioned for us to sit down in the chairs that were lined up against one wall. We obediently took our seats, and then she proceeded to give her report.

As soon as she finished, Judge Malcolm leaned back in his chair with another deep sigh, removed his glasses, and looked directly at Mom and Dad. "I must inform you that I concur completely with Mrs. Porter's findings," he said soberly. "It is, therefore, my decision to have the state rescind your legal custody of Carolyn and Buddy and grant such custody to the State of Arizona until such time as you convince me that you are once again capable of assuming proper parental responsibility for the welfare and safety of these children."

I sat listening, not fully understanding what was going on. Dad smirked and leaned over to Mom, who was staring off into space. "I told you it was a done deal," he said smugly.

The judge turned to Mrs. Porter. "I assume you've made inquiries with regards to a foster home?"

"I have, Your Honor."

The judge then issued a thirty-day restraining order, forbidding Mom and Dad to have any contact with us.

"Is there anything further you wish to say on your behalf, Mrs. Poduska?" he asked.

Mom didn't look up or speak. She slowly shook her head, tears streaming down her face.

"Mr. Poduska?"

Dad also shook his head and said nothing.

"I'll expect the two of you to meet with me again in thirty days," the judge went on. He paused and then added with an air of finality, "This hearing is adjourned."

I felt sick to my stomach. I also had to pee.

Mrs. Porter stood up and walked toward us.

"What's happening?" I asked, turning anxiously to Carolyn.

"I'm not sure," she said, and then she reached out and touched the social worker's arm. "What's going to happen to Buddy and me?"

Mrs. Porter looked down at us, slowly shaking her head. "God only knows, Carolyn. God only knows. But for the time being, the two of you will have to be placed in a foster home."

I looked over at Mom and Dad.

"Say good-bye to your parents," Mrs. Porter went on.

We both ran to Mom and Dad and hugged them. No one seemed able to speak. The social worker nudged us gently, and we were ushered out into the hall. It was over that quickly, leaving me thoroughly confused and frightened.

As we walked down the hall, Carolyn and I began sharing the foster home horror stories that we'd heard at school. We solemnly vowed to do something: fight, run away, anything to avoid having to go to a foster home.

"When will we be able to see our parents again?" Carolyn asked, tugging Mrs. Porter's purse strap.

"Not for some time, I'm afraid," she replied. "The judge wants your parents to solve a few problems first. So, for the time being, you're to come with me."

"Come with you where?" I asked. It wasn't cold, but I was shivering.

"I've found someone to take care of you," she said with a slight smile.

"We're old enough to take care of ourselves," Carolyn protested.

"I'm sure you think so," Mrs. Porter replied, "But I'm afraid that's not possible." The three of us entered another office. "Now, I want you to sit right here while I make a phone call," she directed.

We did as she said. In spite of our vows, we didn't fight, we didn't run, we didn't do anything but sit.

A few minutes later, Mrs. Porter turned toward us and declared, "Good news! I've finalized the arrangements for you to stay at a foster home near St. Bernard's. That means you won't have to change schools."

All I could visualize was an old house with a dungeon from which there would be no escape.

"I don't want to go to no foster home!" I cried.

"Where is this foster home, anyway?" Carolyn asked.

"It's near St. Bernard's. This means you won't have to take the bus; you'll be able to walk to school," she said cheerfully. "You will be staying with a nice elderly couple."

A nice elderly couple, I thought. What could possibly be nice about living with an elderly couple?

"How soon do we have to go there?" Carolyn asked.

"Right away. I'll take you back to your rooms so you can get your things, then we'll go straight to your new home."

Carolyn leaned toward me and whispered, "Can you believe we're going to have to live with a couple of old fogies?"

"I can't believe half the stuff that's been happening," I replied.

Mrs. Porter drove us over to the Imperial Hotel to pick up our clothes. As soon as we got inside, Carolyn reached under the sink and grabbed two empty paper bags and handed one of them to me as we walked into the bedroom. We emerged a few seconds later, carrying our sacks as if they were suitcases.

"That's it?" Mrs. Porter said in surprise.

"We don't have much," Carolyn explained.

Mrs. Porter shooed us out into the hallway and locked the door behind her. "You two wait for me in the car," she called out as we reached the front steps. "I'm going to return the landlady's key and use her telephone to call Father O'Flarity and let him know what's happening." She started to walk away then stopped midstride and turned back to us. "You won't try to run away, will you?"

Carolyn shook her head. I shrugged and looked down at my shoes. "We've got no place to run to," I said quietly.

Chapter 5

ONE OF THE NURSES CAME out from behind the nursing station counter and headed down the hall toward the call light blinking outside one of the rooms at the far end of the hall.

Carolyn put down her magazine and restarted the conversation that had apparently been left unfinished. "So, were you an atheist before you went back to college or did you become an atheist afterwards?"

"Before I went back to college," I acknowledged. "I decided to become an atheist while I was still in the army."

"I'm curious," she continued, "Exactly what led you to make that decision?"

"I guess it was a combination of things," I began. "I was stationed at an army missile range where soldiers from all over the world came to fire their air defense missiles. On one occasion, I had a conversation with a soldier from Pakistan about the Islamic religion. Along with telling me about the basics of his religion, he also shared stories about the trials his family had gone through because of conflicts with the Hindus."

"Did you tell him about the trials that your family had gone through?" she asked.

"No, but this conversation reawakened my interest in how organized religions came about. I began looking into the historical backgrounds of world religions, and while sitting in a small Texas library, I had an epiphany. I suddenly realized *why* there were so many different religions. I sat back in my chair, looked down at the pile of religious books spread out in front of me, and concluded they were all man-made! The Egyptian sun-god, the Greek and Roman mythological gods, Hinduism's Brahma, Christianity—the whole lot of them had been created by the imaginations of men."

"Discovering that must have made you feel like God," Carolyn teased.

"Looking back, it really does sound pretty arrogant," I confessed. "Unfortunately, at the time, I had not yet heard of another young man who had also inquired about the correctness of various religions—Joseph Smith. The important difference between Joseph's approach and mine was that he inquired of the Lord for the answer while I sought the answer in the philosophies of men. As a result of his faith, Joseph Smith had the unique privilege of having our Heavenly Father and his son, Jesus Christ, appear before him and ask him to restore the church that Jesus had established two thousand years ago."

"So, all religions were not man-made after all?"

"No," I admitted, "Jesus established His church during His ministry. After the deaths of his apostles, there was an apostasy, a 'falling away' from the original teachings of Christ. So the fullness of the gospel had to be restored."

My belief that there wasn't a God had left me with a feeling of abandonment, a feeling very similar to what I had felt when we were sent to live in a foster home.

***

Late spring 1947

Phoenix to Mesa, Arizona

The first week at the foster home, I learned that in order to save water, we were expected to bathe in our foster parents' bathwater. Fortunately, Carolyn and I were able to find a way around this 'double dipping.' First, I'd get the washcloth wet in the sink and rub myself all over. Then, while Carolyn was using the washcloth to get herself wet, I'd splash some water on the floor in front of the tub. After we were wet enough, we'd put on the pajamas that some other kids had left behind and go say our goodnights. Invariably, we were scolded for not having dried properly, but it was better than bathing in dirty water.

By the end of the second week, I had learned that because 'children's eyes are bigger than their stomachs' they need to wait to be served, that butter is expensive, margarine isn't good for growing children, and that it would be best to eat my bread and pancakes plain. As a consequence, Carolyn and I ended up feeling hungry most of the time.

One night, Carolyn snuck into the kitchen, found some graham crackers and brought them back to our room. I'm not sure why, but stolen stuff always seemed to taste better. We ate them in bed, left crumbs, and got grounded from playing after school. After that, we waited until we were outside before consuming anything we had stolen.

On one of her nightly excursions, Carolyn discovered some money in a baking soda can and stole two dimes. Toward the end of the week, we stopped at a little grocery store on our way home from school and bought some chocolate cupcakes to celebrate my ninth birthday. We had just come out of the store, when a hand reached out and grabbed Carolyn by the shoulder.

I froze mid-step, sure that we'd been caught in the act. Carolyn put her wrists together, as though she expected to be handcuffed, and slowly turned around.

"Mom!" she cried out in joy.

As she threw her arms around Mom's neck, I bear-hugged Mom around the waist, and the three of us held on for dear life. I wallowed in the familiar aroma of stale cigarette smoke, perspiration, and Mum deodorant.

Mom quickly shepherded us around to the side of the store. Glancing over her shoulder, she explained, "I don't want anybody to see us together."

"How'd you find us?" I asked.

"We don't have time to go into that right now. All that matters is that we're going to be together again."

"Have you come to rescue us?" Carolyn entreated.

Mom glanced nervously back at the street again.

"Come on," I pleaded, tugging at both of them. "Let's go."

"Not so fast," Mom cautioned. "We can't go just yet."

"Why not?" Carolyn asked, impatiently.

"If I take you with me now, the people you're staying with will get worried when you don't come home. They'll have the police looking for you within the hour, and that wouldn't give us much time to get away, now would it?"

"No, but . . ." I stammered, frustrated and confused.

"Then when are you going to rescue us?" Carolyn prodded.

"If we wait until tomorrow morning to meet," Mom explained, "you can hide some street clothes under your uniforms so that you'll have something to change into later. If all goes well, they'll think you're at school and we'll have the whole day to get away before they start looking for us."

"Maybe they'll think we were kidnapped," I interjected.

"I doubt it," Mom chuckled. "Besides, when a child disappears in a situation like this, the first person they suspect is one of the parents."

"But you're our mother," Carolyn protested.

"Once the state has taken custody of children, taking them back without permission is breaking the law. The police call it child stealing. And I could end up being arrested."

Reluctantly, we agreed to spend one more night at the foster home. After a few more hurried hugs and kisses, Mom disappeared around the corner, and Carolyn and I headed back to the foster home for what would be our last night.

Getting to sleep that night was all but impossible. I was lying wide-awake in my bunk, staring at the ceiling, when I heard Carolyn start to giggle. I leaned over the side and whispered, "What's so funny?"

"Can you believe it? We'll be out of this creepy place tomorrow?"

We whispered back and forth for some time. As quiet as we tried to be, sometimes we had to stick our heads under our pillows to muffle our giggles.

Getting dressed the next morning was more difficult than anticipated. I tried to pull one pair of pants over the other and ended up getting stuck. Carolyn had to reach through the legs of the second pair of pants and hold on to the bottoms while I pulled on the second pair. She had to pull one skirt up under her armpits so it wouldn't show below her uniform skirt. Needless to say, it took us twice as long to get ready for school, and our foster parents scared the heck out of me when they offered to drive us to school since we were running late.

After assuring them we could get there on time, we hurried out of the house and began running toward the store. The moment we turned the corner, I spotted Mom waiting for us. The hugs were even more hurried than the day before; once we had made good our escape, there would be plenty of time for hugs.

"Do we have time to change?" Carolyn asked as we headed for the bus stop, walking briskly.

"Not right now. Your father's waiting for us at the bus station downtown," Mom explained.

Fortunately, the city bus we needed to get us there arrived on time, and fifteen minutes later, we got off in front of the Greyhound bus station. Dad was waiting at the entrance.

"Hurry!" he called out. "Our bus is about to leave."

The loudspeaker was already announcing the last calls for several destinations. Dad pointed at the double doors on the other side of the waiting room. "The bus we want is number 1054," he said as we ran toward the open doorway.

The four of us joined the melee of other passengers exiting the terminal to board their buses. A station attendant directed us to our bus, which was parked at the far end of the fleet of Greyhounds. We began working our way through the cramped spaces between the buses.

"Where are we going?" I asked.

"Just look for bus 1054!" Carolyn shouted over the noise.

"I don't mean which bus we are getting on," I shouted back. "Where is our bus going?"

Before she could answer, bus 1054 loomed into view, and I was able to read the word *Albuquerque* on the destination sign above the front windows. "We just *came* from Albuquerque!" I protested, but no one seemed to be listening.

As we climbed aboard, Dad gave our tickets to the driver, who kept motioning for us to hurry. The driver climbed in behind us and swung the door shut. "Get yourselves seated," he said. "I'm already behind schedule."

I grabbed a window seat behind the driver, and Carolyn sat down beside me. Mom and Dad took seats across the aisle from us. As the bus started backing out of its stall, I leaned forward so I could see Mom and asked, "Where did we get enough money to buy tickets to Albuquerque?"

She looked back at me and replied, "We're not going to Albuquerque. We only had enough money to get to Mesa."

"How far is it to Mesa?"

"Oh, about twenty-five miles," Dad answered casually.

"Twenty-five miles! Shouldn't we try to get farther away than that?"

"We don't have the money," Mom replied, with a shrug.

"Then what?" I pressed, terrified of being taken back to the foster home.

"Then we hitchhike," Dad said abruptly.

I slumped down in my seat and stared out the window. "Then we'll hitchhike," I mumbled. Then, loud enough for them to hear, I added, "But I don't know how to hitchhike."

Carolyn and I were sitting directly behind the driver, so it was difficult to see straight ahead. I leaned my forehead against the window instead and stared out at the Arizona desert. We were traveling eastward—

away from Phoenix and Camelback Mountain. We passed uncountable acres of grapefruit and orange groves that abruptly gave way to sagebrush and baked earth.

Several minutes passed in silence before Dad asked the driver, "How far outside of Mesa are we?"

The driver glanced up at the overhead mirror. "'Bout five miles."

"Is the Mesa bus station downtown, or out a ways?"

"Downtown."

"Oh." Dad sounded disappointed.

I could see Dad was frowning and shaking his head as the driver once again glanced up at the mirror and asked, "What's the problem?"

"The people we're going to visit live out near the east end of town," Dad lied. "And we don't have money for a taxi."

"Mesa's not very big. Maybe you could walk."

"I guess so. It's just that my little boy is getting over polio, and he still tires easily."

I glanced at Carolyn. Her eyes were wide with surprise. Then I looked up to see the driver staring at me. Quickly, I let my eyes droop and slid down in my seat.

"Polio," the driver said thoughtfully. "Tough disease. I've got a nephew in leg braces."

"It'd be a lot easier on the boy if you could drop us off at the east end of town."

The driver rubbed his chin. "Well, I don't know . . . it's against the rules." He glanced back at us once more. Dad was wearing a forlorn expression. "Oh, why not. I suppose I could take you as far as the city limits," the driver said then quickly added, "but no farther."

Dad relaxed and sank back into his seat, the hint of a smile crossing his face.

A few minutes later, the bus came to a stop in front of a long brick building. "Mesa," the driver announced. The bus door gasped open, and a burst of hot desert air rushed in. I groaned, and the driver turned to me with a chuckle.

"It's only ten o'clock," he said. "If you think it's hot now, wait until midafternoon." He raised his voice loud enough to be heard by the other passengers. "This is a short stop, and the bus will be full when we leave, so I'd advise you to stay in your seats." After making the announcement, he turned to Dad. "You and the missus will have to put the kids on your laps."

A few minutes later, the driver climbed aboard, did a headcount, and we were on our way again.

I soon spotted a small sign that read "Mesa City Limits—Come back soon." Just past the sign, the bus pulled over and stopped in the middle of the Arizona desert.

"You sure this is where you want to get off?" he asked as the air brakes heaved a final sigh.

Dad nodded and stood up to retrieve our suitcase and cardboard box from the overhead rack.

The driver patted me on the head as I moved toward the door. "You get better, son."

"Thanks," I said in a low voice, as I stepped off the bus. As the bus drove away, we just stood there and watched.

I took in a deep breath. The dry air was charged with the strong scent of sage. I shaded my eyes with my hand and surveyed the desolate, cactus-covered dunes. The silence was eerie, only the hint of a breeze rustling past my ears.

The mountains to the north were covered with sagebrush. The nearest range was a chocolate brown, with each succeeding range getting lighter then fading to gray. A dark row of telephone poles ran parallel to the highway, the bare wires shimmering in the sun. To the south, a jagged riverbed carved its way through the desert, rebounding off a cliff in a deep gorge. The massive, barren expanse made me feel small.

"I had polio?" I asked, looking up at Mom.

"Don't worry, Buddy," she said, putting her hand on my shoulder. "You never had polio." She rolled her eyes in Dad's direction, adding, "Your father must have had you mixed up with somebody else."

Dad looked preoccupied and gave no response. *He's probably trying to figure out what we're going to do next*, I thought as I began to study the telephone pole–shaped cacti growing alongside the highway.

"That one looks like a tall skinny cowboy," I remarked.

"Does not," Carolyn shot back.

"Does too," I insisted. "Look. That one's holding his arms up in the air like he's surrendering to a sheriff."

Carolyn shaded her eyes and stared. "I still don't see any cowboys."

"You can if you try hard enough."

Her hands flew to her hips. "Buddy, things are the way they are and not the way you want them to be."

I frowned and turned back to the desert.

We stood in silence for a while, and then Carolyn stepped closer to me. "Sorry."

"It's okay," I muttered.

"What are you looking at now?"

"Those four over there," I said, pointing toward two tall ones and two short ones.

"They look like a nice, normal family," I said.

"And that's what you think we could be?" she asked.

"Maybe it could happen."

"Not to us, Buddy," she said. "Not to people like us."

She was right, of course. What normal family would be standing in the middle of the Arizona desert with nothing but a suitcase and cardboard box?

"Not much out here," Dad said and then, pointing to the west, added, "Except for that old junkyard."

The junkyard was surrounded by a corrugated metal fence and reminded me of an old western fort.

"I think I'll wander over there and see if anyone can tell us what's on down the road," Dad proposed and then, looking down at me, he asked, "Wanna come along?"

I nodded eagerly and fell in beside him. The pavement was hot, so I changed sides and walked in the gravel. I could feel the small stones through the thin soles of my shoes, but at least my feet had stopped burning.

"Do you think maybe we'll be able to get some food there? I'm real hungry," I said.

"We'll see. But don't go begging. We're not beggars."

The junkyard's "office" was an old truck trailer with the wheels taken off. A sign hanging on the door read, "Closed," but the door was halfway open. Dad pushed it open a little farther and called out, "Anybody home?"

"If that's what ya wanna call it," someone with a raspy voice answered from the darkness.

Dad pushed the door all the way open, and we cautiously stepped inside. The air was thick with dust, and bake-oven heat radiated off the metal walls. There were no windows, and except for a mechanic's light hanging from a hook above a two-burner gas stove, the interior was dark and gloomy. Once my eyes began to adjust, I could make out the form of an old gray-haired man sitting in front of a makeshift counter. He was wearing a ragged, plaid shirt with the sleeves rolled up above his elbows. His pants might have been khaki at one time.

Another unshaven, middle-aged man was standing behind the counter, cooking something. He poured a large can of chili into a frying pan, and then he reached for a can of dog food.

I gasped.

The man turned to me with a sinister grin. "What's the matter, sonny? Never made junkyard hash?"

I shook my head.

"Just mix the chili in with some dog food, add some onions . . ." He paused, smacking his lips, then lifted the pan off the stove and extended it toward me. "Wanna try some?"

I stepped behind Dad.

"No?" he said, returning the pan to the stove. "Well, that's all right. There's not enough to go around anyway." He motioned to the old man. "Throw me that hubcap."

"Get it yourself," the old man replied.

"You lazy old son of a . . ." he muttered, moving to retrieve the hubcap. "Excuse my French, boy," he said, with a noticeable slur. He scraped some of the hash into the hubcap and kicked at a sleeping, mangy-looking dog. "Get up, dog!" He then scraped another portion onto a pie tin. Shoving it toward the old man, he looked up at Dad and asked, "What can I do for ya?"

"We're just passing through, and I was wondering what's on down the road."

"What's on down the road?" the man laughed. "Did you hear that? He wants to know what's on down the road."

The old man snorted and continued eating his hash. His one eye seemed to stare at me from its cavernous socket, while the other stayed focused on his meal. A half-empty whiskey bottle sat in front of him.

"Desert," the cook grunted. "Nothin' but desert."

"Any towns?" Dad pressed.

"Towns?"

"How far is it to the next town?" Dad was beginning to sound irritated.

The two men looked at each other and smiled.

"What about the state line?" Dad asked. "How far is it to New Mexico?"

"I'd guess Gallup's probably about a hundred miles," the old man finally offered, still picking at his hash.

"Maybe farther," the cook added.

Dad prodded me toward the doorway.

"Thanks," he said. "We'll let you get back to your meal."

"No hurry," the old man mumbled. "This stuff'll keep. Can't really tell when it does go bad."

We stepped out of the dark trailer, shielding our eyes from the harsh sunlight. "How can people live like that?" I asked.

"Fate can deal some pretty bad hands," Dad said with a shrug.

I shoved my hands in my pockets, lowering my head. "We're not going to end up like them, are we?"

"Don't know where we'll end up," he replied, "except right here, in the middle of nowhere, unless we get ourselves a ride."

By the time we returned, Mom and Carolyn had decided to use the suitcase as a bench. They were sitting back to back, Mom fanning herself with a scrap of cardboard. Carolyn was bent over, elbows on her knees, and her head in her hands.

Dad unfastened the top two buttons of his shirt and began flapping the edges. "Hot," he said.

Mom gave him a look. "What did you find out?"

"Not much."

"So what are we going to do? Just sit out here and bake?"

"I didn't say that."

"Then how far is it to the next town?"

"You think I've got all the answers? All I know is we've got to get out of Arizona, and New Mexico's that way." Dad pointed vaguely down the road.

Mom shaded her eyes and looked in the direction he was pointing. "That's your plan?" she asked in disbelief.

Hoping to avert an argument, I jumped in. "The men at the junkyard say it's a hundred miles to Gallup."

Carolyn straightened and glared at Dad. "You're not expecting us to walk a hundred miles in this heat, are you?"

"Of course not, but as long as we're in Arizona, the law could catch up with us. If we can hitch a ride right away, we could be safely in New Mexico in two or three hours."

With that said, Dad stepped to the edge of the road and stuck his thumb in the air. Mom, Carolyn, and I picked up the suitcase and cardboard box, walked over to a bush, and sat down in what little shade it provided.

"Mom?" Carolyn said after a few moments of silence.

"Yes, Carolyn."

"It's hot. Can I take off my uniform now?"

"Oh, my!" Mom said, mortified. "I'd completely forgotten you were wearing two sets of clothes. Go behind that bush and change." As Carolyn jumped up, Mom looked over at me. "Are you wearing double, too?"

"Yeah. Double pants."

"Take off the top pair and give them to me."

I had just finished peeling off my outer layer, when Carolyn suddenly came running from behind the bushes, her extra clothes held high over her head.

"What on earth's the matter?" Mom said.

Carolyn pointed behind her. "I just saw a lizard!"

The gravity of our situation was instantly forgotten—at least by me. Lizards! Perhaps things weren't so bad after all.

"Don't go wandering off, Buddy," Dad cautioned. "If someone stops to pick us up, we've got to be ready."

The dormant fear of being left behind instantly surfaced. I dropped my last rock and headed back to the others.

As the day wore on and the sun grew hotter, the traffic became lighter. Undaunted, Dad kept pumping his arm and trying to stare down drivers, but none of the cars even slowed down. I had to keep scooting farther back into the shade of the bush. It was no longer possible to rest my bare hands on the sand. Mom was fanning herself with her hand, and the dark spots under her armpits were growing. Dad wiped his forehead with his shirtsleeve then finally came over and sat down in the shade.

He laid his head back on a rock and closed his eyes. "Doesn't look like I'm having much luck," he said.

"You've got to keep trying," Mom said, trying to sound cheerful. "Sooner or later, someone's bound to stop."

"Maybe we'd have better luck if you tried."

Mom gave him a look again. "You're not suggesting that I should try to thumb us a ride . . . like some kind of hooker?"

"That's not what I meant!"

"Maybe I could lift up my dress up a little, or unfasten a few buttons to show some cleavage."

Dad shrugged.

Mom looked angry for a moment, thought for a moment, and then stood up, ran her fingers through her hair, brushed off her dress, and walked over to the side of the road. Turning toward Dad, she smiled as she extended her hand.

"We'll do it together. That way, no one will get the wrong idea."

Chapter 6

IT WAS NEARING MIDNIGHT, AND the silence in the hospital halls was almost complete, interrupted only by an occasional chime of an arriving elevator or the periodic hum of the drinking fountain's refrigeration unit. Carolyn was concentrating on a crossword puzzle in one of the magazines, and I was alternating between reading scriptures on my Palm Pilot and praying.

Carolyn looked up from her magazine and asked, "What's a seven-letter word that means 'to absolve from payment'?"

"Forgive," I answered without hesitation.

Carolyn made several marks on the page of the magazine and declared with a look of triumph. "That fits!" she exclaimed. "You must do a lot of crossword puzzles to know the answer that quickly."

"Not really," I replied. "It's just that I've been reading about Christ's Atonement for our sins."

Carolyn cocked her head and admitted, "You know, I've been curious about that whole Garden of Gethsemane thing. I first heard about it back when we used to go to catechism classes."

"And here I've been thinking that you seldom thought about religious matters."

"Well, I don't think about religion very often, but I have wondered how Christ could have taken on the pain of someone else's sins. I mean, how would something like that be possible?"

"I often wondered about that myself," I confessed. "That is, until an experience I had while serving as a bishop."

Noticing the confused look on Carolyn's face, I took a moment to explain. "A Mormon bishop is similar to a pastor in the Protestant faiths or a priest in the Catholic faith." Carolyn nodded that she understood, and I continued. "One of the responsibilities of a bishop is to sit in judgment when those in his ward, or congregation, have committed a major transgression. On one particular occasion, a man had made an appointment to see me. However, when I arrived at my office, I found both the man and his wife waiting for me.

"I ushered the two of them into my office and closed the door. The two of them sat down and, not knowing the husband's purpose for making the appointment, I asked how I might be of assistance. At first, the husband remained silent while making sidelong glances at his wife. His wife looked bewildered, as if she had no idea why they were there.

"I once again asked what I might do to help, and in response, the husband blurted out his confession. He had been engaged in an adulterous affair for the past year. At first, his wife's eyes flared wide open, and then her shoulders slowly slumped down as she let out a long sorrowful groan, and then she began to writhe and weep uncontrollably.

"I had never witnessed such agony before. I attempted to console her, but the pain of hearing her husband's confession rendered her inconsolable. She repeatedly struck the sides of her head with her wrists and stomped her feet, while continuing to groan and cry out, 'Why? Why? Why?' Her husband reached out to her, but she pushed him away.

"I sat by helplessly, wanting to do something, anything that might help ease her pain. While I watched her suffer, a deeper understanding of what I was witnessing gradually came to me. Someone who was innocent of the sin that another person had committed was taking on the pain of that sin. I felt tears beginning to form—sorrow for both the husband, who had committed the sin, and for his wife, whose love for him was so great that she was now suffering excruciating pain because of his sin."

"I can see the parallels," Carolyn acknowledged.

"I realize that this incident was not the same as what Jesus endured in the Garden of Gethsemane, but it allowed me to have a greater appreciation of the sacrifice Jesus was willing to endure in our behalf."

Carolyn gazed out the window at the darkness for a moment and then began to reminisce. "It's funny, but when I look back at the time we were hitchhiking, I tend to remember the loving sacrifices Mom made for us rather than just the bad times."

"Me, too," I admitted. "Like when we first started hitchhiking out of Mesa. We didn't know where we were going or what was down the road."

***

Late spring 1947

Mesa to Globe, Arizona

While Mom and Dad busied themselves trying to hitch us a ride, Carolyn and I were constructing miniature roads in the dirt. I had just put the finished touches on a bridge, when I heard the sound of tires skidding in gravel.

A small pickup with an insulated ice box filling the back had pulled over. The driver leaned across the seat and pushed open the passenger door. "I guess I've got enough room to give the two of you a lift," he said.

"That's great!" Dad grinned then turned and beckoned to Carolyn and me.

We stood up and started toward the truck. The driver was a skinny teenager wearing a tan uniform with the name of a dairy embroidered on his shirt pocket, the bridge of his eyeglasses held together with Scotch tape. His eyes widened when he saw us walking toward him.

"I'm sorry, mister," he said, "but there's no way I can fit four of you in here. Besides, I'm not supposed to pick up hitchhikers."

"How about if the missus and the girl sit up front with you, and me and the boy ride in back?" Dad quickly suggested.

"You'd suffocate back there," the driver argued. "It's only got one door, no windows, and three inches of insulation."

"Let's take a look," Dad said. "I'll bet we can work something out."

The driver looked down at his watch and shook his head then climbed out of the cab and led me and Dad to the back of the truck. The rear door had a smaller door in the middle.

The driver touched the smaller door and said, "I use this one to check inside without letting in the heat."

Dad suddenly pulled his belt from the loops in his trousers. I jumped back instinctively.

"What if I were to tie this belt around the handle of the little door . . . like this?" Dad said, demonstrating his idea. "That way, I could leave the door open a little, just enough to let some air in and still keep the heat out."

"I don't know," the driver said, scratching his head. He glanced at his watch again, then looked anxiously down the road. "I could lose my job."

"Nonsense," Dad chuckled. "Who's going to know you stopped and gave us a lift?"

"It's going to be cold back there," the driver argued.

"After standing out here in this heat, cold sounds pretty good to me," Dad countered.

The teenager shrugged his shoulders. "Suit yourself."

At that, Mom and Carolyn grabbed our cardboard box and suitcase and climbed into the cab. The driver yanked open the rear door, and Dad and I climbed into the back.

"How far you going?" Dad asked him as I began groping around in the dimly lit interior for a place to sit among the blocks of ice, boxes of butter, and metal racks of bottled milk.

"My route takes me to the other side of Globe, but I have to make a lot of deliveries to some of the dude ranches along the way," he replied. Then, sticking his head through the small door opening, he added, "Some of them are several miles off the main highway, so it might get a little bumpy when we hit the dirt roads." He backed his head out and threaded the end of Dad's belt through the opening.

Dad grabbed it and wrapped it around his hand. "How far to Globe?"

"About seventy-five miles," the driver called out as he headed for the front of the truck.

"Seventy-five miles," Dad repeated quietly, his face silhouetted in the thin beam of light coming through the small opening. "According to the men back at the junkyard, that should put us twenty-five or thirty miles out of Gallup and the New Mexico border." He turned and punched me playfully in the shoulder. "Got us a pretty good ride, didn't I?"

I tried to smile but couldn't. He wouldn't have seen it in the dark anyway. I sat back against the metal wall, and a quick shiver ran through me. I had no idea where we were or where we were going, but I was pretty certain of one thing: this definitely wasn't a good ride.

Dad's dream ride turned into a nightmare whenever the truck turned off the pavement onto dirt roads. I kept waiting for the milk bottles to shatter from all the jostling they were taking.

"I feel like a marble in a tin can," I shouted, bracing my back against one of the metal crates and wedging my feet against the wall.

"Don't worry, Buddy, it won't be long before we get back to the highway. Maybe then things will smooth out a little."

I was lightheaded and tired from the lack of oxygen. The bouncing seemed endless, but the truck finally slowed, and I felt the smoothness of paved highway under the wheels.

I heard Dad groping around on the floor of the truck. "What're you doing?"

"I'm looking for one of those empty milk crates."

"I think I'm sitting on one." I shoved it over to him.

He picked up the metal basket and began banging on the wall. No response.

"Harder, Dad," I encouraged. Dad swore as he beat against the wall.

All of a sudden the truck slid to a stop, and a case of cheese slammed into the middle of my back. Several seconds passed before the door flew open and a rush of fresh air flooded our dark chamber. Dad crawled out first, leaned against the back of the truck for a moment, and then reached in and lifted me down to the ground.

"Are you all right, Buddy?" he asked, checking a small cut on the back of my head.

A nod was all I could manage.

Dad turned angrily to the driver. "Are you deaf or what? Didn't you hear me pounding on the wall?"

The teenager shrugged. "Don't blame me," he said. "You're the one who wanted to ride in the back."

"Well, not anymore," Dad replied then turned toward the cab. "Gladys! Carolyn! Grab our things and get out of the truck. We're going to get ourselves another ride."

Mom and Carolyn scrambled out and hurried to join us. "What's going on?" Mom asked.

"Nothing—except we're tired of bouncing off walls."

Mom and Dad stepped away and began arguing in muted voices. Dad was pacing back and forth with Mom following. Carolyn and I sat down beside the road and tried to ignore them. In the distance, a small town huddled against the base of a red cliff.

"Where are we?" I asked loudly.

Mom and Dad stopped arguing long enough to turn and look down at me. Then Dad looked around at our surroundings and asked the driver, "Are we out of Arizona, yet?"

"We're just outside of Superior."

"Superior, New Mexico?" Dad prodded.

"No. Superior, Arizona. About fifty miles east of Mesa."

Dad's jaw dropped. "Fifty miles east!" he shouted and then proceeded to spew a string of profanities.

Mom grabbed his arm, in an attempt to calm him, before asking the driver, "How far are we from Gallup?"

"Gallup, New Mexico?" the young man chuckled. "'Bout a hundred and seventy miles."

"Wait a minute," Dad huffed. "There's got to be some mistake. The guy back at the junkyard told me Gallup was only a hundred miles from Mesa. And that was hours ago."

"Well, the guy in the junkyard was wrong," the driver said as he climbed back into the cab. "If you stay on Highway 60, Globe's about twenty-five miles dead ahead. But I'm behind schedule and have to get."

Dad hesitated for a moment before motioning the dairy driver to take off.

"I hope you get where you're going," the youth called out as he pulled back onto the highway.

"Good riddance!" Dad shouted after him then stooped down to pick up the black suitcase.

"Where'd he say we were?" I asked.

"Superior," Dad replied. He pointed at the dilapidated billboard on the far side of the road and read the faded words at the bottom. "Superior, Arizona—Founded in 1882."

"Superior," Mom repeated thoughtfully as she turned to Dad. "Superior to what?"

Carolyn nudged me. "The guy that named the Imperial Hotel was probably the same guy that named this town."

We started giggling but quickly went silent when Dad shot us a harsh look.

"I don't see where there's anything to laugh about," he grunted. "The town may not look like much, but at least we'll be able to get out of the sun." He handed Carolyn the suitcase and shoved the cardboard box into my arms.

The walk into town was long and hot, so finding some shade at an abandoned souvenir stand was all the more welcome.

Superior looked to be about three people away from becoming a ghost town, no more than a small cluster of old weathered buildings at the base of some sheer sandstone cliffs. Why anyone would want to come here in the first place, let alone stay, was beyond me. The few cars we saw seemed to be just passing through; they'd slow as they came to the edge of town then speed up again as they left or turned onto Highway 172. Dad positioned us on the east side of this junction.

"No use wasting my thumb on cars that might turn on to 172," he explained. "Anyone headed to Globe will pass by here."

Like it or not, I was gradually learning the finer points of hitchhiking.

Once we were settled, Mom turned away and started walking toward a small store sitting behind the souvenir stand but farther back from the road.

"Where are you going?" Dad asked, indignant.

"To find us something to eat," she called back over her shoulder.

The store didn't look like much from where we were standing. The sign over the window was so badly faded, the only thing I could make out was the word *Store*, and the screen door was hanging by one hinge. Posters made with butcher paper hung crookedly on the windows, heralding the specials of the day.

Several minutes passed before Mom reappeared carrying a loaf of bread in one hand and a small paper package in the other. I realized my stomach was growling, and I pressed on it with my hand.

"What's in the package?" Dad asked when she got closer.

"Cheese!" Mom replied happily.

Carolyn and I sat down on the ground as Mom began tearing off chunks of bread and cheese. I ate slowly, savoring each bite. I had just finished my last piece of bread and was about to ask if I could go find something to drink, when an old Ford pick-up came chugging up to the junction and stopped right in front of us.

Dad commented that the two men sitting in the cab looked like Navajo Indians. A large woman and two children resembling the men stared at us from the bed. The driver lifted his black cowboy hat off of his head, wiped his forehead with his sleeve, and then nodded at the man sitting beside him.

"If you want a ride, climb in back!" the man in the passenger side hollered, leaning out the window.

Dad hurriedly threw the suitcase in the bed and helped Mom climb in. I wrestled the cardboard box over the sidewall then Carolyn and I scrambled over the tailgate and sat down next to the large woman. She was wearing a long dress of black and red velvet, along with several turquoise necklaces and bracelets. She smiled at us, revealing several missing teeth. The boy and girl sitting next to her were dressed in miniature versions of the adults' clothing. They looked to be about our age, but they didn't speak, and the blank expressions on their faces never changed. They just stared at us.

We were still getting settled when the pick-up suddenly lurched forward and died. I glanced at Carolyn, who rolled her eyes. But the woman kept smiling, and the children kept staring.

The driver hopped out with a wrench in his hand, got the engine running again, and climbed back in. He ground the gearshift into first, and the truck slowly crept forward. Every time he shifted, a loud pop and clouds of black smoke came out of the exhaust pipe. The truck finally settled into what seemed to be its top speed, about thirty-five or forty miles an hour. But at least we were on our way again, and that's all that mattered.

As we started climbing the steep canyon out of Superior, the driver began shifting into the lower gears, and our speed slowed so much that he had to drive on the gravel shoulder to allow the faster vehicles—just about every other car on the road—to pass. I dared a look over the right side of the truck; the tires seemed dangerously close to the sheer canyon drop-off.

I quickly turned my attention to the rugged scenery instead. The canyon was mostly a rust color, speckled with shades of pink, white, and brown. Far below, a peaceful-looking river snaked along the bottom of the canyon, but I had seen enough flash floods in movies to imagine what it might look like after a thunderstorm. There weren't many plants—a few cacti that reminded me of Mickey Mouse ears and some gnarly bushes big enough to be trees.

I saw a large, brown hawk hovering in an updraft, searching for an unwary rodent or sunbathing lizard and hoped he'd have better luck than I did. Tumbleweeds bounced by, ricocheting off a large boulder and rolling down the steep embankment below. The wind driving the tumbleweed carried a mixture of strange, unfamiliar plant smells and the pungent odor of roadkill.

The truck picked up a little more speed as we crossed an old concrete bridge that arched across the middle of the canyon, tenuously connecting its sheer walls. The Indian boy tapped me on the shoulder and pointed at a rock formation in a deep crevasse.

"That's Devil's Canyon," he informed me. As it turned out, those were the only words I would hear him say.

As we approached the crest of the canyon, the wind grew stronger, whipping around the back of the pickup now, tearing at our clothes. Dad pointed at the steam billowing out from under the hood and cupped his hands to his mouth. "I wasn't sure we'd make it!" he shouted.

Mom just nodded, trying to keep her hair out of her face.

The ride was uneventful until we came to the outskirts of a small town named Miami. A loud bang and a cloud of smoke shot out from under the hood. The Indian woman threw up her arms and said something in Navajo. The pickup veered left, across the oncoming traffic, and coasted to a stop near a dry creek bed.

The driver calmly climbed out of the truck and lifted the hood. Huge billows of smoke poured out. He took off his hat and tried waving it away, with little success. He threw up his hands, repeated the same words the woman had said, then looked at Dad and shifted to English. "It is dead."

When the man on the passenger side opened his door and climbed out, the woman and two children climbed over the side; the rest of us got the message and began climbing over the tailgate. Without another word, the Navajos gathered up their belongings and started walking into town.

"Now what're we going to do?" I asked in bewilderment.

"Walk," Dad replied, picking up the black suitcase.

"Walk where?"

Wearily, Mom picked up the cardboard box. "It's getting late, and we have to find someplace to spend the night," she said irritably.

We headed in the same direction the Navajos had. As we crossed the bridge over the creek, I could see a whole series of similar bridges all the way through the old mining town. Tall wooden derricks stood in the distance. Mounds of mining debris threatened to engulf the little houses scattered over the hillsides. As we were walking past an old church with the words "Our Lady of the Blessed Sacrament" painted above the door, Dad commented, "I think we've landed in Purgatory."

"What makes you say that?" Mom asked.

"This town is too religious for hell and too ugly for heaven. And no one would stay here any longer than necessary."

I didn't say anything, but I knew he was right. We had ended up in Purgatory, and there was no one to say Mass for us.

After we'd walked from one end of town to the other, I asked, "Where are we going to spend the night?"

Dad pointed at a sign that read, "Globe—3 miles."

Carolyn groaned, "You're not planning on having us walk all the way to Globe tonight, are you?"

"Not all the way," Dad replied, without slowing his pace.

I didn't know exactly what he had in mind, but already I didn't like it.

As it turned out, we walked about another two miles before we came to one of those desert junctions where a dirt road from nowhere intersects a highway to nowhere. Dad stopped and looked around. Carolyn and Mom sat down on the suitcase, and I squatted down on my haunches. I glanced up at the sky and saw the first star appear. Darkness was falling fast, and we were still out in the open. I was starting to feel scared.

My sense of dread intensified at Dad's next words. "We're going to have to spend the night here."

"Here!" Carolyn cried out, horrified.

"Carolyn!" Mom scolded.

"But we're out in the middle of the cotton-picking desert!"

"It's getting too dark to do anymore hitchhiking," Dad explained. "So this is where we're spending the night."

I jumped up, ready to put in my two cents worth, when Dad pointed a finger at me and I decided to keep my opinion to myself. The decision was final. The desert floor would be our bed for the night.

On the bright side, traveling light made setting up camp pretty simple. Mom cleared out an area between some sagebrush to make it more "livable." Carolyn and I gathered some dry sticks, and Dad had a small fire going a few minutes later.

"Do we have anything to eat?" Carolyn asked.

"Yeah, I'm hungry," I added.

Mom dug into her large makeshift purse and pulled out what was left of the bread and cheese, plus a few cookies she'd secreted away.

Dad pulled a bottle of milk out of the suitcase. "Surprise!"

"Where'd you get that?" Mom asked.

"I swiped it from the dairy truck."

Our dinner was light, but at least we ended the day with something in our stomachs. We weren't so lucky when it came to our sleeping arrangements, though. Since we had no bedding, Mom had Carolyn and me dress double again. Then we lay down between her and Dad in an effort to ward off the desert chill.

I stared up at the huge, star-filled sky again. *This morning I left for school in Phoenix,* I thought, *and now I'm lying in the Arizona desert somewhere outside of "Purgatory."*

What's going to happen tomorrow?

***

Dawn comes early in the desert. Even before I was fully awake, I could hear the call of a meadowlark. I willed one eye open. The first thing I saw was sand then Carolyn's hair, all mixed in together. I pulled myself up on one elbow, my right arm aching from having slept on it all night. The sun was rising, glowing behind the crests of the hills. A crisp morning chill had replaced the heat of yesterday. I sat all the way up and began rubbing my arms, trying to work some warmth into them. Mom was already up, sitting beside the fire pit—watching me.

"Good morning, Buddy."

"Mornin'," I replied without much enthusiasm. An involuntary shudder ran up my back, so I got up and joined her. I held my hands out to warm them but found no relief. "Fire's out," I told her.

Just then, Dad came walking back into camp. "Well, don't just squat there like a dummy," he growled. "Go find some wood so I can get a fire started."

"How come I'm the one that has to go find wood?" I complained.

"Because you're the one with the smart mouth, that's why."

I reluctantly got up and wandered off into the sagebrush. Apparently, our exchange had awakened Carolyn because a few seconds later she caught up with me.

"Sometimes he can be a real jerk," she said.

"He's the King Kong of jerks," I muttered.

With both of us gathering sticks, we soon had a couple of armloads of kindling and returned to camp. Dad acknowledged our efforts with a grunt. Once he got the fire going again, we all just sat there quietly warming our hands and staring at the flickering flames.

Carolyn finally broke the silence. "What's for breakfast?"

Mom looked at Dad. "Don't ask me," he said defensively, holding his empty palms out in front of him.

Mom opened her bag and pulled out the half-empty milk bottle Dad had swiped from the dairy truck. She pried off the cardboard cap and handed the bottle to Carolyn. "Don't drink it all," she instructed. "You've got to share some with your brother."

I watched the movement of Carolyn's throat closely, counting the number of swallows she took before handing the bottle to me. I took exactly four, keeping it even. The milk was warm and chalky, but it was better than nothing.

Once we had emptied the bottle, Dad scooped sand over the fire. "We'd better get going," he said. "We should be able to get some breakfast in Globe. If nothing else, I want to find out for sure how far it is to the state line."

Carolyn and I quickly removed the extra layers of clothing we'd put on the night before and handed them back to Mom. We brushed the sand out of each other's hair while walking back to the highway. The traffic was still light, trucks probably headed toward the Miami mines.

"It looks like it's only about a mile or so to town," Dad remarked. "Rather than trying to get a ride, it'll probably be just as fast if we walk."

In spite of my doubts about the distance, it didn't take us very long to reach the outer edge of Globe. A large railroad yard was on our right, and I wondered if riding the rails might be faster than hitchhiking. But then I realized that, since we weren't going anywhere in particular, the time it took us to get there didn't really matter.

Within minutes, I realized that Globe wasn't a whole lot better than Miami; it had the same Purgatory-like feel. It, too, was an old mining town with streets that seemed to meander aimlessly over the surrounding hills. The only difference I could see was that Globe was bigger and it had a movie theater.

Unfortunately, the first thing Dad saw was the Drift Inn Saloon. "I'll just be a few minutes," he said. "You and the kids go on down the street. I'll catch up with you."

"Honey, we don't have money for booze," Mom pleaded, "and what little we do have has got to last us."

"Just one beer," Dad insisted. "I'll catch up with you in a few minutes."

We'd all heard that line before and knew he'd be spending more than just a few minutes in the bar. Tight-mouthed, Mom folded her arms across her chest and began glancing up and down the street as if she was looking for something to kick.

We walked down Broad Street until we came to an old stone courthouse with a small lawn and a big shade tree.

"This looks like as good a place as any," Mom sighed, so we all sat down on the stone ledge to wait.

By the time Dad finally reappeared, I was really getting hungry. "Are we going to get some breakfast now?" I asked.

Mom turned to Dad. "Bernie, the children need to eat something."

"I know," Dad mumbled.

"I saw a little restaurant when we were coming into town," I offered, jumping down from the ledge. "It didn't look expensive. At least, not from the outside."

At Dad's shrug, the four of us backtracked to the small café. As soon as I opened the door, I was immersed in the familiar smells of hot grease, percolating coffee, cigarette smoke, and stale beer. The cook shoved a plate of food through a rectangular opening at the rear of the café, pulled a tag off a revolving metal wheel, and shouted, "Order up!"

Someone put a nickel in the jukebox and selected "I Love You So Much It Hurts."

"Hey, Gladys, maybe this could be our song," Dad chuckled.

"I don't think the kind of hurt I'm feeling is caused by love," Mom laughed.

Two booths and a counter ran along one side of the room, and three smaller booths nestled against the other wall. Truckers and ranchers occupied all of them, except one. Mom and Dad were still chuckling as we made our way to the empty booth.

I hadn't given much thought to how we must have looked after our night in the desert, but it must have been obvious. From the time we walked into the cafe, the waitress had been watching us. I started to feel a little self-conscious.

"Why do you think that waitress is staring at us?" I asked. "She's looking at us like we're a bunch of Martians."

"Yeah," Carolyn added. "And the guy behind the counter's watching us like he thinks we're gonna swipe something."

Mom pulled a tube of lipstick out of her purse. Using the side of a metal napkin holder as a mirror, she began applying it to her lips. When she was finished, she blotted them with a napkin. "Well? How do I look?"

"You look fine, Gladys," Dad reassured. "But since we don't know anyone here, I don't think it matters how you look."

"Well, I still want to look nice for you."

Dad looked away as if bored.

The waitress finally came over and took our order of two bowls of oatmeal and two cups of coffee. A few minutes later, our order arrived, but it was the big guy behind the counter who brought it.

As the man set Dad's coffee down, Dad asked, "Would you happen to know how far it is to Gallup?"

"Oh, I'd say about two hundred miles."

Dad shook his head. "Talk about a moving target."

He set the bowls of oatmeal in front of Carolyn and me. "I don't mean to pry," he said in a low voice, "but I think there were some people in here last night looking for you folks."

"What makes you think they was looking for us?" Dad asked.

"The guy had a picture of the lady and the kids."

"Police?" Dad pressed.

"Nah, this guy looked like he was government, but I don't think he was a cop."

"Any idea where he might be now?"

"No idea. But he had a good-looking blonde with him."

"I bet that was Mrs. Porter," I volunteered then felt Dad's foot prodding me under the table.

"Anyway," the man went on, "they left here around eight o'clock last night and never came back."

"That was close," Dad said pensively. Then he turned to Mom. "How in the world did they track us to Globe?"

"I have no idea. But that Mrs. Porter can be pretty resourceful."

"Well, if that social worker can do it, the police can do it, too," Dad said nervously as he looked at the prices on the menu and began counting his change. "We'd better eat up and try to get across the state line before they find us."

Chapter 7

SINCE NEITHER OF US COULD sleep, we decided to walk down to the nurse's station to check on Mom's condition. After we were told that there was no change, we wandered back to the waiting room area. I was caught completely off guard when Carolyn said, "You know . . . I considered becoming a nurse once upon a time."

"I never knew that," I confessed, unable to suppress my astonishment. "How come you didn't?"

Carolyn gave a little shrug. "Simple—I never finished high school," she explained. She paused before adding, "Which brings up something that I've always been curious about."

"What's that?"

"How in the world did you not only finish high school but go on to college?"

"It wasn't easy. I couldn't have done it without the help I received along the way. By the time I was in the eleventh grade, I'd all but dropped out of school; I was absent forty-five days during the fall semester. Once my truancy was uncovered, I was sent to the school counselor. When he asked why I had missed so much school, I told him that I had had a mild case of polio when I was younger and that every once in a while it would flare up."

"Old lies die slowly," Carolyn quipped.

"To make matters worse, the counselor pulled out my file and informed me that my Iowa tests scores in grammar and spelling ranked me in the tenth percentile of the nation, which qualified me as functionally illiterate. Paradoxically, my science scores were in the ninetieth percentile, so he authorized a retest. My grammar and spelling scores on the retest were even lower. The counselor asked me how I had managed to get as far as I had in school. I told him that I'd usually get extra points for doing extra stuff, which made up for the points I'd lose because I didn't know how to spell."

"Boy, can I relate to that," Carolyn empathized.

"Fortunately, a kindhearted English teacher heard my predicament and offered to tutor me during lunchtime. 'Sharing sandwiches and participles,' he used to say. We continued to meet every noon hour for the rest of the semester. It was that English teacher that helped me graduate from high school and then finagle a poverty scholarship to Humboldt State College."

"I can't imagine how hard it must have been for you to go to college," Carolyn declared.

"It was horrific," I confirmed. "I struggled through the first year and then transferred to the University of California at Berkeley, where I fell flat on my face. I ended up on academic probation, dropped out of school, and joined the army."

"When did you go back to college?"

"Not until two or three years after I was discharged," I explained. "College was still a challenge, but after working in construction for a couple of years, I knew there had to be a better way. I managed to earn a bachelor's and a master's degree in psychology, but not without some difficulty. In those days, I was still trying to gain control over life's struggles. I was trying to make my will dominate situations. In contrast, after my conversion, and with frequent reminders from my wife, Barbara, I learned to turn things over to the Lord—not my will, but His will be done. Initially, turning it over to the Lord was difficult for me. I wanted to be self-reliant and make things happen. Fortunately, I finally learned to do all I could and then turn it over to the Lord."

"It seems like that would take a great deal of trust," Carolyn noted.

"That pretty much nails it," I agreed. "It's interesting: The word *trust* stems from the Scandinavian language and refers to the ability to feel comfortable while vulnerable. In the early days, a traveler would set out on his journey and walk until nightfall and then look for smoke from a chimney. The traveler would then knock on a door, and those who lived in the home would invite the traveler in, not knowing if they were letting in a thief or even a murderer. The traveler would also be apprehensive, not knowing if he would be robbed in his sleep. But if the hosts and the guest were able to become comfortable, a state of trust was achieved."

"So did you ever learn to trust the Lord?" Carolyn asked.

"I realized that before I would be able to 'turn it over to the Lord,' I would have to learn to trust Him. Of course, not having had an earthly father that I could trust made me somewhat hesitant when it came to trusting God. Yet, in the scriptures, God tells us that He cannot lie and that if we make a covenant with Him, He will keep His part of the agreement. And that's a father that I've learned to love and trust."

Carolyn shook her head thoughtfully. "I still have difficulty trusting."

"Has there ever been someone that you really trusted?"

"Not recently," she replied. "But there have been a few."

"Like who for instance?"

"Well, I trusted that preacher that picked us up when we were hitch-hiking out of Globe."

"Reverend Sanderson," I recalled.

"Yeah. Reverend Sanderson. I trusted him."

***

Summer 1947

Globe, Arizona, to Gallup and Shiprock, New Mexico

Fearing that the authorities might track us down, Carolyn and I ate hurriedly while Mom and Dad gulped down their coffee. We left the café and walked to the other end of Globe, where Highway 60 veered off to the northeast and Highway 70 intersected from the southeast.

"There's nothing for us to the south," Dad said, thinking out loud. "Gallup's to the north, so we'd best stay on 60." He picked a spot just beyond the junction and took up his hitchhiking position, explaining that he'd chosen that particular place because it was far enough away from the junction to allow a car to complete its turn, but close enough to catch it before it had time to gain too much speed.

A few old trucks went by, along with some newer cars, but no one stopped. Heat waves started shimmering over the asphalt, and I saw a water mirage farther down the road. Looking at it made me thirsty, and I began eyeing the milk bottle in Mom's purse. She had filled it with water and was carrying it with the neck sticking out to keep it from spilling. I was contemplating the life expectancy of the cardboard cap when Carolyn tapped me on the shoulder.

"Look, Buddy," she said, pointing at a cloud of dust rising above the desert hills.

From the way the dust was swirling, I guessed that it must be a car driving on a dirt road. It was still a long way off, but it was headed in our direction. Mom and Dad had noticed it too, and the four of us stood there expectantly.

"I don't know why," Mom said confidently, "but I've got a feeling that that dust cloud is our ride."

The dust cloud turned out to be a black, four-door sedan that came to a stop directly in front of us. The driver leaned toward us and shouted, "You folks need a ride?"

"Boy, do we ever!" Dad shouted back.

"Then climb in," the sandy-haired man responded with equal enthusiasm. "I'm Reverend Sanderson, First Church of Christ."

"And we're the Poduskas. I'm Bernie, and this is my wife Gladys." Dad motioned us into the back seat as he completed the introductions. "These two ragamuffins are Carolyn and Buddy."

I didn't appreciate being called a ragamuffin, but I'd been called worse—dimwit came to mind. What mattered was that we were finally out of the sun and on our way to New Mexico.

The Reverend Sanderson was a wholesome-looking man in his midthirties. Like Carolyn, he had lots of freckles. His hair was so fine that it looked as though he didn't have any eyebrows, and his eyes had a twinkle to them.

Reverend Sanderson told us he'd been visiting some church members on the Apache Indian reservations and was heading back to Gallup.

"I don't know how," Mom confided to him, "but the moment I saw that dust cloud your car was making, I knew you were going to be our ride."

The minister smiled knowingly. "The Lord does indeed work in mysterious ways."

The first part of the trip was nothing but idle chitchat and boring scenery. The desert seemed to be getting drier, if that was possible. I saw a lot of the flat, Mickey Mouse cacti, but scrubby-looking trees began dotting the hillsides as soon as we started climbing.

The reverend glanced at the hills on my side of the car and volunteered, "Those are cedar pines. You'll be seeing a lot of those from here to the Salt River Canyon."

Whoop-de-do, I thought as I gazed out at the unchanging scenery. Occasionally I'd see a windmill or an abandoned corral, but not much else.

We continued to climb for several miles, and the engine began to over-heat. But the reverend didn't seem any more concerned than the Indians in the old pickup, so I decided I wasn't going to worry about it either. But then, without warning, the engine died. I sat up and looked at the instrument panel in the dashboard; all the gauges were on zero, including the gas.

"Did we run out of gas?" I cried out in frustration.

"Nah," the driver chuckled. "I always turn off the engine when I get to the top. That way, I can save gas and cool the engine off on the way down."

"But what if your brakes don't last all the way down?"

"Don't worry. The brakes usually hold out till I reach the river, but sometimes the drums overheat and the brakes fade."

As soon as we reached the bottom of the canyon, the reverend turned the engine on and popped the clutch. The engine caught just as we came to a narrow bridge with steel railings and pillars at both ends.

"No brakes," the reverend calmly informed us as we careened across the bridge and started up the other side of the canyon. "But we'll get them back by the time we reach the top."

Just as he'd promised, the brakes returned before we reached the top. We left the brown cliffs of the Salt River Canyon and drove onto flat country, where horses were grazing and little log cabins were scattered among the trees.

"How far is it to the next town?" I asked.

"Getting hungry?" the reverend said with a chuckle then turned to Dad. "Did I tell you I've got six kids of my own? Whenever one of mine asks how far it is to the next town, it's usually because they're getting hungry."

"How far is it to the next town?" I pressed.

"We're probably about fifteen miles out of Show Low."

When we stopped in Show Low for gas, Dad made a halfhearted gesture to help pay for some of it, but the reverend refused. A little ways out of Show Low, we took the left branch at a Y in the road—the branch that led to St. John and Gallup. Complete barrenness stretched to the horizon in every direction. The only break in the monotony came shortly after we passed through St. John, where a large group of Indians were selling jewelry, pottery, and blankets out of lean-tos on the side of the road.

Eventually we turned onto Highway 66. The four of us gave a loud cheer when we finally crossed the New Mexico state line.

Half an hour later, we pulled into Gallup. The town stood on low hills of yellow rock that even the sagebrush seemed to be having a tough time holding on to. Off to our left I noticed a busy rail yard, filled with the sounds of switch engines and cars coupling and uncoupling. To our right was a large cemetery. As we drove past a narrow alley that ran the entire length of the town, Reverend Sanderson told us that the alley served as a runoff creek when it rained, but that it seldom rained.

Many of the houses were built at the top of the steep hills. Most were small with no front yard; the people living in them would open their front doors and step right onto the sidewalks. Between some of the houses stood an occasional trailer, and it turned out that Reverend Sanderson lived in one of those. He honked the horn as we pulled up. The trailer door flew open, and a string of towheaded kids streamed out, reminding me of the circus clowns who keep coming out of a little car. An instant later, the reverend was covered from head to toe with children.

As we were getting out of the car, Reverend Sanderson looked back at Dad and asked, "Do you have a job lined up or a place to stay?"

"No on both counts," Dad replied.

"Well, I don't know what we can do about a job just yet, but I've got a place in mind where you could stay for a while."

Following a flurry of introductions, the reverend explained the situation. "I'm building a house out back, or at least trying to. It's obviously not finished yet, but it's got a roof on it, and the outer walls have been closed in. I'm not hooked up to city water yet, but I could run a hose over and . . . well, what I mean is, you folks are welcome to stay in it till you can find something better."

Dad looked over at Mom, who shrugged her shoulders. He turned back to the reverend. "Are you sure we wouldn't be putting you out?"

"Not at all," the reverend reassured.

"Sounds good to me then," Dad said.

"Anything's better than sleeping out in the desert," I whispered to Carolyn.

"Well, that's one problem solved," the reverend declared, rubbing his hands together. He looked at Mom. "Why don't you and my wife start making a list of what you need to get settled while I talk to your husband about finding him some work?" As the six of us began walking toward the unfinished house, he threw an arm around Dad's shoulders. "By the way, Mr. Poduska, what kind of work do you do?"

"Fry cooking or meat cutting," Dad replied. "And the name's Bernie."

"Well, Bernie, I just might know where you can get a job," the reverend said with a pat on the back.

Construction material was scattered everywhere. The front steps hadn't been built yet, so a wooden plank was propped against the front door threshold. The interior walls were roughed in, but nothing had been drywalled. Carolyn and I began running excitedly from room to room, getting a kick out of walking through unfinished walls.

The reverend took in our sparse belongings and softly said, "The wife and I have some extra bedding and a camping stove we can bring over. Bernie, why don't you ride into town with me? Let's see what we can do about finding you a job."

True to his word, Reverend Sanderson got Dad a job as a fry cook in a local café that was open twenty-four hours a day. However, the shifts turned out to be long, twelve-hour grinds. Near the end of the first week Dad complained, "The owner's a hard man to get along with. Always harpin' about somethin'."

"When do you get paid?" Mom asked.

"Friday, I think."

"I hope so," she sighed. "We're down to our last dollar."

"I know, Gladys," Dad snapped. "I can add same as you."

But Friday came and went without pay. The excuse the owner had given was that Dad had to work for a full week first.

Indignant, Dad ranted, "I don't believe that cock-and-bull story he told me for one minute. But next Tuesday I'll have worked a full week, so one way or another, I'm gonna get paid."

Tuesday night, Dad was late. When he finally arrived, he was swearing under his breath.

"If you'd stop cursing long enough," Mom said impatiently, "I'd like to know what's got you so riled."

Dad calmed down a little. "I hung around after my shift, waiting for the owner to show up and pay me. I waited for over an hour, but he never showed. I got suspicious and asked the other cook what he had been told about getting paid."

"And?"

"And he said that he'd been told that he wouldn't get paid till the end of the month."

"But that's almost two weeks from now!"

"Eleven days, to be exact."

Since there were no walls to muffle their conversation, I was listening but pretending to be asleep. The more they talked, the madder Dad got, until he finally took off.

I don't know when he got home, but Mom didn't bother to wake him the next morning until it was almost time for his shift. When he did get up, he was really hung over, telling Mom how he had shown the owner of the café a thing or two. Mom was telling him how she hoped he hadn't done anything foolish when he began waving a fistful of money. He told her that he had finally gotten paid. Unconvinced, Mom kept asking questions.

"Okay! Okay!" he shouted. "Get off my back! So I took the money from the cash register. He owed it to me. If I hadn't taken it, he never would've paid me."

"I'm sure you're right, honey, but what you did was the same as stealing. The owner could have you arrested. What would me and the kids do if you got thrown in jail?"

"So that's what you're really worried about? Taking care of your own skin?"

"That's not what I meant, and you know it," Mom sighed in frustration. "You always twist what I say."

Dad shifted uneasily. "Well, the money won't be counted until this morning, so we're safe for a while."

We began folding the blankets the Sandersons had loaned us and stacked them in a corner. Mom piled some cans of food on the floor beside me and told me to pack them in the cardboard box. I was coming to realize that the box was *my* responsibility.

I was still packing it when I heard a car pull up in front and the sound of a door slamming. My heart started racing; I was convinced that the police had come to arrest Dad.

"I think the police are here!" I yelled.

Dad immediately started toward the back door and Mom ran to the window.

"Wait!" she shouted. "I think it's one of the waitresses from the café."

Dad came back and looked out the window. "It's only Velma," he sighed in relief and then opened the front door.

"Bernie! You've got to get out of town!" Velma pleaded.

"What happened?"

"The owner found out about the missing money and called the sheriff. Jan told him that you'd taken only what you had coming to you. He called the sheriff's office anyway. He said you were going to get twenty years for this, and no dumb fry cook was going to outsmart him. I've never seen him so mad. You'd better get out of town while you can."

"Thanks, Velma," Dad called out. "We're on our way."

"Jan's covering for me, so I've got to get back," she yelled back, as she hurriedly returned to her car. "Good luck."

Mom wrote a quick thank you to the Sandersons and began cleaning what would someday be the kitchen.

"Let's go! We don't have time for that," Dad protested.

"What kind of housekeeper will Mrs. Sanderson think I am, leaving the place looking like this?"

"Who cares what she thinks? We'll never see her again."

"It's not just what *she* thinks of me. It's what *I* think of me," Mom explained while cautiously following us down the plank.

We scrambled down the hill and across the railroad tracks to Highway 666, which ran north toward Shiprock. Dad's plan was to cross into Colorado north of Shiprock on the way up to Durango.

"We're going to run out of states pretty soon," Mom noted.

"Hey, I'm not the only one they're looking for," Dad reminded her. "You're the one who swiped the kids."

"We're turning out to be a couple of real desperadoes," Mom said dryly and then paused when she noticed a small café up ahead. "I don't know about you, but I sure could use a cup of coffee."

"There's no time," Dad cautioned. "I don't like the idea of standing out here by the highway while the sheriff's looking for me, but we're going to have to risk it."

Reluctantly, we walked across the gravel parking lot to the edge of the highway. The highway traffic was pretty heavy, but most of the drivers just stared straight ahead as they drove past, as if we were invisible. Dad said that once you made eye contact, it was harder for them to keep going, so we should try to make eye contact.

We'd been standing there for about half an hour, when a sheriff's car pulled into the café's parking lot. Dad had seen it too and was watching it nervously. But then he smiled as he spotted an old truck turning toward us out of the parking lot, piled high with household goods and furniture. Although its engine was racing, the truck was barely moving— underpowered and overloaded.

By the time it reached us, the truck was still moving only a little faster than a man could walk. Dad and I began jogging beside it. The man on the passenger side was facing straight ahead, but he was watching us out of the corner of his eye.

"How about giving us a lift?" Dad called out.

The man rolled down his window and put his hand to his ear.

"How about giving us a lift?" Dad shouted a second time.

"Sorry! No room!" the man shouted back.

"We can ride in the back," Dad shouted.

The passenger looked over at the driver, who shrugged his shoulders and let off the gas, much to my relief. My side was beginning to ache, and I was falling behind.

As soon as the truck stopped, Mom and Carolyn picked up our meager belongings and hurried to join us. The passenger got out to help us with our things, and as he busied himself making room in the back of the truck, I saw Dad giving him the once-over. From the look on his face, I could tell he didn't like what he was seeing. But he didn't say anything.

The desert wind had started to pick up, and the tarp covering the front half of their load began flapping noisily.

Unexpectedly, the man nodded toward Mom. "Since it's so windy, why don't the little lady ride up front?"

Dad looked uneasy. "What do you think?" he asked Mom, giving the man the once-over again.

"I don't care where I ride," Mom said, practically shouting to be heard over the noise of wind and the engine. "Just as long as I can get out of this wind."

Dad glanced back at the sheriff's car in the parking lot. "Okay, Gladys, you go ahead and get in front." He grabbed the side rail and pulled himself into the back of the truck with us. Mom settled herself between the two men, and the driver turned around and shouted through the steel grid opening where glass should have been. "All set back there?"

"All set," Dad called back even though we were still trying to get under the tarp and out of the wind.

Just then, I heard a car burning rubber. The sheriff was coming up behind us, red lights flashing.

The patrol car caught up with us in a matter of seconds. And then it roared past. Dad let out his breath. "He must be going to an accident or something."

Once I was sure the sheriff was gone, I turned my attention to the task of getting comfortable. Unfortunately, the mattresses loaded in the truck had been packed standing up. I spotted a few sofa cushions, wedged between a chest of drawers, and a quilt that was being used to protect the mirror. I decided I was more important than the mirror, so I pulled the quilt around me and helped myself to one of the cushions.

As the road gradually descended from the mountains into the desert, the wind began to subside. Carolyn fell asleep first, then Dad. I divided my attention between the rainbow of color reflecting from the chipped glass knobs on the chest of drawers and the monotonous black ribbon of road disappearing into the desert behind us. I was just starting to drift off when I thought I heard a faint voice in the distance. I listened closer, and just when I was about to dismiss it as a quirk of the wind, I heard it again. It sounded like Mom.

I pulled back the edge of the tarp and stood up, trying to see into the cab through the jumble of furniture. Frustrated, I started climbing over furniture. I still couldn't see much, but I could hear the voices more clearly through the metal grill in the window at the back of the cab.

"Come on, lady. You don't want ol' Ralphy here drinkin' alone, do you?" the man on Mom's right was saying, offering her a half-empty bottle of whiskey.

"I told you I don't want any," Mom snapped at him, pushing the bottle away. "Now leave me alone."

The man shoved the bottle at the driver. "How 'bout you, Zack? Wanna another drink?"

But the driver seemed to have lost interest. "Hey, Zack, ain't she the pretty one," he said, stroking Mom's hair.

"Get your filthy hands off of me!" Mom shouted, jerking away.

"She's a spunky one, ain't she, Zack?"

"I like my women with a little spunk," the driver said, putting an arm around Mom.

"Leave me alone!"

But the driver pulled her closer.

I scrambled back through the jumble of chairs and lamp poles. I shook Dad by the shoulders until he woke up.

"Dad! You've got to do something! Those two men are messing with Mom!"

He was on his feet in an instant and climbing over the furniture. When he saw what was going on up front, the veins popped out on his neck. With more anger than I'd seen in a long time, he untied one of the ropes securing the tarp and climbed onto the roof of the cab. The tarp blew off, and the wind began hitting me full force.

Holding on to a rope, Dad laid down on top of the cab, reached through the side window, and tried to punch the driver. The driver ducked his head and then started to laugh as he began rolling up the window, forcing Dad's arm out.

Dad spun around on the roof of the cab and kicked at the side mirror until it broke off. Then he kicked the roof of the cab with the heels of his shoes. Frustrated, he finally climbed back down to the bed.

"What's going on?" Carolyn asked, fully awake now.

"We've got to do something!" I gasped.

"I know, but what?" Dad hollered back. "I tore one of the mirrors off, but they don't seem to care about their truck."

"How about their furniture?" Carolyn suggested.

Dad considered that for a moment, and then he pulled out one of the dresser drawers and handed it to Carolyn. "Start throwing this stuff over the side!"

We all began pulling drawers out and throwing them off the truck. As they hit the asphalt, they exploded into a swirl of splinters. Dad got behind the chest, braced his back against a refrigerator, and pushed. Once the chest started to slide, Carolyn and I moved to help him. When it went over the back, it skidded sideways and then tumbled end over end on the road.

The lamps were next, and then a set of twin-size box springs, followed by three sofa cushions and the sofa.

The truck began swerving. "Hold on!" Dad yelled. "I think we got their attention!"

A moment later, I heard the sound of gravel on the underside of the truck. I stuck my head over the side rail and looked ahead.

"There's a gas station coming up," I called back to Dad. "I think they're pulling in."

As the truck skidded to a stop, Dad quickly lowered Carolyn and me to the ground, and then threw down our box and suitcase. We didn't stop to pick them up; as soon as our feet hit the ground, we were running toward the gas station.

I dared a glance back and saw the two men leaping out of the truck and running back toward Dad. In the next instant, Mom jumped out and began running toward us.

Two gas station attendants, who had been leaning back against the wall in their chairs, leapt to their feet, sending their chairs flying.

"Is that truck gonna blow up?" one of them shouted.

"The truck's okay," Mom said breathlessly, "but those men are trying to hurt my husband. You've got to help him!"

I turned around to see Dad perched on the back of the truck, wielding a baseball bat.

Staying a safe distance from the bat, the driver yelled up at Dad. "Throwin' our stuff off the truck was a big mistake, mister. I still owe on some of that stuff."

"Yeah? Well you made a bigger mistake trying to mess with my wife," Dad shouted back.

By now, the two attendants were cautiously approaching the arguing men. Mom, Carolyn, and I were right behind them.

"You want I should call the sheriff?" the first attendant called to Dad.

"I don't know," Dad replied, never taking his eyes off the two men below him. "What do you two think?" he said to them. "You think the sheriff might want to find out how much you've been drinking before you get back on the road?"

The driver took a few steps back, put his hands in the air. "I don't want no trouble with the sheriff," he said, his anger instantly vanishing. "We stopped to give you a ride, and it didn't work out. Let's just part company and let it go at that."

"Sounds fair to me," Dad said, without lowering the bat.

Motioning the other man back to the truck, the driver went on. "We'll go back and salvage what we can and be on our way."

His friend wasn't ready to give up so soon. "Come on, Zack. I could take this guy with one arm tied behind my back."

The driver nudged his drunken companion to the cab. "Cool it, Ralph. It's three against two now."

As soon as the cab doors closed, Dad jumped down from the truck. But he held on to the bat. With a big sigh of relief, I watched the truck make a U-turn and pull back onto the highway.

We watched until it was completely out of sight and then walked back to the gas station with the attendants. "You folks all right?" one of them asked, finally breaking the silence.

"Yeah, we're okay," Dad replied lightly. "Just a little misunderstanding." Then he turned to the rest of us. "One thing's for sure. That's the last time we'll ever accept a ride in a truck."

"Amen to that," Mom sighed, collapsing on an old wooden bench on the side of the office.

A few minutes later, Dad wandered out to the two gas pumps in front of the station, leaned against one of them, and just stood there staring at the desert. We knew he was in one of his moods, so we steered clear of him. Carolyn sat down beside Mom with her knees up under her chin, looking bewildered. No one seemed to know what to say, so we said nothing.

The attendants were tinkering with a car in the garage now, and I'd found a shady place to sit where I wouldn't be in anyone's way. I felt frustrated so I threw a rock at a can.

One of the attendants came outside, wiping a wrench with a dirty red cloth. "What seems to be the trouble, sonny?"

"Nothing," I replied without looking up.

"Well, I don't know about a lot of things," he said, "but I've got a son about your age, and when he throws a rock like that, there's usually something troubling him."

I hesitated and began tracing a line in the dirt with my finger. "I don't know . . . it just seems like hitchhiking's a hard way to get anywhere. We do a lot more hiking than hitching, and when we do get a ride, something usually goes wrong."

"But you know, kid, hitchhiking might be a lot like life," he offered kindly. "Both are mostly a struggle. There are times that it's sort of easy, usually just before the next struggle begins." He smiled down at me for a moment. "Where are you headed, anyway?"

"I think Dad said something about Durango."

"Durango," the man repeated thoughtfully. "Why don't you just come with me while I have a little talk with your pa."

He put down his wrench and started toward Dad. I slowly got up and followed, dragging behind a little ways, curious to find out what he was up to.

Dad was still leaning against one of the pumps. The attendant leaned casually against the other pump and began staring out at the desert. A full minute or two passed.

"God must like deserts," he commented.

"What makes you say that?" Dad asked.

"Because He always makes them so big."

Dad nodded. "Yeah, and they seem even bigger when you're trying to get across one."

"Well, you haven't got too much farther to go. Your boy said you might be headed for Durango."

Out came the usual lie. "Got a job waiting for me. That is, if I get there in the next two days."

The attendant stared out at the desert for a while, as if mulling it over, then turned to Dad. "A church bus carrying a bunch of kids broke down nearby a couple of days ago. We had to wait for parts to come out of Albuquerque, so some of the kids' parents picked them up. I told the preacher I'd bring the bus into town as soon as I got it running." He paused for a moment before adding, "So I'll be taking it into Farmington in the morning. Be glad to give you and your family a lift."

"Farmington's a lot closer to Durango than we are now," Dad replied casually. "Are you sure there'll be enough room?"

The attendant laughed. "Plenty. It's a surplus army bus. We'll leave around eight. By the way, friends call me Jake."

"We'll be waiting, Jake," Dad assured him.

With the ever-pressing task of getting a ride taken care of, Dad turned to me with a shrug. "We might as well gather up our belongings and start looking for a place to sleep."

The shadows were growing longer, fingers of darkness inching their way from one clump of sagebrush to another. I looked around for someplace to spend the night. Except for Jake's trailer, there was nothing but empty desert.

We camped behind the station, in the shelter of a shallow indentation in the desert, providing some protection from the wind. Dad built us a fire while Mom rummaged around for something to eat in the box I'd been carrying. We ended up with a can of creamed corn, which we passed around till it was scraped clean. I was still hungry, but I didn't want to complain. Mom was sensitive about having us go to sleep hungry.

The air was already getting chilly, so Carolyn and I crawled under the large piece of cardboard that Dad had dragged to our sandy hollow behind the gas station. Mom and Dad slipped in as best they could on either side, and we huddled together.

Sometime after the fire had burned out, I realized Mom was crying. She was quietly blowing her nose, and I knew she didn't have a cold.

The next morning, she acted as though nothing was wrong. She stirred up oatmeal and made some fresh coffee. Dad punched a hole in a can of condensed milk, and breakfast was served. We didn't have sugar, but again, no one complained. So far the rules seemed to be 1) don't notice what's missing, and 2) if you do, don't say anything about it.

After breakfast, we buried the cans, brushed the sand off, and headed back to the gas station. Jake and an old army-green bus were waiting for us at the pumps. He finished pumping gas and pointed at the small trailer I'd seen the night before.

"Me and the missus live over there," he said. "Sorry it's not bigger."

"Doesn't matter," I said. "We're getting to be pretty good campers."

He smiled, unfolding a red-and-white checkered napkin to reveal a pile of golden biscuits. "The missus cooked up a batch of these to take with us," he explained. Mouth watering, I climbed aboard the ugly green bus with the others, and we started up Highway 550.

Riding in that converted old school bus was the most fun I'd had in a long time. We could choose any seat we wanted, and when it got hot, we opened the windows, but then the adults started complaining about the wind, and we had to close them.

We also got to eat fresh biscuits. Jake's wife had cut them in half and put a little dab of jelly in the center of each one. I was starving but didn't want to look, as Mom would say, like an animal, so I deliberately took my time eating. I'd take a slow bite, lean back in the seat and savor it, then smile over at Carolyn and take another bite.

We arrived at the little town of Shiprock about midmorning, turning east into the sun. About half an hour later, Jake pulled over at the junction of Highways 550 and 64. He pointed to the north. "Durango's 'bout forty miles. You shouldn't have too much trouble catching a ride."

Mom began gathering up our belongings. "Make sure you don't leave a mess," she told us. "I don't want Jake having to clean up a bunch of half-eaten biscuits."

I handed him the cloth napkin with the last three biscuits. "I promise, Mr. Jake, we didn't leave anything half-eaten."

Jake smiled. "I'm sure you didn't," he said then unfolded the napkin and shuffled the biscuits around before handing the parcel back to Carolyn. "Why don't you take these with you?" he offered, still smiling. "I can always get more."

Carolyn thanked him, and we stepped off the bus.

"Y'all be careful now," Jake called out, pulling the door shut. We waved as the bus slowly pulled back onto the highway.

"How are we going to divide up three biscuits?" I asked, snatching the bundle from Carolyn.

"Don't be so grabby," she scolded.

Ignoring her, I unfolded the napkin. "You guys can keep the biscuits," I laughed. "I'm going to keep this!" pulling out a five-dollar bill and waving it over my head. Dad looked as surprised as I was. We all turned to wave at the rapidly receding bus. Jake must have been watching in his rearview mirror because the travel lights blinked on and off in an unspoken, "You're welcome."

We crossed the highway, munching on the leftover biscuits, and took up our hitchhiking position just beyond the junction.

Around noon, when it was really starting to heat up, a large Trailways bus slowed as it approached the junction. After waiting for the oncoming cars to pass, it turned onto the road where we were standing. I expected it to pick up speed as it passed by, but it slowed again and pulled off the road, stopping right in front of us.

The door swung open, and the driver stepped out. "You folks need a ride?"

"Yes," Dad replied, "but we don't have money for the bus."

"Where you headed?"

"We're trying to get to Durango, but—"

"Would fifty cents apiece be too much?" he asked.

Dad turned to Mom. "We can afford two bucks, can't we?"

Mom grabbed the black suitcase. "We're taking it, even if we can't."

Dad reached in his pocket and handed the driver the five-dollar bill I'd found in the biscuits. The driver made a show of taking the money. He gestured toward the bus with his thumb. "The formula for calculating distance and ticket prices is complicated," he explained quietly. "Some of the other passengers might not understand, so I'd appreciate it if you didn't say anything about what I charged for your tickets."

Dad nodded then the driver threw our things into the luggage compartment, and we climbed aboard.

Chapter 8

I TRIED GETTING COMFORTABLE BY placing my feet on top of the waiting room coffee table, but the back of my knees began to ache, and so I took them down. Carolyn tried to get comfortable by placing her legs over mine, but comfort no longer seemed possible for either one of us. Carolyn was the first to voice her discomfort. "This has got to have been the longest night I have ever had to endure."

"I don't know; we experienced a few nights trying to sleep under newspapers that would rival this one," I countered.

"I didn't like sleeping on sand, but right now I'd gladly trade it for the hardness of these chairs."

"It's funny how our views of things change over time," I said thoughtfully. "I often wonder about how the value we place on things changes as we go through life. For example, when we were living on the road, I tried not to get too attached to any particular toy, but stuffed animals were hard not to love. Stuffed animals were considered non-essential and all non-essentials had to be left behind. But before I could leave it behind, I'd find a secret hiding place and promise to return."

Carolyn nodded her head. "I remember you carrying around that teddy bear, pretending it was a pet."

"You'd outgrown stuffed animals. But since having a pet was out of the question, I often substituted stuffed animals as make-believe pets, so they came to mean a lot to me. When we were gathering our stuff to go to the foster home, I hid my teddy bear above the attic access hole in the closet. I promised I'd come back—but I never did. There is still a small part of me that feels a little sad when I think of that teddy bear sitting patiently in the dark, waiting for me to keep my promise."

"It's funny what we get attached to," Carolyn remarked.

"Yeah, there was a time when cap pistols and tricycles were important, but not anymore."

"The most important thing right now is what's going to happen to Mom," Carolyn agreed.

"That's because we've grown to appreciate what's *really* important."

I gently pulled Carolyn's legs off mine and got up to get a drink from the water fountain. After drinking my fill, I stood there for a moment, contemplating the dilemma involved in trying to determine what is really important. I imagined two sets of parents sitting way up in a press box overlooking a basketball court. Their child is ushered in at one end of the court and told that he or she can select any *one* item on the court. The items on the basketball court start out with squeeze toys, stuffed animals, balls and such—things that a small child might like. The items progressively become more valuable on the way to the other side; things like bicycles, then cars, boats, gold, private jets, etc. However, interspersed among these worldly goods are things like the scriptures, temple sealing, happy marriages, healthy children, and loving relationships. While watching their child grope through the variety of items, one set of parents might say to themselves, "Please don't pick the bicycle," or "Don't choose too soon; wait until you get to the gold!" However, the wiser set of parents, knowing what things are truly valuable in life, might be thinking, "Please, don't pick the worldly goods. Pick the scriptures or a temple sealing or a happy marriage."

"Those would be some tough choices," I murmured to myself.

Returning to Carolyn in the waiting area, I shared, "I sometimes imagine that our Heavenly Father is looking down on us as we choose what we think is valuable—praying that we will choose that which has eternal value. Because God loves us, He knows what we need, in contrast to what *we* think we need."

"That sure beats the kind of father we grew up with," Carolyn declared. "He didn't seem to care about anything."

Shaking my head, I added, "Unfortunately, most children's first impression of what God is like is usually based on what their father is like. If their father is authoritarian, then they will tend to see God as someone who makes rules and punishes those who disobey. On the other hand, if their father is kind and considerate, they expect their Heavenly Father to be a loving and understanding God."

"That may be," Carolyn rebutted, rolling her eyes, "but no god could be as bad as our Dad—lying, drinking, in and out of jail. Even I have a better opinion of God than that."

***

Summer 1947

Shiprock, New Mexico, to Grand Junction, Colorado

While we were riding the bus to Durango, Dad told Carolyn and me that Durango had a miniature train—a narrow-gauge railroad—that was still carrying people and supplies to the mining camps. Since Dad lied a lot, I told Carolyn that I bet her an arm punch that there wouldn't be any miniature train. She upped the bet to two arm punches—I lost.

Unfortunately, the miniature railroad would be about the only thing I'd like about Durango. Neither Mom nor Dad was able to find a job right away. So we were forced to seek refuge in an old work camp located just outside the city limits.

To get there, we had to follow a narrow dirt road with weeds and bushes growing in the middle. As we rounded a bend, a ragged collection of run-down sheds came into view. A tired-looking woman with a naked toddler on one hip eyed us suspiciously and prodded a small child inside.

"She sure looks old for someone with such young kids," Carolyn commented.

"Poverty has a way of making people look older than they are," Mom sighed, perhaps thinking of herself.

Dad walked over to the woman and asked, "Who do we see about getting a place to stay?"

"Don't need to see nobody," she replied. "Just find one that's empty and claim it."

"Who collects the rent?"

"Nobody," she replied and then nodded toward the other sheds. "These were abandoned some time ago. Health department comes 'round once in a while, threatens to tear 'em down."

"Much obliged," Dad said, and we continued on our way. A stray dog walked up and sniffed at my leg.

"Don't pet that dog," Mom cautioned. "No telling what you might catch."

Carolyn tugged on Mom's sleeve and pointed at a shed that stood a little ways off from the main cluster. Mom nodded her head and then nudged me in the back. "Buddy, run over there and see if that one's empty."

I hurried over to the shack and knocked on the door. When no one answered, I ran to the side and stood on my tiptoes, wiped the grime off the glass, and peeked through the window. "Looks empty!"

Carolyn ran to the door and shoved it open wide enough to squeeze through. "Yuck!" she cried out from inside.

As I squeezed in behind her, my hands went to my nose. The smell of urine was almost overpowering, and piles of trash and garbage filled every corner of the one-room shack. A variety of spiders and mice had made nests in the corners, and where the floorboards were missing, weeds were growing through the holes.

"This place smells like the back door of the Imperial Hotel," I complained.

"Worse!" Carolyn said, backing out of the doorway.

Moments later Mom and Dad walked up. They pushed the door all the way open.

"Oh, my Lord!" Mom said, visibly shuddering. "We can't live in a place like this!"

"I'm afraid we're going to have to, at least for the time being," Dad grunted as he forced open a window. "Once we slosh some bleach around and air it out a little, it won't be so bad."

"Carolyn, go back to that woman we just talked to and see if she has a broom," Mom urged. "Buddy, go find me some water."

It took us several days, but we finally got the shed cleaned up enough to be livable. Mom found a waitress job at a small café and had to leave for work while we were still asleep. The owner of the café let us come there for breakfast.

School was already out for the summer in Durango, so Carolyn and I didn't have to face the nightmare of being the new kids at school. We would sleep late, get up and get dressed, and then walk into town to eat. We liked to explore, so each morning we would take a different route.

On one of these mornings, we were walking down the tree-lined meridian on Third Avenue when we passed four or five boys playing basketball in a driveway.

One of them stopped the ball and called out, "Hey, Okies! Got any cooties?"

I knew what cooties were, but I had no idea what "Okie" meant, so I came back with the only thing I could think of. "We don't have no cooties, and we're not Okies neither."

A second boy picked up the taunt. "Don't you know nothin'? All you Okies got cooties."

"We're not Okies," Carolyn snapped.

"You are too!" an older kid yelled.

"Oh, yeah? Well, you're an Okie too!" I shouted back.

The teasing instantly stopped. And they stared at me in disbelief.

One of them started toward me, and the others quickly followed. The first boy stopped in front of me, about a foot away, feet spread, both hands on his hips.

"What did you just call me?" he said.

Unwittingly, I continued along my path to destruction. "I called you the same thing you called me."

"You calling me a Okie?"

"If the shoe fits." I shrugged.

He hit me. Then he wrestled me to the ground and hit me again. A moment later, a woman came rushing out of the house. "You two stop that fighting right this minute! You hear me?"

One of the boys pointed at me. "He started it."

"He did not," Carolyn protested.

The woman managed to pull us apart and then yanked us to our feet. She gave me the once-over and frowned at Carolyn. "I don't recall seeing you two before. Do you live around here?"

"We live just outside of town," Carolyn replied.

"They're from Okieville," one of the boys sneered. "They're Okies!"

"We ain't either," I insisted, still not knowing what it was that they were calling us.

The woman pointed a finger at me. "We don't like your kind sneakin' around our neighborhood."

"We weren't sneakin'," Carolyn insisted, tears coming to her eyes.

"Don't sass me, you little hussy. You've got no business mixing with regular folks."

"I'll bet you sleep with your sister," one of the boys interjected.

"So what if I do?" I replied defensively.

The entire group, including the woman, burst out laughing.

Carolyn tugged at my arm and began pulling me down the sidewalk with her.

"Why were they laughing at us?" I asked, once we were out of earshot. "I do sleep with you. What's wrong with that?"

"That's not what they meant, Buddy," she said with a shake of her head. "Just forget it."

But I wasn't about to forget it. The encounter had left me with a sense of shame that I didn't understand.

We walked in silence for a few minutes, and then I looked up at her. "What's an Okie?"

"Okies are poor folks. People who don't have a home and wander around looking for work."

I thought about that for a while. "Then I guess those kids were right. We *are* Okies."

"Good grief, Buddy; we're not either. Sometimes you just think too much."

I didn't say any more, but I couldn't help but think, if the shoe fits . . .

By the time we arrived at the café, I had managed to put the humiliating incident behind me. Eating a fresh donut was now my only concern. We climbed up on the stools at the far end of the counter, and Mom brought us cake donuts and milk.

A row of booths stood opposite the long counter. About halfway down the row was the doorway to the bar, with strings of colored glass beads hanging down in the opening. Dad spent most of his time in the bar section, nursing a beer and playing penny-ante poker with Mom's tip money.

Our daily routine didn't vary much. After finishing breakfast, Carolyn and I would spend a few hours in the bar playing shuffleboard. But the air was always a cloud of cigarette smoke and Mom would shoo us outside. We'd wander around town for a while and then go back to the bar, where we would spend the rest of the day bumming sodas.

Shortly after she finished her shift one night, Mom told us she was exhausted and wanted to go home. We sat down at the bar, knowing it would take her a while to talk Dad into leaving.

"Let's go, honey," she pleaded. "I've been on my feet all day, and I'm tired."

"As soon as I get even," Dad said distractedly, laying his cards on the table. "Stick around, Gladys. You bring me luck."

Mom threw up her hands and sat down at the bar. She asked the bartender for a draft and began counting out her tip money.

A man sitting a few bar stools down from her held up a dollar bill. "I'll get that," he offered.

"Thanks, but no thanks," Mom began, glancing up to acknowledge the stranger. He was a tall, slim man dressed in a clean khaki shirt and faded Levis. Mom suddenly brightened and, with a shrug, smiled back at him and acquiesced. "Why not? Sure beats being ignored."

The man put the dollar on the counter, calling out to the bartender, "Two Coors," then stood up and moved closer. "Coors okay with you?" he asked.

"Doesn't matter to me. Just as long as it's cold."

I poked Carolyn to make sure she was paying attention to what was going on. She was as wide-eyed as I was. Dad caught my eye and motioned Carolyn and me over to his table.

"Who's that talking to your mom?" he asked, with a nod.

"Don't know," Carolyn said. "I've never seen him before."

"Well, I don't like his looks," Dad said suspiciously. "Keep an eye on him . . . and on your mom."

"Keep an eye on them yourself," Carolyn shot back. "She's *your* wife."

At that, we hurried off to the shuffleboard. "What do you think's gonna happen?" I whispered to Carolyn.

"Beats me. But if Dad's getting in one of his moods, there's probably going to be trouble."

A few minutes later, I heard Mom laugh. I looked over at Dad. His face was turning red.

"Count me out of the next hand," he said, standing up. Then he walked over to Mom and the stranger.

"You two seem to be having a pretty good time," he said sarcastically and then took a wild swing at the stranger. Other customers soon joined in, and the fight quickly turned into a full-fledged brawl. The bartender grabbed the phone from under the bar just as a chair bounced off the wall right over our heads.

The fight was the most excitement I'd had for a long time, but I was still relieved when I heard the wail of sirens and the screeching of tires. Seconds later, the sheriff and his deputies came bursting through what was left of the beads in the doorway. "All right, let's break it up!" the sheriff shouted.

The fight was quickly brought under control, and after a quick survey of the damage, the sheriff turned to the bartender and asked, "How'd this get started?"

Without hesitation, the bartender pointed at Dad. "That guy over there took the first swing."

The sheriff looked over at his deputy and then nodded toward Dad. The deputy cuffed Dad's hands behind his back.

Mom didn't seem all that surprised. "This isn't the first time your father's ended up in jail," she sighed. "Nor is it likely to be the last."

"Do we have enough money to bail him out?" Carolyn asked.

"Not really." Mom frowned. As it turned out, bail was set at twenty-five dollars, and Mom had to hock her wedding ring at a local pawnshop to get the money.

The jail was in an older brick building with "La Plata County Sheriff's Department & Jail" printed across the front door. Mom paused outside, a worried expression on her face. When I asked her what was wrong, she confided, "I'm worried somebody might've checked on your dad for outstanding warrants—possibly robbery charges out of Gallup."

I thought we'd gotten away, but Mom's words once again reminded me that it's never completely safe, no matter what.

The three of us stepped inside the jail. A long counter stretched across the front of the room. Mom cautiously approached the deputy sitting on a stool behind the counter.

"Mornin', ma'am," the officer said cheerfully. "Something I can do for you?"

"My name's Mrs. Poduska," she said, handing the deputy some papers. "The judge said you'd release my husband if I paid the twenty-five dollar bail."

"Your husband wouldn't happen to be the one who was brought in last night after the fight at the Silver Mine Café?" the deputy asked as he began shuffling through a stack of papers.

"I'm afraid so," Mom replied. "How soon can be released?"

"As soon as I finish the paperwork and you sign these forms," the deputy replied without looking up.

Mom's shoulders sagged with relief. After Mom signed the form, she set the twenty-five dollars on top and slid the stack back across the counter. The deputy quickly reviewed the form and placed the money in a metal box. A few seconds later, he pressed a buzzer, a door swung open, and Dad came into the room. One of his eyes was black, his nose was bent slightly to one side, and he had several cuts and bruises on his cheeks.

"You're free to go, Mr. Poduska," the deputy said, shaking his head. "I sure hope the other guy looks better than you do."

Dad put his arm around Mom's shoulders for support, and we started down the street. "Where to next?" he asked.

"You look like you could use a cup of coffee," Mom replied. "Let's go over to the Silver Mine."

"After what happened last night," Dad commented, "are you sure I'll be welcome there?"

"Honey, we don't have any money, so if you want a cup of coffee, that's where we're going to have to go. Colleen and I have become pretty good friends. I'm sure she'll be good for a couple cups of coffee."

Not only was Colleen good for a couple of cups of coffee, she also gave us two glasses of milk and a couple Danish rolls.

After gulping down my milk, I spun my stool around and watched Colleen work. As she wiped off the tables near the front windows, I noticed two deputies come out of the police station, run to the corner, and begin looking up and down the street. They exchanged a few words, and then one of them headed straight for the Silver Mine Café.

"You didn't by any chance *bust* your husband out of jail, did you?" Colleen asked Mom, her eyes on the approaching deputy.

"No, I paid his bail," Mom replied. "Why?"

"Because there's a deputy headed this way, and I don't like the way he's coming." Colleen turned to us. "Quick! Everyone get to the storage room in back."

"But—"

"Don't argue. Just get! We'll sort this out after I find out what's got those deputies all riled up," she said, shoving us toward the back room.

We made it to the back room but left the door open a crack so we could still see out. A moment later, the deputy burst into the café. He stood there for a moment, scanning the customers, before asking. "Did that new waitress and her husband come in here a few minutes ago?"

"Calm down, deputy," Colleen chuckled. "What do you want with those two? Did you let her husband go by mistake?"

"It's not her husband we're looking for," he replied, still looking around the café. "It's the woman we're after."

"Gladys? Why in the world would you be after her?"

"Turns out there's a warrant for her arrest out of Phoenix. She's charged with child stealing," the deputy explained. He turned to leave and then added, "My partner's checking the bus station right now. They haven't had time to get very far, so they've got to be around here someplace. If she does show up, call me at the sheriff's office."

"That's the first thing I'll do, deputy," Colleen said to the closing door, but her tone was sarcastic.

Once he was gone, she hurried back to the storeroom. "Did you hear what he said about the child-stealing warrant?"

"It was an awful place and we hated it," I declared. "Besides, Mom didn't steal us. She rescued us."

Colleen smiled reassuringly. "Don't worry. I'm on your side." She glanced back at the front door, adding somberly, "But what I think and what the law thinks don't always agree. What we have to do now is get you out of town."

"How?" Mom entreated. "The deputy said they were watching the bus station. Not that it matters, since we haven't got enough money to buy a ticket anyway."

"Never mind about the money," Colleen said, taking off her apron. "You folks wait here. I'm going to go see my boyfriend, Murray," she said with a sly smile, "who just happens to be a Trailways bus driver." At that, she rushed out the front door.

Colleen returned half hour later with four bus tickets, having arranged for her boyfriend to pick us up on his way out of town.

The highway out of Durango toward Grand Junction cut through a wide valley of green fields that contrasted sharply with the bright red cliffs rising to meet a forest of dark green pine trees. About ten or fifteen miles out, we climbed out of the valley and into the Rockies. The higher we climbed, the worse the road became, until it was little more than a bulldozed path. The bus had to weave around workmen and heavy machinery chiseling stone from the sides of the sheer granite walls. Unguarded cliffs dropped hundreds of feet to the Animas River, rushing through the narrow gorge below us.

The driver informed us that we were traveling on the Million-Dollar Highway, named for the million dollars a mile it was costing to build.

A sign at the summit read, "Coal Bank Hill Pass—10,640 feet." After that, much of the road was just one way. At one point, I stuck my head out the window and discovered that I couldn't see the road below us— just air and huge outcroppings of rock hung over the roadway above us.

While maneuvering our way around a particularly sharp curve overlooking a deep valley, a small town came into view. I leaned toward the driver. "What town is that?"

"That's the historic town of Silverton," the driver answered with a nod of his head.

Silverton was a town out of the Old West, with buildings dating from the early 1800s. Unfortunately, Silverton was only a fifteen-minute rest stop, and we were soon following a twisting road over Red Mountain Pass and down through a narrow gorge.

Several hours later, the bus swung around the last of the *S* curves at the bottom of a box canyon and pulled into an old mining town on the north side of the San Juan Mountains. As the bus came to a stop, the driver called out, "Ouray. This is a thirty-minute stop. The restrooms are at the rear of the café, and if anyone is hungry, you'd better get something to eat now. This will be the last stop until we get to Grand Junction."

The only thing I had eaten all day was the breakfast roll Colleen had given me that morning, so I looked over at Mom and Dad expectantly.

"I could eat a little something," Carolyn said casually.

While the other passengers were getting off the bus and going into the café, Mom began rummaging through our food bag for something to eat. Unfortunately, the dishwasher who Colleen had sent to get our belongings hadn't picked up the cans of food we had put on the window-sill.

Mom gave up the search and nudged Dad. "Any idea what we're going to do about something to eat?"

"Just leave that to me," Dad said, as though he'd been thinking about the situation for some time. Mom merely sighed.

The restrooms were crowded, and we had to wait in line. Once we'd finally taken our turns, we worked our way back outside to meet Dad. But when we stepped out of the café, we found our suitcase and box sitting on the sidewalk, with Dad nowhere in sight. I was about to ask Mom why our things had been taken off the bus, when I spotted Dad coming out of the small grocery store across the street.

He walked up to us, and said, "Well, I managed to get us some money for food and . . ."

"And a bottle of whiskey," Mom pointed out. I, too, had noticed the brown paper bag sticking out of his coat pocket.

"Don't push me, Gladys," Dad warned. "I got banged up pretty bad back there, and I needed a little something for the pain."

"Ha! If you're drinking for the pain, then you've been hurting since the day I met you."

"Back off, Gladys. I'm not in the mood."

Mom eyed him suspiciously. "Just out of curiosity, where *did* you get the money?"

"I turned in our bus tickets for a partial refund," Dad replied nonchalantly.

Mom threw her hands up in the air. "What in the world got into you, Bernie? Now how are we supposed to get to Grand Junction, or anyplace else for that matter?"

"I suppose we'll just have to—"

"Bernie, don't you dare say we'll just have to hitchhike. Don't even think about it. I've had it up to here with hitchhiking. If we have to be on the road, I want to travel like normal people, not like a bunch of gypsies."

"Hey, don't be too hard on the gypsies," Dad said. "You'll see . . . Things are going to work out. So why don't we talk about this after we've gotten something in our stomachs?"

Mom glared at him, but I knew she'd already lost. The situation had pretty well been determined the moment Dad had turned in the bus tickets. If we were going to get out of Ouray, we were going to have to hitchhike.

Along with the booze, Dad had bought some canned goods, a loaf of bread, and a few slices of bologna. So we all ate a bologna sandwich, then wandered down the near-empty streets of Ouray. With the high mountains on both sides of town, it got dark early. I was soon rubbing my arms to warm them.

Carolyn was feeling the chill, too. She pointed at the black suitcase and asked, "Mom, could you dig out my blouse?"

We sat down on the curb to wait as Mom pulled the old black suitcase to her and started digging through it when a woman's voice came out of the darkness. "From the looks of things, you folks could use a little help."

"My name's Emma McNally," the voice continued as she stepped into view. "I'm headed for Gunnison but can give you a lift to Montrose, about thirty-five miles north of here."

"We're trying to get to Grand Junction," Dad explained, "but Montrose is thirty-five miles closer than we are now."

The ride to Montrose passed quickly, and once we got into town, Dad made a broad sweeping motion with his hand and said, "You can drop us off just about anywhere."

"Are you sure?"

"We'll manage," Mom interjected. "We always do."

The lady dropped us off at the next corner. We waved good-bye as she drove away; then we gathered up our belongings and started looking for a place to spend the night.

We stayed off the main streets, afraid that the sheriff in Durango had notified the authorities to be on the lookout for us. We were walking past a high school gymnasium when Dad noticed that one of the side doors wasn't completely closed.

He bent down and removed a small rock from the base of the door. "Some kids probably propped it open," he concluded. "Probably planned to come back to shoot some baskets." He pulled the door open a little farther and we went inside.

We slept in luxury that night on gym mats and were awakened the next morning by the clatter of metal pails. A janitor was mopping the hallway right outside the gymnasium doors. We had slept in our clothes, so we quickly picked up our shoes and slipped out unnoticed.

Still mindful of the possibility of being spotted by the police, we kept to the side streets and alleys as we made our way back to the main highway. As we were walking down one of the alleys, we came across a delivery truck loaded with trays of fresh glazed donuts. No one said a word, but we all slowed down and then stopped, gazing silently at the mouthwatering pastries. I took a deep breath, inhaling the sweet smell.

Just then, a man came out the back door of the bakery carrying another tray of donuts. He stopped when he saw us and stared at us for a moment. Then he looked down at the tray in his hands, walked over to us, and lowered the tray until it was waist-high to Carolyn and me, all the while never saying a word. We looked up at Mom, then back at the man. They were both smiling. So we reached out and took a donut.

"Two," the man said softly. We dropped our bundles and took another donut with our free hand.

The man raised the tray up to Mom and Dad. "Two," he said again with a nod.

Mom and Dad smiled politely and took their donuts. Then the man walked over to the delivery truck, slid the half-empty tray onto a rack, climbed into the cab, and drove off.

"Two" was the only word he had spoken, but I would never forget the man's kindness, his lack of hesitation in deciding what to do when he saw us standing there by his truck. The brief encounter left me with a lump in my throat, and I had to wait a while before I could eat my donuts.

They were still soft and warm, and since we couldn't carry our stuff and eat at the same time, we sat down on the back steps of the bakery to savor our good fortune. Once we had swallowed the last bite, we licked the frosting off our fingers, picked up our bundles, and continued on our way.

"How far are we gonna walk, anyway?" I asked, after we'd gone quite a distance.

"As far away from town as possible," Dad replied. "If we get far enough out, we'll look like we've been abandoned. Drivers will feel sorry for us and pull over."

"I've felt sorry for us for the last three miles," I muttered.

Walking ahead of me, Carolyn turned around to face me and began walking backwards. "I'm going to ask Mom if she can get Dad to stop for a while." Then she turned around again.

I caught up with her, and we quickened our pace until we drew even with Mom. I added drama to Carolyn's request for a rest by clutching my throat as if I were dying of thirst.

Mom smiled, ruffled my hair, and called out to Dad, "There's a gas station up ahead, honey. Why don't we rest for a while?"

Dad didn't turn around, but he gave her a thumbs-up. The end was in sight, even if it was only temporary.

As we got closer, I nudged Carolyn and pointed at the cool convertible parked in front of the gas station. A teenage boy was standing beside it, arguing with the attendant. He didn't have money to buy gas but needed to get to Grand Junction.

"Looks like we're not the only ones with problems," Dad commented, reaching into his pocket and pulled out some change. "I've got a dollar and eighty-two cents. Will that buy enough?"

"You bet!" the boy laughed, as he took money from Dad and handed it to the attendant. "Here. Now give me some gas."

Once the gas was pumped, Mom, Carolyn, and I climbed into the back seat of the souped-up convertible. Dad took the shotgun position in the front. The driver vaulted over the side and slid into the front seat. The engine came to life with a roar, and we were on our way.

We reached Grand Junction in what had to be record time. The car's exhausts echoed off the bridge girders as we crossed over the Colorado River and down the slight incline into town.

Dad tapped the driver on the shoulder. "You can let us off at the next corner." The exchange of good-byes was brief, and the teenager drove off, leaving us standing on the corner.

"That looks like it could be a park or something," Mom said after a minute, pointing at a cluster of trees down the street.

"Probably as good a place as any," Dad sighed.

The park was only a couple of blocks away, but it was hot, and the corners of the cardboard box I was carrying kept collapsing from the sweat on my hands. Once we got there, Carolyn and I raced each other to the water fountain. The water was warm, but we took turns gulping, nevertheless, pausing just long enough to catch our breath, then gulping some more.

"Don't drink too fast now," Mom called out.

Dad commented, "This was a good idea. Sitting here, we look just like any other family enjoying a day at the park."

"As long as it's daylight," Mom frowned. "But what about when it gets dark?"

"I've been giving that some thought. Let's scout around a little. See if we can find someplace off the beaten path."

Reluctantly, we gathered up our things and began walking down Colorado Street. Eventually we found ourselves in front of St. Mary's Hospital, an isolated three-story building.

"Nuns are usually an easy touch," Dad said matter-of-factly. Sure enough, they were glad to feed a hungry family.

We left the hospital an hour later, sleepily full, and walked down to the railroad yards a couple of blocks away, where we met up with an old tramp stumbling along the tracks. The man's gray whiskers were tobacco stained, and I couldn't see more than one tooth in his lower jaw.

"Do you know of any out-of-the way place where we could bed down for the night?" Dad called out to him.

The man's back was badly bent, so looking up at Dad took some effort. "I just came from the river over there," he replied in a raspy voice.

With a shaky hand, he pointed over his shoulder. "It's pretty tricky getting through the willows, but once you get to the river, there's lots of places to make camp."

Dad thanked him, and we made our way to the stand of willows on the other side of the yard. After probing several dead-end paths, we finally found one that led all the way down to the Colorado River. Dad walked a little ways out onto the sandbar that ran parallel to the river and dropped the suitcase.

I dropped my box right beside it. Mom collapsed there too, folded her arms around her knees, and began to cry.

I knelt beside her. "What's the matter, Mom?" I asked.

"I'm just tired. Tired of being on the road," she said, wiping her cheeks with her wrists. "I just want to go home."

"Where's that?" I asked in surprise.

"South Dakota." She began to cry even harder. "I'm tired of hitch-hiking. I'm tired of being poor. I'm tired of being grown-up. I just want to go home and be a little girl again."

Dad stood a few feet away, looking disinterested. "There's no going back, Gladys," he said impatiently. He took a quick swig from the whiskey bottle. "It's never like it used to be."

"I don't care," Mom argued. "I still want to go home."

"Be reasonable, Gladys. The Utah state line's only about twenty-five or thirty miles from here."

"Honey, the kids and I are exhausted," Mom insisted. "I'm not sure how much longer we can go on like this."

Dad gave Carolyn and me a sidelong glance. "The kids look okay to me."

"It wouldn't have to be for very long," Mom continued. "Just long enough to get some direction back in our lives."

Dad sat down on a nearby rock and pulled the bottle out of his coat pocket again.

"I wish you wouldn't," Mom pleaded.

"Wouldn't what?" he snorted.

"Drink so much."

"I don't drink half as much as I'd like to," he said and then took an extra-long swig.

"As if getting drunk is going to help," Mom scoffed.

"Getting drunk's about the only thing that does help. Look, Gladys, I'm heading west in the morning. You and the kids can go whatever direction you want. Go to your farm in South Dakota. Go to Utah with me. Go to blazes, for all I care."

"And just what do you mean by that? I thought you cared about us, but all you really care about is . . . your bottle."

"Get off my back!" Dad shouted, staggering to his feet.

I felt scared and remembered what Mom had said the day we were evicted in Albuquerque. "It doesn't really matter where we go, just as long as we're able to stay together."

I watched Dad stumble off toward the riverbank. He lost his balance on the slippery rocks at one point, but after some exaggerated arm swinging, he managed to recover.

Carolyn nudged me. "We'd better gather some wood before it gets dark." Mom was still sitting there crying, but letting her cry it out seemed to be all the help we could offer.

By the time we got the fire going, it was dark, and Dad still hadn't returned. No one said it out loud, but I'm sure we were all considering the possibility that he might not return.

Mom opened a can of pork and beans out of the groceries Dad had bought back in Ouray. She set it down on a rock near the edge of the fire, trying to act as if everything was normal, but I wasn't quite sure what normal looked like anymore.

She brushed her cheek with a quick swipe of her hand and continued going about her duties with forced cheerfulness. "Carolyn, will you get some plates out of the box?"

"How many?" Carolyn asked.

"Four, as usual," Mom answered, ignoring the implication.

As soon as the label burned off and the beans started bubbling, Mom pulled the can off the fire. Dinner was served.

I was just reaching for a piece of bread to go with them when I saw Dad staggering out of the darkness, clutching his wrist. Blood covered the side of his pants and he had a blank look on his face. He took a few more steps and collapsed.

Mom leaped up. "Bernie! You've got blood all over you!"

"I was holding the bottle . . . fell," he said in a whisper.

I wasn't breathing and was starting to get frightened.

"How bad is it?" Mom asked.

"Don't know. Too dark . . . I think it's pretty bad."

"Let's get your hand over here by the fire," Mom said in a take-charge voice. Painfully, Dad rolled a little closer to the fire and stuck his hand out.

Carolyn and I gasped simultaneously at the sight of the wound. Blood was pouring out everywhere, making a hissing sound as it fell on the hot rocks near the fire. Mom started tearing up one of Dad's shirts.

"Carolyn, cut me some more bandages," she ordered, as she began wrapping one of the torn strips around Dad's palm.

He howled in pain as she applied pressure. "I think there's still glass in my hand!"

Mom held his hand closer to the fire. "There's just too much blood." Pointing at the bottle of water, she shouted, "Carolyn, pour some water over his hand. I'll look for glass."

Carolyn quickly grabbed the bottle and started pouring.

"Not too fast," Mom cautioned, gently exploring the wound with her fingernail. "I think I see something," she said. Then she began digging in his palm. Dad started swearing, but Mom kept at the task and finally pulled out a large sliver of glass. As soon as it was removed, more blood started gushing out.

"Bernie, can you hear me?" Mom said loudly.

Dad nodded.

"Honey, we've got to do something to stop the bleeding."

Dad nodded again.

"You're going to have to hold your hand over the fire."

Dad's eyes widened for an instant.

Mom grabbed the shirtsleeve she'd just torn off, twisted it, and said, "Put this between your teeth and hold on to me."

Dad bit down on the twisted fabric, shut his eyes, and stuck his bleeding hand right over the flames.

The smell of singed hair filled the air. A few seconds with his hand in the flames, and Dad let out an animal-like howl as he fell backward. Mom quickly wrapped his hand with strips of the torn shirt and then gathered him into her arms, both of them sobbing convulsively.

I knew Dad needed medical help, but unable to find the path through the willows, we were trapped until daybreak.

I watched silently as Mom rocked Dad in her arms. "Is Dad going to die?" I whispered to Carolyn.

"I don't think so," she whispered back. "There's a hospital nearby. If he was supposed to die, it would've happened somewhere else."

As I drifted off to sleep, the boulders tumbling in the river helped drown out Dad's moans.

Chapter 9

A JANITOR WAS STEADILY WORKING his way up the hall with a wide dust mop. As he passed the waiting area where Carolyn and I were gradually becoming part of the furnishings, he smiled and continued on down the hall toward Mom's room and the nurses' station. I noticed Carolyn was watching the janitor's slow progression. "How would you like to have a job like that?" she commented, shaking her head.

Surprised by the rather disparaging tone of her question, I asked her if her question had been rhetorical.

Somewhat taken aback by my interest, she explained, "I was just commenting on what it might be like to be in a dead-end job like being a janitor."

"I was a janitor for three years while I was going to school," I informed her.

"Well, that was different," she countered. "You went on to become a professor."

"God is no respecter of persons," I declared.

"God . . . what?"

"God is no respecter of persons," I repeated. "That means God doesn't care whether someone is a janitor, professor, farmer, or soldier. These are merely the outward trappings of what kind of work we do. God is more concerned with what kind of person we are on the inside—the nature of our character, our desire to live righteously, and our capacity to love."

"Maybe so, but I would still prefer to be doing something a little more important than pushing a dust mop," Carolyn scoffed.

"Sometimes what may appear to be trivial can actually be very important," I counseled. "It reminds me of a story an English teacher told me.

"This story takes place during World War II. The US Army had set up a weather station on a desolate highland mountain peak near the northern coast of Scotland. It was a barren, windswept place, but it was also the first place storms made landfall as they moved down from the Arctic.

"The station consisted of a couple of wooden buildings and a diesel generator. The only connection to the small village was a narrow dirt road that wound its way down the side of the mountain. The station was manned by a sergeant, who was also a meteorologist; a corporal, the acting radio operator; and a private, who was supposed to maintain the diesel generator.

"There was excitement in the air because the greatest amphibious assault in the history of warfare would soon begin. The private wanted to be a part of the invasion. He would look south and complain about his rotten luck to be stationed in the 'backwaters' of the war. The others would tell him, 'We've all got a job to do,' but he wanted to be doing something important instead of being a diesel jockey.

"The private reasoned that if his job wasn't *important*, it wasn't worth doing. As a consequence, he didn't maintain the generator and, in the middle of a rainstorm, the generator stopped working. Without the generator, the radio was useless.

"The next morning the sergeant was concerned about how they were going to get their daily weather report to London. Their orders were clear and specific: transmit information on current weather conditions each morning at 0600.

"Fortunately, the sky was clearing as the storm moved south toward London and the channel. So the sergeant climbed on a rickety bicycle and headed down the mountain to the village and a phone. In spite of the mud and swollen streams, the sergeant managed to reach the village and hurriedly called his weather report into London while wondering if it had really been worth the extra effort.

"In London, General Eisenhower had been up most of the night. A steady rain was still coming down through the gray dawn. The weather on the English Channel had deteriorated and the condition of the men on the troop ships had worsened. The decision to postpone the invasion or to commit thousands of lives to the shores of Europe had to be made soon. Their fate hinged on a weather report due in from northern Scotland.

"When a messenger rushed into the staff room holding a piece of paper, General Eisenhower quickly read the note and announced, 'The weather report from the highland station indicates that there's going to be a break in the weather over the channel in twenty-four hours. Gentlemen, the liberation of Europe will begin tomorrow.'

"General Eisenhower had a view of the big picture and knew how vitally important the mission assigned to the men at the weather station was to the success of his plan. As did the private, many of us might think that what we do in our everyday lives is unimportant. And yet, since God has a view of the big picture, what we are asked to do can be vitally important to the ultimate success of God's plan."

"Perhaps you're right," Carolyn cautiously acknowledged, "but I'm still not certain what I'm supposed to do with my life or what my mission is. Sometimes I feel like I might as well just go along with whatever others want me to do. So many times, others seem to know where they are going and why, and I'm just along for the ride, like when that farmer gave us a ride to Utah."

***

Summer 1947

Grand Junction, Colorado, to Spanish Fork, Utah

We broke camp at first light and made our way back through the willows. Since Mom had to help Dad, Carolyn and I carried the black suitcase, while juggling the box and bag. The going was slow, but luckily the hospital was only a couple of blocks beyond the tracks.

A nurse met us as soon as we stepped through the emergency room entrance.

"My husband cut his hand real bad," Mom explained.

"It looks like his face got pretty banged up, too," the nurse said, already pushing a gurney toward Dad. "Have him lie down on this," she went on, "and I'll call Dr. Metcalf."

Just as she finished making the call, Dad passed out and fell over onto the gurney. The nurse quickly put down the phone and raced back to help.

"He's lost a lot of blood," Mom cried, trying to loosen Dad's clothing.

Just then, a man in a white coat and stethoscope hurried in. He lifted one of Dad's eyelids and shone a small light into his eye. A nurse was already taking Dad's blood pressure.

"Eighty over fifty, Doctor," she reported, her voice filled with concern.

"When did this happen?" the doctor asked, glancing up at Mom as he unwrapped the makeshift bandages on Dad's hand.

"Last night," Mom said worriedly. "Right after dark."

The doctor began shouting commands. "I want a blood type ASAP! Get an IV started, and someone get me a sutures tray."

A nurse soon arrived with a tray of syringes. "This may take a while," she told Mom, "so it would be best if you wait in the lobby." We were starting to leave when she added, "While you're waiting, you'll need to fill out some insurance forms."

"We don't have any insurance, do we?" Carolyn asked Mom in a low voice, pushing our way through a set of swinging doors.

"No, we don't," Mom sighed. "I have no idea how we're going to pay for all this."

When we arrived at the lobby, there was a man in a plaid shirt and faded coveralls talking to the receptionist. We sat down to wait our turn. The man in the coveralls was telling the receptionist that his daughter had just given birth to his first grandchild, and he had driven over from Utah to be with her.

The receptionist looked up and noted, "I see that your daughter has been moved to a private room, so I'll have to wait for additional information before I can finish your paperwork."

"Just make sure you include everything," he smiled. "My daughter and her husband don't know I'm paying for all this. They're just getting started, and I want to help out a little."

He picked up his western-style straw hat from her desk and set off in our direction. He sat down beside us in a theatrical flourish, and with a wide grin, he pulled out a pack of gum and held it out to us. "I don't smoke cigars, so if a stick of gum will do, you can help celebrate my first grandson."

Mom nodded her approval, and Carolyn and I quickly accepted the kind offer. A moment later, the receptionist motioned for Mom to come to her desk.

"My name's Lundquist," the new grandfather offered by way of introduction. "And who might you be?"

"I'm Carolyn and this is Buddy."

"And what brings you folks to the hospital this morning?"

We told him about Dad's accident, about what a long and awful night it had been. Lundquist listened quietly with an expression of genuine concern on his face. He talked to us openly about life on his small farm near Spanish Fork, Utah.

"Mom says that everyone from Utah's a Mormon," I declared.

"Well, I don't know about *everyone*, but a lot of folks from Utah are Mormon." He grinned.

"What's a Mormon?" Carolyn asked.

The farmer laughed good-naturedly, slapping his knee. "Ah, the golden question," he chuckled. "For now, let's just say that a Mormon is someone who shares my religion."

Mr. Lundquist went on to tell us all about how his ancestors were among the first pioneers to settle in Utah, that he was a third-generation farmer, and that he harvested fruit from trees that his father and grandfather had planted. "Where might you folks be from?" he finally asked.

"We're not from anywhere," I replied, a little embarrassed.

"Is that so? And here I've been thinking that everyone was from *somewhere*."

He was about to say more when Mom came back and sat down.

"Mom, this is Mr. Lundquist," I said excitedly. "He lives on a farm in Utah."

"That's nice," Mom replied halfheartedly.

"Troubles, ma'am?" Mr. Lundquist asked.

"Troubles with a capital *T*."

A doctor came through the swinging doors and inquired, "Mrs. Poduska?"

Mom stood up quickly, with a worried look. "Yes?"

"Mrs. Poduska, your husband has lost a great deal of blood. I'd like him to stay in the hospital until tomorrow."

"We couldn't afford that," Mom sighed, wringing her hands.

"Mrs. Poduska," the doctor said kindly. "Your husband needs time to rest and recuperate."

"What if he doesn't stay?" Mr. Lundquist interjected.

"It's hard to say for certain," the doctor replied cautiously, "but his chances for recovery would improve if he was to stay in the hospital overnight."

At that, Mr. Lundquist volunteered to pay for Dad's hospital stay. He also paid for a room for us to sleep in at the motel where he was staying.

The next morning, Mr. Lundquist drove us over to the hospital, and the nurse brought Dad out to the lobby in a wheelchair.

"You've lost a great deal of blood and suffered a pretty severe beating," the doctor cautioned. "You need a couple of weeks of bed rest to allow your body time to heal."

Dad chuckled as he looked up at Mom. "What do you think, Gladys? Think a couple of weeks of rest might do me some good?"

"A couple of weeks of rest would probably do all of us some good, but I don't see how you're going to get it."

Mr. Lundquist stepped forward with another offer. "I've got a home big enough for all of you and plenty of extra beds."

"That's nice of you, Mr. Lundquist," Mom said, smiling sheepishly, "but you've already done more than enough."

"If there's more to be done, then I haven't done nearly enough."

"Given Mr. Poduska's condition," the doctor interjected, "I'd strongly recommend that you take the gentleman up on his offer."

So we accepted Mr. Lundquist's kindness again, and the five of us left the hospital in his pre-war Ford station wagon. After leaving Grand Junction, we followed the Colorado River until it left us somewhere in the vastness of eastern Utah. We turned north at Green River, followed Highway 6 through Price and then Helper—a small town named for the extra engines that were added to help the long coal trains over the windswept pass called Soldier's Summit. The railroad and the highway competed with the Price River for space, climbing through a narrow gorge, finally reaching the summit, and then quickly dropping down through Spanish Fork Canyon. Mr. Lundquist's farm lay a few miles west of Spanish Fork and just south of Utah Lake.

"Well, this is the farm you've been hearing so much about," Mr. Lundquist said proudly as we turned onto a dirt road. A uniform line of fruit trees stretched into the distance with irrigation ditches flooding the ground beneath them.

"That's my youngest boy Alma working the water gates," Mr. Lundquist explained, honking as we drove past the young boy standing beside one of the ditches. "Got another boy, Jared. He's on a mission in Italy. He won't be home for another year."

We drove past a huge barn with wooden bins stacked in front of it, and then a large farmhouse came into view—a big two-story farmhouse with large gables. Mr. Lundquist pointed at a young girl coming out the front door. "And that little gal is Martha. She was down with the flu when I left. That's why my wife wasn't able to come to Grand Junction with me. But she looks healthy enough now. She's about your age, Carolyn, so the two of you ought to hit it off." The farmer turned to us and winked. "I guess you're the newest members of the family."

"Then shouldn't we be using first names?" Dad chuckled.

"Oh, my heck, you're right. My wife tells me I've got the manners of a goat, butting into people's business without properly introducing myself. The name's Hyrum, and that pretty young lady coming out on the porch is my wife, Sarah."

Sarah was indeed a pretty woman. Waves of auburn hair cascaded onto her shoulders, framing her face and accenting her incredibly green eyes. She had a slender athletic look about her.

Their reunion was all laughter and hugs, and I watched with longing. For the second time, I was witnessing a happy and loving family. I didn't know for sure why they were so different from us, but both Reverend Sanderson and Mr. Lundquist were kind, religious men, and maybe that made a difference. Mr. Lundquist's wife had a twinkle in her eyes, just like her husband, and her laugh had the same unguarded playfulness.

Once the introductions had been made, Sarah invited us into her kitchen. It had high ceilings, and some of the walls were off-white, while others were decorated with bright, cheerful wallpaper. A big wooden table stood in the center of the room, covered with flour, mixing bowls, and an assortment of bread pans. As I drank in the sights and smells, a deep sense of longing returned.

"How long have you guys lived here?" I asked.

"Hyrum was born in this house," Sarah replied, "and I've lived here ever since we got married. Twenty-eight years now."

She bent down to take two loaves of golden brown bread out of the large oven. "Would anyone like some fresh-baked bread?"

Feeling self-conscious, I hesitantly took a slice of the hot bread from her hand and sat down at the end of the table.

Sarah offered the plate to Mom, and at first she didn't respond. Then, looking as if she'd been caught daydreaming, she helped herself to a slice with a grateful smile.

"You looked like you were deep in thought," Sarah observed. "Care to share?"

"I was just savoring the smells of your kitchen," Mom confessed. "It reminds me of the kitchen I grew up in on my parents' farm. Ours was smaller, but the stove is the same."

During the first day or two of our stay, we merely watched Alma and Martha do their chores. But they soon asked us to join in. I think they wanted us to help because they wanted us to feel more at home.

After finishing the chores early one afternoon, Carolyn and I raced Alma and Martha back to the house. Carolyn got to the back porch first, the rest of us scrambling up the steps behind her. While we were sitting there, I heard Sarah humming in the kitchen, then Hyrum coming into the kitchen a few minutes later. He started joking around with her, making her laugh.

Carolyn was sitting beside me on the steps, leaning back on her elbows as she stared out at the orchards. We sat there in silence for a while, and then I said softly, "At first I thought they were just putting on an act to impress us."

"Me too," she agreed, and then she turned to Martha. "Are you guys always like this?"

"Like what?"

"You know . . . laughing and getting along with each other. Stuff like that."

"Most of the time," Martha said, scratching their little mixed-breed dog's ears. "Every once in a while one of us gets mad, but it doesn't last very long."

"Where'd you get him?" I asked, nodding at the dog lying beside her.

She ruffled the dog's ears. "Frisky? He's just some old stray Dad picked up. Dad's always bringing home strays."

The words were out, and there was no way of retrieving them. With a hurt look, Carolyn asked, "Strays like us?"

Martha quickly tried to apologize, but Carolyn couldn't hold back her tears and ran down the steps into the orchard.

Martha apologized again that night, and Hyrum assured us that his daughter hadn't intended to offend. I knew she hadn't meant to hurt, but it was true—we were strays. We didn't belong in their world and probably never would.

The next day, Dad thanked the Lundquists for everything and explained that it was time for us to go. Hyrum asked about our plans. Dad told him that he wanted to go north to Salt Lake City, where he might find a job and get us back on our feet.

Besides giving us a ride, Mr. Lundquist suggested another way that he might help. "You know, I've got a brother-in-law who manages a hotel in Salt Lake. He owes me a favor, so I should be able to talk him into letting you stay there for a while—on the house."

After Hyrum had made the arrangements for the hotel, Mom asked if she could make a collect call to her sister in California. I didn't need to hear the conversation; whenever Mom called her sister, it was about borrowing money.

While talking, Mom gestured at Dad, making a circle with her thumb and forefinger. "You're a lifesaver, Francis," she said gratefully. "Wire it to the Western Union office in Salt Lake City." Then she paused for a few seconds before continuing. "Password?" Another pause. "Hitchhikers!" she exclaimed. "Use *hitchhikers* for the password." Then she hung up the phone and turned around with a look of triumph.

***

The drive from Spanish Fork to Salt Lake City took about an hour. For the most part, conversation was limited to comments on the scenery and the quaintness of the numerous small towns we passed through. Once we reached Salt Lake City, we drove down State Street toward the capitol building and then took a left.

The Pioneer Hotel looked to be an older five-story brick building with a wing on each side. The entrance featured wide steps leading up to a double set of doors.

Mr. Lundquist parked the car in front of the hotel and insisted on coming in to properly introduce us. The moment I saw his brother-in-law, I sensed there was going to be trouble. He had slicked-back hair and a thin mustache that was neatly trimmed; he strutted like a peacock.

I nudged Carolyn and whispered, "Get a load of that."

"Oh, brother!" she moaned, rolling her eyes.

"Darrel, these are the Poduskas," Mr. Lundquist said.

"Indeed," the manager responded, taking a small step backward, while giving us the once-over.

Don't worry, mister, I thought, *we ain't got no cooties.*

He looked around the lobby as if he was afraid someone might see him talking to us. "Look, Hyrum," he went on, "I know I told you that we could accommodate your . . ." He hesitated, looking us over again. "Your friends, but . . ."

Mr. Lundquist placed his hand on his shoulder and in a low, serious voice said, "Darrel, you owe me this favor."

The debt must have been big because Darrel immediately threw up his hands in surrender. "Very well, but they can only stay for two nights. Now, let's get them up to their room."

After we had said our good-byes to Mr. Lundquist, we were whisked up to the fourth floor and down the hall to our room. The manager opened the door and then dropped the keys in Dad's hand without entering. With barefaced arrogance, he informed us that the bathroom was down the hall and that he hoped our stay in the hotel would be a pleasant one.

Carolyn began mimicking his swagger as he walked away.

"Carolyn!" Mom scolded under her breath. "Shame on you!"

"Well, he had it coming," Carolyn retorted.

Our small room was meagerly furnished, with only one double bed, a chest of drawers, and a couple of nightstands. Mom pushed the long drapes to each side, opened one of the two windows, and began pulling out a pile of dirty clothes from the suitcase.

Dad looked annoyed. "What're you up to now?"

"I'm going to do the wash. There's no telling when I'll have water and a sink again."

Dad shook his head in disbelief. "Why didn't you do the wash while we were at the Lundquists?"

"Sarah and I were taking turns. I was going to do mine today. How was I to know we'd be leaving so suddenly?"

Dad grunted. Mom merely carried an armload of clothes over to the small sink and started doing her washing.

Once the clothes had been scrubbed and rinsed, she laid them over the chairs and draped them on the windowsills. Then she pulled the bedspread and sheets off the bed and held them up in front of us. "I've got to wash what you've got on, too. So strip to the skin and wrap yourselves up in these."

We did as we were told, but not without considerable giggling and horseplay. After handing Mom our clothes, we wrapped ourselves in the sheets, climbed on the bed, and started dancing and whooping like Indians.

Mom shushed us. "You two are making way too much noise."

"Oh come on, Gladys," Dad said playfully. "Let the kids have a little fun."

"It won't be much fun if we get evicted."

But Dad seemed to be in an unusually good mood. Ignoring her warning, he wrapped the other sheet around him, folded his arms across his chest, and said in a deep voice, "I'm Chief Snot-in-the-Face, and you are my booger braves."

We all started laughing, even Mom. It wasn't like Dad to clown around.

"I want to welcome you to my tepee," Dad continued. "And it is our custom to exchange boogers as a sign of friendship." He pretended to pick his nose and then extended his finger toward us. "Here's mine!" he cried.

Carolyn and I screamed and jumped off the far side of the bed. Dad climbed up after us and jumped off too. Since we were all wrapped up in bedding, none of us could run very well. Everyone kept falling down, which made us laugh all the more.

Our free-for-all was suddenly cut short by a loud banging at the door. Mom opened the door, and there stood Darrel with an exaggerated look of shock and dismay on his face.

"Really!" he huffed when he saw us. "I mean, really. This kind of hooliganism is not what our hotel guests are accustomed to." Then he looked around the room and added, "Nor is this hotel used to being turned into a Chinese laundry!"

By this time, Dad had stood up and put a sober look on his face. He walked toward the manager with his hand outstretched. Darrel seemed to relax a little at the gesture.

"Hey, we're sorry we let things get a little out of hand," Dad said sincerely. "What do you say we exchange boogers as a sign of friendship?" Then his outstretched hand shot up to his nose, and the look of dismay on Darrel's face turned to horror.

"Well, I never!" he exclaimed, and then he turned on his heels and hurried down the hall toward the elevator.

Dad shut the door behind him with a self-satisfied grin. Carolyn and I were rolling on the bed with laughter. Mom just stood there in front of the sink, shaking her head.

***

The next afternoon, Mom went to the Western Union office. As soon as she returned with the money, Dad insisted that we all go out and celebrate.

"Come on, honey," he urged. "We've all been through some pretty rough times. We deserve a little fun."

Carolyn and I were all for it, but Mom was hesitant.

"I don't want us to end up penniless again."

By this time, Carolyn and I were giving her pleading looks.

"Oh, all right," she finally conceded, "I guess we deserve to have a little fun once in a while." She paused before adding, "But that doesn't mean we have to go hog-wild."

In honor of the special occasion, Carolyn and I both combed our hair and washed our faces. Too excited to wait for the others, I hurried out the door ahead of them and ran down the hall to the elevator. We'll be just like the Lundquists, I thought, as I pressed the button.

"I want to push the button," Carolyn called out, as she came running down the hall.

"Too late," I yelled back, full of self-importance.

I was still feeling giddy when we walked out of the hotel, but the feeling quickly left as we neared the movie theater. Dad stopped, reached into his pocket, and handed us each a quarter.

I stared down at the coin in my hand. "We're not going to the movie as a family, are we?" I asked softly.

"Your mom and I have already seen this one," Dad lied. "You two go ahead. We'll meet you back here after the show."

Carolyn sensed my disappointment and put her arm around my shoulders. "How many times do I have to tell you, Buddy? We're never going to be like other folks. It'll never happen."

"But I sure want it," I said, wiping my nose with my sleeve.

"I know you do, Buddy," she said softly. "But wanting and getting are two different things."

I sniffled and then quickly wiped the tears off of my face so that no one would see that I'd been crying.

Mom and Dad met us after the show. I could tell that they'd already had quite a bit to drink. Hungry, I peeked into the grocery bag Mom was carrying. It held six bottles of beer and a bottle of soda pop. "What's for dinner?" I asked.

"We're going to stop and pick up some Chinese food on the way back to the hotel," Dad said, slurring noticeably.

Once we got back to our room, Mom had us get ready for bed while she dished up the Chinese food, and Dad made a trip down the hall to the bathroom. Since we slept in our underwear, getting ready for bed merely meant getting undressed. We were just sitting down to eat, when there was a pounding on the door.

Mom hurriedly opened the door. It was Dad.

"Shush!" she scolded, as she stepped aside to let him in.

"Someone was using the bathroom, and I almost wet my pants," Dad snickered, and then he reached into the sack and pulled out a bottle of beer. Mom offered him a dish of food. "You need to get something in your stomach besides beer," she said.

He dismissed her with a wave of his hand. "Give it to the kids. I'm not hungry." But I knew that what he really meant was that he could get drunker on an empty stomach.

It was already late, but Dad still turned on the radio, found a station that was playing Benny Goodman, and asked Mom to dance. Then Dad turned up the volume, and seconds later, the people in the room next door came over and asked him to turn it down. Dad suggested that they stick their fingers in their ears because he was celebrating and slammed the door in their faces. Then he turned the radio up even louder. An instant later, the neighbors started pounding on the wall again.

Dad responded by putting his thumb over the top of his beer bottle and banging it on the wall. But his thumb wasn't enough to contain it, and foam spewed all over the room. Mom screamed as the spray hit her, and Carolyn and I scrambled under the bed.

Dad was yelling obscenities at the wall, when he suddenly grabbed his groin and began hopping up and down. "Whoa, Nellie! That beer went right through me, and nature's calling. Wooee!"

I couldn't make out anymore because of the loud music and the pounding on the door. I was turning the doorknob when Dad yelled, "Don't open the door!" But the warning came too late. The hotel manager was standing there with a look of rage that quickly turned to stunned disbelief when he looked past me. "You're nothing but animals!" he shouted.

I turned around to find out what he was so upset about and saw Dad leaning against the wall, urinating into the sink.

"Animals!" Darrel repeated. "Favor or no favor, I want you out of my hotel."

Mom stood in front of Dad, trying to shield him from view, but there wasn't much to do but wait until he was finished.

"I should never have let Hyrum talk me into letting trash like you in here in the first place," the livid manager continued. "I want you out of here."

"Okay," Mom replied, trying to calm him down. "You've made your point. We'll leave first thing in the morning."

"Not first thing in the morning! Now!"

"What do you mean, now?" Dad asked, turning around as he zipped up his pants.

"I mean I'm calling the police. And if you're not out of my hotel in fifteen minutes, I'll have them throw you out." At that, Darrell turned on his heels and walked off.

Dad closed the door, and Mom began gathering up our laundry and hurriedly stuffing it back into the suitcase. No one said much. We took one last look around the room and then left without closing the door behind us.

As we were walking to the elevator, a woman in the room next to ours yelled, "Good riddance." None of us looked back.

Once we reached the street, Dad cuffed me on the back of the head. "I told you not to open the door!"

"I didn't hear you."

"Don't give me that. You heard me, all right," and then he cuffed me on the back of the head again.

"Stop blaming the boy," Mom said in my defense. "He wasn't the one who turned up the radio or pounded on the walls."

"Or peed in the sink," Carolyn added defiantly.

"So you're all going to blame this on me," Dad lashed back.

"Look, it doesn't matter who's to blame," Mom argued in a lower voice, attempting to restore peace. "Fact is, we're out on the street, so we've got to find a place to spend the night."

We wandered the streets for a while before stumbling onto a small park with a few benches and lots of trees.

Dad announced, "This looks like as good a place as any." Carolyn and I headed for the nearest bench and lay down, exhausted. Mom took some clothes out of the suitcase to cover us, and then sat down on a nearby bench with Dad.

I watched some fireworks exploding in the distance, but I didn't feel much like celebrating. "Happy Fourth of July," I said without much enthusiasm to no one in particular.

"Yeah, I'd forgotten what day it was," Carolyn replied.

I turned my head away from the bursting rockets and slowly drifted off to sleep.

Chapter 10

A HOSPITAL SECURITY GUARD WAS making his way up the hall, checking to see if the doors that were supposed to be locked were indeed locked. He stopped for a few minutes to joke with the night nurse before continuing on his rounds. As he was passing the waiting room, he smiled and pointed out the obvious. "Looks like you folks are spending the night with us."

Carolyn chuckled. "It looks that way."

"It's our mother," I volunteered.

"I'm sorry," the guard said with sincerity. "I'll say a prayer for her while I'm checking the hospital chapel."

"Thank you. We'd appreciate that," I said with a slight wave as he headed on down the hall to complete his rounds.

Carolyn looked out the window for a few seconds before commenting. "When he said that he was going to pray for Mom, I realized that I wasn't sure what I want him to pray for."

"What do you mean?"

"I mean, did I want him to pray that Mom will recover? But then I thought, what if she ends up an invalid? What kind of life would that be? But I certainly didn't want him to pray for her to die. I'm so confused. I don't know what to pray for."

"Sometimes it's not so much a matter of what we want, but what God wants," I proposed.

"Now it's my turn to ask what you mean."

"When Jesus was asked how we should pray, he said, 'Our Father which art in heaven, Hallowed be thy name. Thy kingdom come. *Thy* will be done in earth, as it is in heaven.' The Lord's Prayer is very specific that *His* will is to be done both here on earth and in heaven."

"But how can we possibly know what God wants?" Carolyn countered.

"Ask Him," I exhorted. "It is truly amazing how our lives can be transformed when we are willing to inquire of the Lord what it is that He wishes us to do rather than trying to persuade Him to do our will. At first we may merely ask him to grant us our desires: 'Help me get this job,' or 'Prompt a certain person to marry me.' However, if too much time passes without our request being granted then we usually begin to barter."

"Barter?"

"By barter, I mean we offer to give God something in exchange for God giving us something in return. 'Please dear Lord, if you will do this one thing for me, I will . . . read my scriptures every day, I will become a full tithe payer,' and so forth."

"What happens if God still doesn't grant your wish?" Carolyn asked.

"If there is still no satisfaction, then we usually return to the bargaining table. 'Dear Lord, I'll not only read my scriptures every day and pay a full tithe, if you will but grant me what I want, I'll'—and here's where we up the ante—'I'll promise to write in my journal every day and go the temple every month.'"

"I don't see anything wrong with that," Carolyn noted.

"The problem with this kind of an approach is that we apparently believe that God has a price and that if we can make it worth His while, we can get God to do our bidding. What a travesty it would be to attempt to maintain a relationship with our Heavenly Father on such a basis."

"Then what are we supposed to pray for?"

"Rather than praying that our will be done, pray to have His will revealed to us. For example when my son Ryan got engaged, he and his sweetheart were desperately trying to find a decent apartment to live in after they got married. They were both working and going to school, so they had very little money. Ryan repeatedly prayed for God to help him find an apartment that they could afford. He wanted to rent something near where his fiancée worked. Weeks went by without finding a place to live. Then, as he was about to get on his knees once more, a thought came to him. Perhaps he was praying for the wrong thing. He had been praying that what he wanted would be granted, that his will be done rather than God's will. He changed his prayer and asked God where He wanted them to live, where God needed them to be at this time in their lives. The next day, they found a wonderful, and affordable, apartment."

"So God might have a better idea of what's good for us than we do?"

"Think of it this way: If a father asks his three-year-old what he wants for Christmas, and the child says, 'I want a 12-gauge shotgun,' would a loving father give his three-year-old son a shotgun just because he wants one and is begging and pleading? However, when the father says no, the child will probably get mad and accuse his father of not loving him. Hopefully, after the child matures, he will better understand his father's wisdom."

Carolyn thought about that for a moment. "I can see where, in that example, getting what he wants might not be best for the child, or for his family—or for the people living in the neighborhood, for that matter. But we live in an instant gratification kind of world, so people don't take it very well when the answer is no."

"I completely agree, so even if the answer is yes but delayed, people get upset with God. One of the things we must consider is that things will be done when He wants them to be done and that, more often than not, His time frame will not correspond to the schedule that we have in mind. There's an old saying, 'We become *patient* when we are willing to accept God's schedule. We become *impatient* when things aren't being done on our schedule.'

"Sometimes we must wait for a long period of time before our prayers are answered and during such times we may feel abandoned and alone. However, Jesus Christ promised that He will never abandon us in our time of need. 'Peace I leave with you, my peace I give unto you: not as the world giveth, give I unto you. Let not your heart be troubled, neither let it be afraid.' The Lord, in His wisdom, will always see that we have that which is sufficient for our needs."

Carolyn cocked her head to one side and furrowed her brow. "When I think back on the time when we were hitchhiking, we never had much, but we usually had enough to get by. And that usually came from the kindness of others."

"Like when we were dropped off outside Salt Lake City and tried to hitchhike out of Utah?" I asked. "If I'd known then what I know now, that's the time I would've started praying."

"Praying for what?"

"Praying to know what God had in mind for us," I admitted.

***

Summer 1947

Salt Lake City, Utah, to Elko, Nevada

We had been kicked out of our hotel and forced to spend the night sleeping on park benches. When I woke up the next morning, Dad was sitting on a nearby bench stretching out the kinks. He rousted the rest of us, pointed at the bag and box, and said, "Grab your stuff. We're getting out of here."

Mom quickly picked up the clothes we had used as blankets and put them back into the suitcase. I grabbed my box, Carolyn grabbed her bag, and we headed west across the railroad tracks.

A few blocks beyond the tracks, we came to a main thoroughfare and started hitchhiking. Before long, we were picked up by a man on his way to work at the Kennecott copper smelter near the Great Salt Lake. As a favor, he drove a little past the smelter and let us off at a place called Lake Point Junction—about twenty miles west of Salt Lake City.

The Great Salt Lake stretched out to the north horizon, waves lapping on the barren shoreline. Behind us, the Oquirrh Mountains soared into the sky. No one said anything as we picked up our belongings and began hiking west. The sun, now high above the Wasatch Mountains, felt good on my back.

Unfortunately, there wasn't much traffic, and the sun kept getting hotter. We tried all day to hitch a ride without so much as a hint of getting one, so we just kept walking.

When we reached a Y in the road, called Mill's Junction, Dad finally gave up and decided to pitch camp beside a large cluster of rocks. We were about ten miles from where we had started and another ten miles short of the small community of Grantsville. Mom warmed up the leftover Chinese food from the night before while Carolyn and I opened a bottle of soda pop.

Once again, I found myself sleeping under newspapers and listening to the forlorn howl of coyotes.

The next morning, the Oquirrh Mountains shielded us from the rising sun. The newspaper Mom put over us had blown away during the night. A thin layer of sand covered my face. None of the others were stirring. So I quietly eased myself out from between Mom and Carolyn. I climbed one of the large rocks, and from my vantage point, I could see that except for a few small buildings in a cluster of trees, there was nothing but desert.

Hearing the others begin to stir, I climbed down from my perch to find Mom in the middle of her morning ritual—searching through her bag for something to eat—but this time she didn't come up with anything. So she opened the suitcase and began rummaging through it, until she found an old undershirt rolled up in one of the corners. "I've been saving this until we got good and hungry," she explained as she unrolled it.

Until we got good and hungry? When hadn't we been good and hungry?

Mom gave the shirt one last flick, and a small jar of peanut butter dropped out. "I'm afraid there's not much peanut butter in a small jar like this, but . . ."

"It's better than nothing," I declared, my mouth watering.

One by one we dipped a finger into the jar until it was empty. Then we broke camp and began walking toward Grantsville.

We hadn't gone far when we came upon the small cluster of trees and old buildings I'd seen from the top of the rock. The largest building looked like an old mill of some sort, but I couldn't imagine what they would've had to grind out here. When we reached the far end of the building, we discovered that part of the first floor had been converted into a small café.

Dad tapped on the window with the tips of his fingers.

A tall woman with her hair wrapped in a bun yelled, "We're not open yet!"

"How soon then?" Dad hollered back.

The woman put the tray down then walked over to the door and unlocked it. "The deliveries haven't been made yet," she explained, opening the door. "Be another hour or so before the milk truck arrives." She spoke in an unhurried tone.

"That's okay," Dad said. "We can wait."

"But I'm hungry," Carolyn pleaded.

"Me too," I added.

"Beggars can't be choosy," Mom said in jest, but it struck me that she was right—we *had* become beggars.

Making do with what was available until the delivery was made, the woman prepared a breakfast of Wheaties with sour milk and no sugar. It tasted like cardboard, but I was hungry, so I ate it. After we finished, we thanked the lady and got up to leave.

"Which way you headed?" she asked as Dad reached the door.

"West," he answered.

"The guy pulling up in that delivery truck has come to drop off some supplies, but he'll be heading into Grantsville as soon as he's finished here. I can ask him to give you folks a lift."

"Beats walking," Dad said gratefully.

The delivery truck was a small, paneled Chevrolet with only two seats in the front. Dad climbed in next to the driver. The rest of us sat in the back with the produce.

We were dropped off at the west end of Grantsville, which was little more than a small cluster of houses in the middle of nowhere. Traffic seemed steady in both directions, so I thought we'd be able to get a ride without too much trouble. I couldn't have been more wrong. We spent the entire day roasting in the desert heat across from a small gas station.

"This is the part I hate the most about hitchhiking," I complained. "I hate the waiting with nothing to do."

Mom and Dad looked bored. They would alternately lean against an old cottonwood tree, sit down for a while, and then stand up and lean against the tree again. At first, Mom would brush the dirt off her dress each time she stood up, but as the day wore on she no longer bothered.

When I commented to Carolyn how pointless it was for Mom to try and keep her dress clean, Carolyn explained, "It's just something left over from when it did matter."

We sat as close to the road as possible while staying in the shade of the cottonwood tree. As usual, we faced the oncoming traffic, but as the day wore on, there was less and less traffic in either direction.

Dad waited near the highway, drawing in the dirt with a stick. He'd stand up from time to time, look down the road, and then squat back down. "Midday traffic's bound to be light in this kind of heat," he said, as much to himself as to anyone. "Since it's the middle of July, only hardy souls or dumb fools would even try to cross the Great Salt Lake Desert during the day."

What's that make us? I thought.

I sat staring at the small gas station on the other side of the highway. It was a single-bay building with a sign on the bay door that read, "No Mechanic." The two old gas pumps had faded Texaco signs painted on them, and a red Coca-Cola cooler sat in front of the office. An A-frame sign near the edge of the highway boldly declared, "Last chance."

Carolyn was also staring across the highway. "I wonder if that sign out front is trying to tell us something," she said.

"Like, 'Turn back now or you're going to die'?" I scoffed.

Somewhere around noon, the gas station attendant came out of his office. He was a tall, lanky man, and his Texaco uniform didn't fit very well. He pulled four bottles of Nesbitt's orange out of the cooler, popped the caps off, and started across the highway. When he didn't give so much as a glance in either direction, I quickly looked both ways for him.

He must have noticed my concern. "Out here, you can hear 'em coming before you can see 'em," he laughed.

"I've been watching you folks waiting over here," he began, "and I figured you could use some refreshments."

He held up the bottles. I looked back at Mom and Dad. They alternately looked at each other and then at the stranger.

Dad's initial reaction was suspicion. "That's awful thoughtful of you," he said carefully, "but we're a little short on money, and what we do have is mostly for food."

And booze, I added silently.

"Don't worry about it," the man smiled. "These are on me."

Dad thanked him for his kindness and then nodded his approval to me and Carolyn. We scrambled to our feet and grabbed a bottle. It wasn't until after we'd taken our first drink that we simultaneously remembered to say, "Thanks, mister!"

The bottle was cold and wet, so I held it to my face when I wasn't drinking from it. The others were doing the same.

For a long while, we silently sat there, savoring our drinks. Then the man from the gas station turned to Dad and asked, "How long you been on the road?"

"We left Durango about a month ago," Dad replied.

"Where you headed?"

"West coast."

"Might be a little tough getting a ride out of here. Folks don't like to pick up hitchhikers this far out. Once you leave here, towns are few and far between. There ain't nothing but desert for over five hundred miles, so you can't just abandon someone beside the road. If you pick 'em up, you're stuck with 'em. Like it or not."

Dad nodded as if in agreement but maintained his belief that most drivers would stop when they saw a woman and kids.

"Actually, having four of you probably works more against you than for you," the attendant went on. "You and your family take up a lot of room, and most folks traveling this road are fully packed. It'd be hard to make room for the four of you, let alone what you're carrying."

Dad didn't respond, and the man grew quiet for a few minutes. Then he slapped his knee and said, "I've said too much as it is. I don't want to meddle in your private affairs any more than I have already." As he stood up, he mentioned that he wasn't in any big hurry but that he'd like to have the bottles back when we were finished with our sodas.

All too soon the bottles were drained, and the man was collecting the empties. We all thanked him again as he started back across the highway. Halfway across, he waved the empty bottles over his head and called back over his shoulder, "Good luck, and God bless." But as he got closer to the gas station, he was shaking his head, which is something I had gotten used to seeing with most of the people we'd met on the road.

Somewhat refreshed, I settled back into my vigil of watching for oncoming cars. In the distance, the highway looked like it was covered with water. The heat waves coming off the asphalt distorted everything, so I wasn't sure if what I was seeing was actually a car or just some sagebrush near the road.

But then Dad yelled, "Heads up. There's a car coming."

I squinted, but I still couldn't tell for sure until I heard the distant drone of an engine. "I hear something!" I called out. "You can hear 'em before you can see 'em."

The engine had a high-pitched whine to it. Whatever it was, it was coming fast.

Dad walked over to the shoulder. "Get out here and get your thumbs up!" he shouted back at us. Mom grabbed the suitcase, and we hurried over to join him.

The oncoming car turned out to be a black Buick Roadmaster with a large chrome grill. As it got closer, I could hear the tires tearing themselves free of the sticky asphalt. The Buick began to drift toward the center line then straddled it, as if the driver was trying to stay as far away from us as possible. I knew it wasn't going to stop. But when it roared by, two boys in the backseat stuck their tongues out at us.

For a while, I just stood there staring after the car, turning away from the wind and dust that always follows speeding cars and large trucks. No one said anything until Carolyn finally broke the silence. "Why do people have to be so mean? Stop and pick us up or keep on going. How simple is that?"

"I'm glad they didn't stop and pick us up," I added. "It probably would've been a crappy ride anyway."

Nothing more was said about the Buick, but if I'd felt bad before, now I felt even worse.

Once again, we settled back into the shade. The heat and the constant buzz of the grasshoppers began making me sleepy, and my chin slowly dropped to my chest. But when I heard Dad yelling, my head jerked up.

"What's happening?" I asked groggily.

"Dad says there's a truck coming," Carolyn said, helping me to my feet.

"What kind of truck?"

"How should I know? A truck."

Dad shaded his eyes. "It looks like there's more than one truck," he said. "It looks like it might be a . . . It is! It's a convoy!" he shouted. "It's an army convoy!"

The convoy wasn't moving very fast, but even from a long way off, the roar of the engines was loud. As the lead truck came closer, Dad announced, "They're army deuce-and-a-half's! This is probably our best chance, so keep your arms up and your thumbs pumping. Don't stop for anything. Just keep pumping." He also reminded us to smile and make eye contact.

All four of us assumed the hitchhiker position: arms up, elbows bent, thumbs extended— each with our own pumping style.

Before long, the lead truck was abreast of us. There were no doors on the trucks, just scalloped openings. I desperately tried to make eye contact. The driver waved with one hand but kept a tight grip on the steering wheel with the other.

The soldier riding shotgun just stared at us as the truck passed by without slowing. I quickly shifted my attention to the second truck, just as the tornadoes of wind hit me. I was rubbing my eyes when the second truck roared by carrying only a driver. He shrugged his shoulders as he drove past.

The third truck was coming up now, and still no one was slowing down. The driver in the third truck looked surprised and started shaking his head in that all too familiar way.

The dust clouds grew progressively worse with each passing truck. By the time the fourth truck passed by, I was finding it hard to breathe. I turned away coughing, and then I looked up in the direction of the trucks that had already passed. The brake lights of the lead truck blinked on. In quick succession, the brake lights of the succeeding trucks lit up.

I yanked on Mom's sleeve and shouted above the roar of the engines. "Mom! Dad! They're stopping! They're stopping!" By the time the last of the five trucks was driving past, the first truck had pulled off the highway and stopped on the shoulder. The drivers climbed out of their cabs and gathered near the lead truck. Then one of the soldiers started walking toward us.

He introduced himself as Private Hansen. "The captain sent me over to find out if you folks were in some kind of trouble."

Dad shook the soldier's hand and then turned to Mom. "Gladys, you and Carolyn gather up our belongings. Buddy, grab your box." Then he added offhandedly, "You and I are going to go have a little talk with the head man."

Dad, the private, and I walked over to the group of soldiers still milling around the lead truck. Dad had given the private our names while we were walking, so as soon as we arrived, he began introducing us to his captain.

"From the looks of things, you might be having a little trouble," the captain commented.

"Little is a relative term, Captain," Dad said, motioning Mom and Carolyn to join us. "Let me introduce the rest of my family," he continued, "my wife, Gladys, and my daughter, Carolyn."

The captain leaned toward Dad and said in a low voice, "At first, I wasn't going to stop. According to Corporal Ross, the legal-eagle behind me," he continued, gesturing with his thumb over his shoulder, "it's against regulations to pick up hitchhikers. He's kind of nitpicky, if you know what I mean."

"I heard that," the corporal objected. Corporal Ross was mousy looking, with small wire-rimmed spectacles and a high-pitched voice. "And I'd like to remind the captain that 'for purposes of safety and security, army regulations strictly forbid the use of military vehicles for the purpose of providing transportation for nonmilitary personnel.' In addition, regulations specifically prohibit the unscheduled stopping of a military convoy, except for repairs or in case of an emergency."

"Ross?"

"Yes, sir?"

"Why don't you put those regulations where the sun don't shine," Captain Foster said nonchalantly. He turned back to Dad. "What are you doing out here in the middle of nowhere?"

"Trying to hitch a ride."

"I can see that. What I meant was how did you end up out here in the middle of this desolate wasteland?"

"I'm not quite sure," Dad answered truthfully.

The captain turned back to his driver. "What do you think, Corporal? Think we should give them a ride?"

"Picking up hitchhikers is against regulations, sir."

"Like I said before, Corporal . . ."

"I know, sir. Put it where the sun don't shine."

"You're learning, Ross. You're learning."

"I didn't know if I was doing the right thing or not by stopping, but seeing you people standing by the side of the road . . . well, it looked like you needed some help."

One of the other drivers stepped forward and addressed the captain in a low voice. "Sir, according to what Ross said about army regulations, someone needing help could qualify as an emergency . . . so that would justify stopping the convoy."

Corporal Ross rolled his eyes.

The captain chuckled. "I know I'm bending the rules a little, but the way I see it, regulations are meant to be bent."

After the chuckling subsided, the captain's face took on a more serious look. "Just where you folks headed?"

"I've got a job waiting for me in Reno," Dad lied, as usual, "but they'll only hold it for me till Friday."

The captain grimaced. I don't think he liked the idea of being stuck with us all the way to Reno. He paused for a moment and then shrugged his shoulders. "Well, none of us are getting any closer to Reno standing here."

The challenge now was to figure out exactly how to transport us. The lead vehicle was the only truck that had full seating for both driver and passenger. The other four trucks had only a driver's seat. After some discussion, it was decided we'd each have to ride in a separate truck, using the drivers' duffel bags for seat cushions. Problem solved, Dad threw the suitcase into the cab of the second truck and climbed in. A driver helped Mom into the third truck. Carolyn climbed into the fourth, and my box and I climbed into the cab of the fifth.

Without further delay, the drivers took up their positions behind the wheel and started their engines. I was too short to see out the front window, so I leaned my head out the scalloped doorway in order to see what was happening up ahead.

"Hey, kid, don't lean out too far. I don't want to lose you before we even get started."

"I'll be careful," I reassured him, continuing to monitor the trucks in front of us. I knew where the others were, but I still didn't like the idea of being separated from them.

The captain climbed up on the running board of the lead truck, looked back at the convoy, rotated his arm above his head a couple of times, and then pointed forward. The lead truck pulled back onto the highway, and the others followed one by one.

We were on our way to Reno.

Once the driver got through the initial gear shifting, the engine roar became more tolerable, and brief conversations could be held with minimal shouting.

"What's your name, kid?" the driver yelled.

"Buddy," I replied, looking up at him. He appeared to be in his late teens. He had blonde hair that was shorn into a crew cut and wore his dog tags on the outside of his army-brown T-shirt. His blue eyes and freckles gave him a wholesome look.

"Mine's Pierson," the driver volunteered. "Michael Pierson. But everyone calls me Mike."

I soon discovered that Mike liked to talk. He told me that the convoy had originated at an army depot near Denver and that they were hauling jeeps to Fort Ord. I didn't have to say much; having someone to talk to seemed to be enough for him.

I watched the bleak landscape go by. Even the sagebrush was becoming sparse. A dust devil snaked across the desert. A hot wind blew into the open cab, causing some candy wrappers to whirl around the floor before being whipped out of the truck.

We began climbing out of one of those long inclines on either side of the shallow desert valleys. After shifting three times in rapid succession, Mike shook his head. "Danged if this desert won't fool you. I can't tell we're climbing most of the time. But I'm still losing speed with the pedal to the floor."

"Yeah, it looks pretty flat," I agreed, leaning my head out the door. A moment later, the pitch of the engine increased.

"How 'bout that, kid!" Mike laughed. "We made it to the top. No desert's going to beat this baby!" The words were barely out of his mouth when his eyes opened wider; his tone grew serious, and he tapped me on the shoulder. "Maybe I spoke too soon. Take a gander up ahead."

I grabbed the handle on the dash and pulled myself up. I could still barely see, but what lay ahead left me speechless. I'd seen a lot of desert before but never anything like this. The vast white flatness of the Great Salt Lake Desert stretched before us. There were no trees, no cactus, no sagebrush, just some stubby telephone poles poking up out of the salt.

"I'm sure glad I don't have to walk across that," I gasped.

We soon left the low desert hills and drove out on the salt flats. The initial wonder I'd felt gradually turned to boredom from the monotony of the unchanging scenery. Coupled with the heat, staying awake became more and more difficult.

I don't know how long I'd been sleeping, but the sensation of slowing prodded me awake.

"Why are we slowing down?" I asked, rubbing my eyes.

"I'm not sure," was Mike's response.

Since he didn't seem to know any more than I did, I leaned my head out the open doorway. We were climbing out of the salt flats into a low mountain range. Small billboards, advertising attractions in Wendover, Nevada, pockmarked the landscape.

Ahead of us, the first truck was pulling off onto the shoulder. As soon as it stopped, the captain jumped down from the cab and signaled the second truck—the one Dad was in—to keep going. But then he signaled the third and fourth trucks, the ones Mom and Carolyn were in, to stop. When he signaled our truck to keep moving, Mike looked confused.

"Well, for heaven's sake, make up your mind," he said as he began the gear-shifting process all over again. We had slowed to a crawl and had to wait until we were clear of the trucks that had stopped in front of us before he could pull around them and get back on the road. As we coasted by, I saw Mom climb down from her cab and walk back to Carolyn's truck. Carolyn took her hand and jumped to the ground. As we came abreast of the lead truck, the captain was climbing back into his cab. Black smoke belched from the exhausts of all three trucks as they slowly began moving forward in unison.

I didn't have the foggiest idea what was going on. All I knew was that Mom and Carolyn were being left behind. I jumped.

I hit the ground hard, scraping my hands, elbows, and knees on the gravel. Mike yelled something, the air brakes hissed, and the tires screeched. Then silence.

Mom reached me first. "Did you break anything, Buddy?" she asked, nervously feeling my arms and legs. "Where does it hurt?"

"I think . . . I'm okay," I said, trying to catch my wind. I could hear Carolyn crying in the background and Dad telling her that I was going to be just fine. Personally, I wasn't completely convinced. But considering that I'd just jumped out of a moving truck, I didn't feel all that bad.

The drivers were all gathered around me. Someone had grabbed a first-aid kit out of one of the trucks. Once they'd determined that nothing seemed to be broken, they sat me up, and Mom washed the gravel and dirt off my scuffed palms with warm water from the milk bottle.

"It all happened so fast," Mike was explaining. "I didn't have a chance to grab him."

Corporal Ross sounded especially upset. "Don't say I didn't warn you . . . this is exactly why we have regulations. We should never have picked them up in the first place. I knew something like this would happen. I knew it."

Once Mom was satisfied that I wasn't seriously injured, she started in with the third degree. "Do you realize you could've been killed? Whatever possessed you to jump?"

My response to her flurry of questions was simply, "I thought they were leaving you and Carolyn behind."

A few mouths fell open, but no one said anything.

Mom found her voice first. "Leaving me and Carolyn behind?" she echoed, and then a smile of understanding came to her face. "We weren't being left behind, honey. We were just asked to walk a little ways, and then get back in the trucks."

The captain turned to Corporal Ross, pointing his finger in his face. "Because of your obsession with following regulations . . . it's your fault the kid ended up jumping."

Looking more confused than ever, Mike asked, "How is it Ross's fault?"

"Halfway across the salt flats," the captain began, "this legal-eagle started telling me about some anti-prostitution law called the Mann Act and wouldn't shut up about it." He paused, apparently trying to compose himself before continuing. "He told me that it's against the law to transport women you're not related to across a state line. It's a violation of the White Slave Act or some such nonsense. It would be a federal offense that could land us all in Leavenworth prison." The captain kicked a rock in frustration. "So I figured if the gals walked across the state line between Utah and Nevada, I wouldn't actually be transporting them, so we wouldn't be breaking any law."

Dad assured the captain that no real harm had been done and that he was sure nothing like this would happen again. The captain didn't look convinced, but with a shrug and a wave of his hands, we all climbed back into our trucks.

Before Carolyn climbed into her truck, she paused long enough to ask, "Are you sure you're okay?"

I waved off her concern, but I appreciated it.

Mike would glance at me nervously every once in a while. "Your mom told me to keep an eye on you," he explained, "in case that scrape on your head turns out to be more than a bump."

Or in case I got the urge to jump again, I added silently.

By the time we reached Wells, Nevada, Mike had started complaining about being hungry. "I see a sign for a café up ahead on the left," he said, then mumbled in a low, prayerful tone, "Come on, Captain, pull that baby over."

His prayer was soon answered. A cloud of dust billowed up as the lead trucks began pulling off the highway onto a narrow strip of dirt between the road and a set of railroad tracks. As he slowed, Mike asked with a smile, "No more jumping?"

I grinned sheepishly and shook my head, and he smiled back.

The captain climbed to the ground and gathered the drivers around him for a short conference. Then he came over and spoke briefly to Dad. Dad explained what was happening as we gathered. "The captain's afraid that if we go into the café with the rest of them, someone might put two and two together and report them for transporting civilians. As a precaution, he wants us to wait here for a few minutes before we go in. Once we're in the café, we're to act like we don't know them."

We all nodded and then sat back and waited a few minutes before crossing the highway.

As soon as we walked in, Mom nudged us toward an empty booth in the back. We sat down, and she handed out the menus.

I was pretending to read mine and didn't notice that a waitress had walked up to our booth.

"Are you folks going to be ordering anything?" she asked, looking right at me, sounding more curious than dubious.

I didn't know the answer, so I shrugged.

She patted me on the head and chuckled. "Guess that stray cat that's been hanging around here got your tongue." She had what Mom called a full figure, so she jiggled when she laughed. "You folks ready to order?" she pressed, giving us the once-over. *Probably wondering if we'll be able to pay*, I thought.

"You bet," Dad said. "Any suggestions?"

"Our special today is meatloaf. We're out of chicken-fried steak, and the soup of the day is vegetable."

"How much is the meatloaf special?" Dad asked.

"Special's a dollar. It includes mashed potatoes, green peas, and bread," she replied, vigorously chewing her gum.

Dad looked in his wallet, then put it away and took out some change. While he slowly added up the coins, the waitress leaned over a little, straightening up when he finished adding. She gave me a wink and a smile. I blushed and smiled back.

"There's no sales tax in Nevada," she offered calmly.

Dad looked at Mom. "How hungry are you?" he asked.

Mom answered casually, but it sounded forced. "Oh, I'm not very hungry. Just order something for you and the kids."

"Can't do it," he replied in a low voice. "I've only got enough for one."

"Then order one."

Dad looked up at the waitress, who had her order pad and pencil at the ready. "We'd like one meatloaf special, please."

"That's it? Just one?"

"I'm afraid so," Dad said apologetically.

The waitress turned her head and called out, "One special!" before returning to her post behind the counter. After pouring more coffee for the soldiers, she returned to our booth with four glasses of water and some silverware. She set the water down first and started arranging the silverware. "If you don't use the silverware, don't worry about it. Someone else will."

A few minutes later, a small bell rang, and the fry cook yelled, "One special up!"

The waitress went to pick up the order but then said something to the cook and he took the plate back. When she walked past again, she explained, "Your order wasn't quite right, so I sent it back."

Before long, the little bell rang again and the fry cook yelled, "One special up!" This time, the waitress picked up the plate and delivered it to our booth.

The plate was piled high with four slices of meatloaf, mashed potatoes, and peas. Dad asked, "All this for a dollar?"

She winked. "I told you the meatloaf was today's special."

Dad pushed the overflowing plate of food to the center of the table, and we all dug in.

We had just finished scraping the plate when our waitress reappeared. "Did I mention that dessert was included in the special?" she asked, her order pad and pencil at the ready.

Mom looked up in surprise. "You've got to be kidding!"

The woman hesitated for a moment, chewing her gum thoughtfully, then confessed, "Well, yeah. Dessert's not really included, but one of those soldiers slipped me something on his way out. Said he wanted to pay for your desserts. Some people are hard to figure."

Mom nodded slightly. "Yeah, they sure are."

"So anyway, we have apple pie, cherry pie, vanilla ice cream, or caramel custard. What's your pleasure?"

We each ordered something different and then ate quickly, knowing the drivers were waiting for us. We had barely finished our desserts, when the waitress came back and put the bill on the table. "No need to bother with a tip," she said, already walking away. "The soldier took care of that, too."

Dad turned over the bill. "One meatloaf special—one dollar," he said while carefully counting a dollar in change.

On our way out, Mom walked over to the waitress and took her hand. "Thanks," she said. "Thanks for everything."

The woman put her other hand on top of Mom's. "I've got a couple of kids about the same age as yours. Believe me, there's been times when we've had to scrape the bottom of the lard barrel." She patted Mom's hand. "You take care now, ya hear?"

Mom's eyes were all watery. I was about to say something when Carolyn nudged me, shaking her head. So I held my tongue.

As we were crossing the highway, I tugged Carolyn's sleeve. "Which driver do you think paid for our desserts?"

"I don't know, and for sure they'll never tell us," she said. "So I guess we'll just have to like 'em all."

As soon as we were all seated again, the truck engines roared to life. The captain leaned out and gave the signal to move out. After the familiar gear shifting and smoke belching, we were back on the road.

The sun set, and the twilight gradually faded. Except for the faint glow of the dashboard, we were in total darkness. Mike was the first to spot the lights of Elko in the distance.

Once we reached the edge of town, the lead truck slowed and then turned into a motel parking lot. The rest followed, each one pulling in beside the other with their front bumpers lined up in a neat military row. The captain got out and walked back to Dad's truck. As it turned out, the army had reservations at the motel, but only for the five drivers and the captain.

"Where are you guys going to sleep?" the captain asked.

"Don't worry about us," Dad said, putting a hand on his shoulder. "You've got your men to look after. We'll manage. We always do. There's a train depot near the center of town. We can sleep there. You won't leave without us, will you?"

"We won't leave without you. But you'll need to be ready to go at 0600 hours. Did you get everything out of the trucks?"

"We've got it all," Dad nodded. "See you in the morning."

Dad looked at me and let out a sigh. "Well, we'd better start walking. If I remember right, the station's not too far."

I followed the others into the darkness. I didn't like walking beside highways at night. The passing cars blinded me, so I ended up tripping and stumbling a lot.

We soon arrived at the train depot. The station itself was an old redbrick building with large, wood-framed windows. There was a large parking lot in front with a couple of streetlights.

"I hope they haven't locked the doors," Dad muttered as we approached the building. "Buddy, try that door in the middle."

I ran to the door and pulled. "It's open!" I hollered.

"Keep the noise down!" Dad pleaded.

The station was empty. A sign announced that the depot opened at eight a.m. The clock on the wall showed ten thirty.

It's been a long day, I thought as we each claimed one of the high-backed wooden benches as our own. Mom pulled some clothing out of the suitcase for pillows and covered us with newspaper. Although it provided little protection from the chill of the night air coming through an open window, the paper felt comforting—familiar.

As my eyes grew heavy, I was drawn to the single light bulb hanging above me and a sign on the wall. "Welcome to Elko."

Chapter 11

CAROLYN STOOD UP, GLANCED TOWARD the nursing station, and arched her back. "I don't know how you're feeling, but right now, I've got an ache in my back that I'm not sure will ever go away."

"I know what you mean," I replied with empathy.

Carolyn sat back down and asked, "Do you think Mom knows that we're still out here?"

"Hopefully she's getting some sleep, which is more that I can say for the two of us. But if she is awake, she probably knows we're nearby."

Carolyn sat silently, looking concerned. "I wouldn't want Mom to feel like she's all alone or that nobody cares."

"God is always there, and He cares," I offered.

"That's not what I mean," she countered. "You can't see God, and I'm still not sure He'll be there when I need him."

"O ye of little faith," I said jokingly.

Carolyn laughed and then added, "So I don't have as much faith in God as you do."

"You remind me of the story of a pilot who was shot down over the South Pacific."

"What pilot?" Carolyn asked, and then with a look of anticipation, she added, "Another story might help pass the time."

"Okay, during World War II, an American fighter pilot was engaged in strafing attacks on a Japanese-held island. His plane was hit by anti-aircraft fire, and the pilot turned toward the coastline in hopes of bailing out over the relative safety of water rather than over land.

"Fortunately, his plane remained in the air long enough for him to reach the coast, but just barely. The pilot bailed out only a few hundred yards offshore. As soon as he hit the water, he inflated his life vest, but the Japanese were firing at him from the shore, so he didn't inflate his lifeboat. To his horror, he found that the current was pushing him toward the beach and certain capture. He immediately began swimming parallel to the shore in hopes of freeing himself from the current.

"He soon tired and rolled over on his back to just float. After a few minutes, he realized that he was no longer drifting toward shore. The pilot continued to float until nightfall. Once it was dark, he inflated his one-man rubber craft and climbed in. During the night, he steadily paddled with his hands, hoping to be far from the island by daybreak. However, when the glow of sunrise crept over the horizon, the pilot realized that he hadn't moved very far.

"Convinced that if he did not keep paddling he would be captured, the pilot continued to paddle throughout the day while searching the horizon for signs of a rescue party. Night came and went, and still there were no signs of a rescue. The pilot grew weary and began to have doubts that anyone would even bother trying to rescue him. After all, who was he that others should risk their lives to save him? Besides, as close as he was to shore, any rescue attempt would come under heavy fire, and someone could die in the attempt.

"Tired and thirsty, the discouraged pilot entered his third night aware that the possibility that he might die at sea was now just as great as was the possibility that he might die in a prison camp. In the middle of the night, the pilot's rhythmic paddling was interrupted by the sound of water churning and splashing nearby. Afraid he was about to be eaten by sharks, he pulled his hands out of the water. In spite of the darkness, the pilot was able to make out the shape of a large black mass in front of him and concluded that a large whale had surfaced. Then he heard the sound of a soft voice calling to him through the darkness. He realized that the dark shape was a submarine and the voice was that of a fellow American. Once the pilot was safely aboard, the submarine slipped below the surface.

"As soon as the pilot had something to drink, he spoke to the captain. 'I thought I was a goner for sure. I've never felt so alone and abandoned. I thought no one really cared about me and that I wasn't worth having someone else sacrifice their life in order to save me.'

"The captain looked at the weathered pilot and replied, 'You were never alone. You couldn't see me, but I was always nearby, and I never once thought of abandoning you. From the time you got into trouble, I was watching over you. But I couldn't come to you while you were still in shallow waters. So, I had to wait for you to come to me.'"

"Is that how you think of God?" Carolyn asked. "Always nearby even though you can't see him?"

"Very much so," I assured her. "And like Jesus, the captain of the submarine was willing to sacrifice his life to save someone else. And like the pilot who was in trouble, we must come to God in order to be saved."

Carolyn nodded and then spoke quietly. "There have been times in my life when I have felt like that downed pilot—completely abandoned."

"Like when the army convoy dropped us off in Reno?" I suggested.

"Yeah, like then."

***

Fall 1947

Elko to Reno, Nevada

A night of fitful sleep in the Elko train depot came to an end with the sound of air brakes early the next morning. I rubbed the sleep from my eyes while Mom and Dad went to greet the army convoy.

A few minutes later, Mom hurried back into the depot and started giving orders. "The two of you go to the restroom and wash up. The drivers are waiting, so don't waste any time."

"Good morning to you, too," Carolyn muttered.

"We'll hurry," I said as we headed into the restroom.

"I wish we had something for breakfast," Carolyn said wistfully as we finished washing and headed back to the lobby.

"I'm hungry too, but I don't think we'll get a chance to eat anything. Everyone seems to be in too big of a hurry."

Mom was waiting for us. "Your father's already taken the suitcase out," she said. "Buddy, be sure to check your box."

I double-checked the contents of the box, which still contained only the bare essentials. The rule was simple: if it has no useful purpose, leave it behind. To my way of thinking, as long as I was carrying the box, I was being useful and wouldn't get left behind.

As soon as I stepped outside, Mike greeted me cheerfully. "Good morning, Buddy."

"Mornin'," I replied as I climbed into the cab and onto his duffel bag. I tried to match his enthusiasm, but after sleeping on a wooden bench all night, I didn't feel all that chipper. I placed my box on the floor and had barely gotten myself seated when the captain gave the signal to move out.

Once the convoy pulled back onto the highway, Mike reached under his seat and pulled out a pink box with the aroma of fresh donuts drifting out of it. I had to keep swallowing because my mouth kept filling with spit. He then pulled a bottle of milk out from behind him and triumphantly exclaimed, "Voila!"

I stared silently at the box.

"You're a proud little bugger, aren't you." Mike grinned, shaking his head. "Half-starved and a foot away from a box of donuts, but you won't beg." He opened the box. "In case you're wondering, the captain bought us some milk and donuts to eat on the way." He paused, nodding his head in the direction of the box. "But he bought way too many. I'll never be able to eat all those myself. So, since you're my truckin' buddy, maybe you could help me eat some of them?"

I hesitated for a moment then cleared my throat and tried to sound casual. "I might be able to help you with a couple, but I'm not very hungry. Which one do you want to eat first?"

"Don't matter to me. One's as good as another."

"I think I'll try this one," I said, carefully extracting one of the chocolate donuts.

"I'll take the one that's covered with sugar," Mike said.

Later that day, I learned that the captain had bought way too many donuts for the other drivers as well.

For the most part, the trip from Elko to Reno was uneventful and boring, with only an occasional pit stop to buy gas, use the restroom, and get something to eat. We finally reached the outskirts of Reno late in the afternoon, and as the intersections passed by, a familiar hurt started to well up. The good-byes were getting nearer. I hated good-byes.

The lump in my throat continued to grow as the inevitable drop-off point drew near. Leaning out as far as I dared without alarming Mike, I monitored the lead truck's movements. My heart sank when I saw the pullover begin. One by one, the trucks eased over to the curb and stopped. The drivers silently got out and joined us on the sidewalk. They had left the engines running, so I knew the good-byes were going to be brief.

Mike pulled me to one side and reached into his shirt pocket. "I have this extra collar insignia," he said. "It ain't worth much, but I want you to have something to remember me by."

"Gee, thanks!" I said, rotating it in my hand to reflect the sunlight. Then I looked up at him sadly. "I don't have anything to give you to remember me by."

Mike ruffled my hair. "Don't worry, kid. I guarantee I won't ever forget you. You've been a good truckin' buddy. Just talking to you made that last stretch seem a whole lot shorter."

"Thanks for sharing your donuts," I said, keeping my eyes on the ground so he wouldn't see that they'd gotten all watery.

Suddenly, Mike turned around. "Hey, you guys!" he shouted. "I just got a great idea. Since we'll be making this same run for the next six months, how 'bout we meet each other four weeks from today at this same corner?" He turned to Dad then and asked, "Do you think you guys could do that?"

I doubted that we'd still be in Reno in another month, but Dad surprised me by saying, "Don't see why not."

"Okay with you, Captain?" Mike asked, and the captain nodded his approval. "Then it's all settled. Four weeks from today, we'll have ourselves a rendezvous." The plan to meet again softened some of the hurt.

We picked up our belongings and crossed the street so we could wave at the drivers as the convoy pulled out. As the trucks began moving out, someone yelled, "See you next month!"

The trucks were swallowed up in the traffic with an unexpected suddenness. Like so many things in my world, I wondered if they had ever really existed. Looking bewildered, Mom finally asked, "What are we going to do now?"

"Get something to eat," Dad said decisively. "I'm not sure what we'll do after that, but first things first." He picked up the black suitcase and started walking toward the railroad tracks, which, judging by the sound of the train whistles, weren't too far away. Mom followed, and Carolyn and I fell in behind.

"How about that!" he yelled, pointing at a sign arching over the street, 'Reno—The Biggest Little City in the World.'"

I didn't get it. To me, "biggest little city" sounded like a fancy way of saying "medium-sized."

The discussion about the sign continued until we reached the Salvation Army headquarters near the railroad depot. "You three wait out here while I check things out," Dad said as he stepped inside. Not knowing how long this might take, Carolyn and I sat down on the curb to wait.

Dad soon reappeared carrying a brown paper bag. "Fried chicken sound good to anyone?" he asked, holding up the sack.

No one ever had to call me twice when it came time to eat. "I want the drumstick!" Carolyn and I called out in unison.

"Most chickens have two legs, so there's one for each of you," Mom teased, lowering the bag so we could see inside. Appearances didn't mean much to any of us anymore, so we sat there on the curb and ate our chicken as people passed by. Some stared at us curiously, some critically, but I didn't care. The chicken tasted too good to let anything bother me.

Dad wiped his hands on his trousers and said with his mouth half-full, "Go ahead and finish off the rest of the chicken while I see if the Salvation Army can put us up for the night."

We all glanced up, nodded our approval, and then quickly turned our attention back to our meal. While chewing on a wing, I noticed how tired Mom looked. It had been four days since any of us had had a good night's sleep, and it was beginning to take its toll. When Dad came back, he was carrying a slip of paper.

"Well?" Mom prompted.

"They gave us a voucher for a room in the State Hotel across the way," he replied, pointing at a two-story brick building on the other side of the tracks. It was old and crumbly looking, with a faded cigar advertisement on one side.

"How many nights?" Mom asked.

"The voucher's good for a week, but we can get an extension if we have to."

Mom stared at the dilapidated hotel and shook her head. "Let's hope we don't have to."

We didn't bother to go back to the street crossing; we just started walking across the tracks. "I don't want to see you kids crossing these tracks like this," Mom said. "You both have to promise that you'll stay off these tracks while we're here."

"Sure, Mom," I replied automatically.

"We promise," Carolyn added.

The hotel had no lobby, just a narrow hall and a square opening in the wall a few feet inside the front door. The opening had a countertop with a little bell sitting on it. Dad rang it, and we waited. The hall smelled musty and old, and a two-year-old calendar from a radiator shop hung on the wall.

"Be just a minute!" someone called out from behind the opening. There was no place to sit, so we just stood there. An elderly man in a bathrobe finally appeared. He nonchalantly put his hands on the counter and asked, "What can I do for you?"

Dad shoved the slip of paper across the counter. "The people at the Salvation Army said to show this to the man in charge. Is that you?"

"Yep, that's me, all right. I'm the manager and janitor, so I guess that makes me in charge. How many of you are there?"

"Just the four of us," Mom volunteered.

"Four of you," the manager said, rubbing his chin. "We usually just get single fellows and an occasional couple down on their luck. But four . . . Wait there a minute while I check something out with the wife." He hurried through a side door, and I could hear him asking someone about beds. He reappeared a few seconds later, looking smug.

"Problem's solved. I can put you up in 204. It's on the second floor and faces the street. It's only got one double bed, but I'll get a rollaway up to you. The kids can sleep on it." He handed Dad a key and pointed to the narrow staircase. "Room 204. Turn left at the top. Can't miss it."

The room was small. The bed took up most of the floor space. A mirror with cracks fanning out from one side hung above a small sink in the corner. A chest of drawers stood on one wall, and a small table and two wooden chairs sat between the windows. Two metal hooks next to the door served as the closet.

Carolyn flopped down on the bed with a big sigh. "I think I'll just lay here forever."

"Not alone you won't," Mom teased, collapsing on the bed.

Curious about what could be seen out the windows, I put my box down on the table and pulled back the curtains. Spread out below me was a large freight yard filled with railroad cars.

"Wow! I can see the whole rail yard from up here!" I cried. All and all, it had turned out to be a pretty good day.

***

As things turned out, we didn't get just one extension on our room but several, and by August it was blistering hot. Dad was supposed to be looking for a job, but most of the time he just lay on the bed in his underwear complaining about the heat. When he did leave to look for a job, he usually came back half soused. I have no idea how he got money for booze, but he obviously found a way. Mom passed the time by playing solitaire or napping. As long as the Salvation Army was providing room and board, neither of them seemed very concerned about finding work. Carolyn and I got bored in the room, so we spent as much time as possible outside, which often meant sneaking down to the hobo jungles to spy on the hobos.

The hobo jungle in Reno was one of the biggest around. Dad said they were leftovers from the depression days when bums used to ride the rails looking for jobs. But nowadays, they were mostly filled with drunks and crazy people. That's why we weren't allowed to go into them.

Nevertheless, Carolyn and I would sneak across the maze of steel ribbons in the forbidden freight yard. We had promised Mom that we would stay off the tracks, but Carolyn rationalized that we would be keeping our promise by stepping *over* them. What she said seemed to make sense, but she was starting to sound a lot like Dad. Much of what she said seemed to be only half-truths.

Summer was over far too soon. As the days got shorter, the nights got colder. Our room had a steam radiator by the window, but it didn't work. Mom complained, and still we didn't get any heat. She asked the Salvation Army for some extra blankets, but they told her they needed all they had to keep up with the increased demand at their transient facilities. On the really cold nights, we'd all sleep in the same bed—Mom and Dad with their heads at the head, Carolyn and I with our heads at the foot. It was crowded but warmer.

Unfortunately, with fall came school. I dreaded school. Being in a different state, I'd probably be behind. And I'd be the new kid. The new kid doesn't know any of the rules: what to wear, what to say, who to play with. I knew I'd get picked on and teased, no matter what. I hated being the new kid.

Mom went to see the principal before school began. He told her that Carolyn didn't seem ready for the sixth grade and that it might be better for her to re-enroll in fifth grade. Since Carolyn had been held back a grade, Mom argued that it would be devastating for her daughter not to be allowed to enroll in the sixth grade. So the principle reconsidered and permitted Carolyn to enroll in sixth grade on a trial basis.

The week before school began, Mom bought us some school clothes at Goodwill. I got a wool jacket, a flannel shirt, corduroy pants, and a pair of high-top shoes. Carolyn got a long tweed coat, a dress, a pair of brown-and-white shoes that were going to be hard to keep clean, and a used binder. Mom would have gotten us more, but it would be another week before she'd get her first paycheck from her new job, so she used her tip money to pay for our clothes.

When the dreaded first day of school arrived, I got up reluctantly, dressed, and combed my hair. Unfortunately, when I was eating my Cheerios out of a tiny box, I tore the wax paper inside, and the milk dribbled out on the table. While I cleaned up my mess, Carolyn waited with her hand on the doorknob.

"Ready?" she asked as I finished.

"Ready as I'll ever be," I answered.

"Then let's go," she said impatiently, opening the door.

The school was only about five blocks from the hotel, but we had to cross the busy highway to get there. We were used to the traffic, though, because we had to cross the highway once a month to meet up with the convoy. We'd faithfully kept our promise and met them at the corner each month, even though we had to wait for hours sometimes before the trucks finally came through. Some of the drivers were new, but everyone seemed to have heard about us and waved anyway. I knew he wasn't supposed to, but Mike would honk as he passed by. Those days in the truck with him, eating donuts and hanging out the window—even my jump out of the truck—had been good days.

Dad's drinking was getting completely out of control, and fights became more frequent. The fights were usually over Dad drinking too much, not working enough, or Mom being "tired of living like this." But it didn't really matter what the fights were about, they were all scary.

Mom and Dad had their biggest fights when they had been out drinking. They were out drinking tonight, so Carolyn and I were worried. The longer they were out, the worse it would be.

"I wish Dad wouldn't drink so much," I said as we lay there in the darkness.

"Me too," she replied. "Dad gets drunk almost every day."

I propped myself up on my elbow and confided, "I think Mom goes to the bars just to get out of this room."

"When do you think they'll get back?" Carolyn asked in a low, serious voice.

"How should I know? When the bars close, I guess."

"Does Dad have any whiskey left around here?"

"I think there's a bottle in the cabinet above the sink."

"We should get rid of it," Carolyn said matter-of-factly.

"Dad would kill us if he found out!" I declared.

"We could pour it down the drain. He'll probably be so drunk he won't be able to remember if he had any stashed here or not." Carolyn paused for a moment before adding, "Let's do it!"

"Do what?" I asked cautiously.

"Get rid of the booze."

"How?"

"I already told you. We'll pour it down the sink."

I was feeling more anxious by the second. "What if we get caught? Remember what happened when I threatened to dump his whiskey down the sink in Phoenix?"

"Don't be such a worrywart. We won't get caught. I'll watch for them from the window, while you pour it down the sink.

"While *I* pour it down the sink?"

"Oh, for Pete's sake, Buddy. I'll be watching from the window." She climbed out of bed and sat down on the windowsill.

"Okay," I sighed, "but you'd better keep a sharp eye out." I turned on the light, climbed up on a chair, and opened the cabinet. "See anyone coming?"

"No, the coast is clear."

I took the pint bottle of Four Roses out of the cabinet and unscrewed the cap. "Are you sure?"

"Just a couple of winos over by the corner," Carolyn said nervously. "But hurry up. We don't have all night."

"I'm hurrying as fast as I can," I said as I started pouring whiskey down the drain.

Suddenly the door swung open, and there stood Mom and Dad.

"What in the . . . ?" Dad gasped. Then he began shouting obscenities as he lunged across the room.

I fell back against the wall, dropping the bottle in the sink. It shattered instantly, splashing whiskey on the walls.

"You stupid little . . ." The rest of the curse was interrupted when his fist sent me flying off the chair, against the wall, and onto the floor.

I could taste blood in my mouth, and my ears were ringing so badly that I could barely hear Carolyn screaming, "I didn't see 'em coming! I didn't see 'em coming!" A sharp crack sounded as Dad backhanded her across the face.

"Shut up, or I'll really give you something to cry about!" Dad shouted.

Mom grabbed Dad's arm. "Bernie! They're just kids!"

Dad's elbow caught her right above the left eye. She went flying backwards onto the bed, blood running down her face.

Dad reached down and picked me up by the front of my undershirt and pulled me close to his face. I could almost taste the stink of the whiskey on his breath.

"Just who do you think you are? You good for nothin'. . ."

Carolyn got to her feet and began pulling on Dad's arm.

Without loosening his grip on me, Dad grabbed her by the throat with his left hand. Her eyes bulged as he squeezed her windpipe. I reached desperately for the top of the table, groping for something to hit him with. I felt the handle of the porcelain hotplate, got a firm grip on it, and smashed it against the side of his head.

Instantly, he let go of us both and fell to the floor, blood flowing from the open wound on the side of his head. Carolyn lay sprawled beside him, gasping for breath and clutching her throat.

Mom struggled to her feet and asked Carolyn if she was okay. Carolyn nodded, and Mom knelt down beside Dad. I just stood there, the hotplate dangling from my hand.

"Is he dead?" I finally dared. "Did I kill him?"

Dad moaned and rolled his head. "Well, he's still alive," Mom sighed, "but you two had better not be here when he comes to."

"Where'll we go?" Carolyn managed, getting to her feet.

Before Mom could answer, someone began banging on the door.

"You folks okay in there?" the manager called out.

"We're okay," Mom lied. "Just a family squabble."

"You sure now? I can call the police," he offered.

"No need," Mom assured him through the door. "We're okay."

"Well, if you need anything, we're just downstairs," he said, sounding unconvinced.

"Thanks for the offer, but really . . . we're okay," Mom reassured. Then she pulled us close and whispered, "Go with him. Ask if you can spend the night. I'll take care of your dad. Maybe he'll be more settled in the morning."

"I don't want to leave you alone with him," I argued.

"I'll be all right. Just get me a cold washcloth for his head. How about you?" she asked as I went to fetch the washcloth.

"I'm okay," I replied, exploring my mouth with my tongue. "I've got a loose tooth, but I think that's all."

Dad moaned again and rolled over.

"You two had better hurry," Mom whispered. "Your dad's starting to come to."

"Forget it, Mom. We're not going anywhere without you," Carolyn said bravely.

By now, Dad was sitting up, holding his head with both hands. Mom wrapped a towel around his head, and then he crawled onto the bed and fell asleep. She turned the light off, and we sat there in the dark, listening to his breathing. I was alert to any change in the rhythm. I finally dozed off, but when I heard Dad stirring sometime before dawn, I snapped awake. Mom reached over and turned on the light.

Dad covered his eyes with his arm and groaned, "What happened to my head?"

"You fell against the radiator," Mom lied.

"No I didn't. You must have hit me with something."

Slowly, I began easing my way toward the door then froze when Dad got up and stumbled to the sink. He leaned against it, staring at his reflection in the broken mirror. Then he swore under his breath and turned to Mom. "I've had it," he declared.

Mom tried to go to him, but he pushed her away and opened the door. "In fact, I'm through with the lot of you!" he shouted, slamming the door behind him.

A few minutes later, someone knocked on the door.

"Who is it?" Mom asked cautiously.

"It's the manager. I need to talk to you."

"Just a minute," Mom replied, hurriedly trying to remold her hair and straighten her dress before opening the door.

As the manager stepped into the room, he gestured toward Mom's eye. "That's one doozy of a shiner you've got there. You ought to have somebody take a look at it. Looks pretty painful."

"That's all right. I heal fast," Mom said.

He looked down at Carolyn and me. "How are you two?"

"We're okay," I answered.

Mom sat down by the window and sighed. "My black eye's not what you came to talk about, is it?"

"No, ma'am. It isn't."

"If it's about the racket last night, Bernie's gone. You don't have to worry about that happening again."

"That's just it, ma'am. I'm sorry I have to tell you this, but, well . . ."

"Well what?"

"They told me not to extend your room voucher anymore," he said apologetically.

"What do you mean? Why? Bernie's been looking for work. He's just had a run of bad luck, but he'll find something."

"Well, it ain't just that. It's a lot of other things," the manager said, squirming.

"Like what?" Mom demanded.

"Like the fighting . . . especially last night. Other people in the hotel have been complaining."

"Complaining! A lot they have to complain about! I've heard more than one midnight argument through these walls."

"Yeah, but that's just it. They're just arguments. Things aren't getting broken, and people aren't getting beat up."

"So what are we supposed to do?"

"I don't rightly know, ma'am," the manager said kindly. "All I know is they aren't going to extend your room voucher, so you'll have to be out by Saturday."

"By Saturday!" Mom said, her voice rising in panic. "But that's only three days from now! How am I supposed to find another place in just three days?"

"I don't rightly know, ma'am," the manager said helplessly.

"Well, we'll just see about that," Mom said indignantly as she pulled Carolyn and me close and then slammed the door.

"What's happening, Mom?" I asked, but I knew that my fragile world was about to fall apart again.

"We have to move."

"Move where?" Carolyn asked.

"I don't know, but we'll have to find someplace. It's almost winter, so we can't stay out on the streets," Mom lamented, staring out the window at the overcast sky.

The eviction was enforced on Friday, shortly after we arrived home from school. Mom had tried to find something in town, but either the rent was too high or they wouldn't take children. She'd finally found a makeshift trailer for rent just outside the city limits.

The small trailer sat on concrete blocks in the middle of a field. A section of the back had been torn off, and a clapboard lean-to had been built over the opening. In some places, you could see daylight between the boards, so I stuffed newspaper into the cracks. The roof was nothing more than overlapping sheets of tar paper. An outhouse sat twenty feet behind the trailer, and a clothesline stretched between it and the lean-to.

We used a small oil stove for both heating and cooking, but it didn't do either very well. For water, there was a hose that ran from a spigot near an animal trough to the trailer; it froze at night. It wasn't much, but Mom said that the owner was letting us stay there for almost nothing, whatever that meant.

All three of us slept on a queen-size mattress on the floor of the lean-to—no box springs or frame, just the mattress.

Dad was nowhere to be found. Mom was worried that he would not be able to find us. Personally, I hoped he never would.

I was feeling rather melancholy one day, thinking that carrying my box hadn't kept me from being left behind after all. Carolyn and I were looking out the window, watching the first heavy snow of winter. Although the snow seemed to float as it fell, I sensed a heaviness to it, and I found myself wondering what it would be like to be buried underneath it. I'd heard stories about the Donner party; anyone who'd lived in Reno for any amount of time was familiar with that ill-fated wagon train.

"Do you think we're going to starve to death out here, like the people in the Donner party?" I asked Carolyn.

Carolyn looked over at me in surprise. "Don't be silly, Buddy. What makes you think we're going to starve to death?"

"My teacher told me how the people in the Donner party got caught in the snow trying to cross the mountains. Most of them starved to death," I explained, swallowing hard before continuing. "She said that the survivors turned into cannibals."

"Well, we're not going to starve to death, and we're certainly not going to turn into cannibals."

"Just what do we have to eat?"

"I'll check," Carolyn offered as she began opening and closing the cabinets. She then turned to me with her hands on her hips. "It looks like we're going to be eating pancakes."

"But we had pancakes for breakfast."

"Doesn't matter. That's all there is." She climbed up on the couch and resumed watching the snow come down. "Today's the day the convoy comes through," she said thoughtfully.

I ran my fingers over Mike's army insignia in my pocket. "Yeah, I know. I hope Mike doesn't think I forgot him."

"He knows we'd be there if we could, but we can't," she said. "But we met them quite a few times, didn't we?"

The familiar hurt had started to swell in my chest again, and a lump had come to my throat. I hated good-byes.

Chapter 12

CAROLYN TRIED USING HER JACKET as a pillow, but not very successfully. I offered to ask one of the nurses if there was a spare pillow she could use, but she didn't want to bother them.

"A pillow might make things better," I prompted.

"Now, you're sounding like Dad," she mumbled. "When things were absolutely miserable, he'd always say that they were going to get better."

"For instance?"

"For instance, I'd hoped things would get better after we left Reno, but they didn't. Dad promised us it would be better in Eureka, California," she continued, "but it turned out to be no different than any of the other towns we'd been through."

"The 'nice place to live' that Dad had promised turned out to be nothing more than a single room in the back of a long-past-its-prime hotel," I added with a tired sigh.

"And we were evicted one week after we arrived."

I shook my head as I remembered. "It wasn't all that long before Dad wanted to leave again."

Carolyn sat up straight and added, "That's when Mom told Dad that she was too tired to go back on the road and that she wanted to stay put for a while. She wanted to give us a chance to go to the same school two years in a row."

"So, Dad left town without us," I said matter-of-factly, "but eventually he did come back, at least for a while. I remember coming home one day and hearing you and Mom yelling at each other. Mom was shouting, 'Carolyn, you're only fifteen.' You were yelling about being old enough to get married."

"Boy, that's a day I'll never forget," Carolyn sighed, rolling her eyes. "Mom had just found out that Dad was considering giving his permission for me to get married, and she was furious. I'm just glad we eloped so I wasn't around when she found out he had actually signed the papers."

I shrugged and recounted, "With you and Dad both gone, and Mom working all the time, I became somewhat of a loner. Mom found an old dilapidated trailer sitting in a field south of town. It was a small eighteen-footer with a water hose connecting it to a standpipe in a neighbor's garden, and with an outhouse behind the trailer. Once again, Mom had to walk a mile to the bus line to get to work."

"Memories of Reno must have been unavoidable," Carolyn interjected. "Things just never seemed to change. That's why I tried to escape by getting married. But what did I escape to? My husband didn't have a job, and he didn't want to get out of bed to find one. We had to live in someone's crummy attic. A few months later, he was arrested for robbing a Safeway store. He went to jail, and I went on welfare—three months pregnant. The only good thing about it was that by having a child I qualified for a small apartment in the federal housing project."

"Whatever happened to your husband?"

"He got out of jail, I got pregnant again, then he broke the law again and was sent back to prison. The third time, I had my third child adopted and divorced him."

"Mom was right when she said that you'd had a tough life."

"I sometimes wonder what my life would have been like if I'd been born into a different family," Carolyn mused.

"I used to think about that," I confessed. "However, after my conversion, my view of my life changed."

"In what way?"

"Well, for one, I came to understand that my life on earth was merely a stage of existence, that I had a pre-mortal existence prior to coming to earth. It wouldn't surprise me if someday I was to find out that in the pre-mortal existence I had made a promise to do something while I was here, and until I embraced the gospel, I wasn't doing what I had promised."

"Considering how hard my life has been so far," Carolyn grumbled, "I don't think I would have complained too much if I'd been given a different life to live."

"Maybe . . . maybe not," I cautioned. "I found something in the Gospel of John that has had a major impact on my way of thinking about my life. Perhaps it will help you understand your life a little better. You may be familiar with the incident when Jesus was arrested in the Garden of Gethsemane. Peter drew his sword in an attempt to defend Jesus, but

Jesus told him to put away his sword then said, 'The cup which my Father hath given me, shall I not drink it?'"

"What did he mean by that?"

"Jesus meant that each of us is given a mission, a 'cup to drink' here on earth. The cup Jesus Christ was given to drink was to suffer and die for our sins. In a like manner, each of us has our own special cup to drink. The opportunities and challenges we encounter as we live our lives can help us fulfill our missions and become stronger. We don't have to look very far to see that the 'cup' someone else has been given might be more difficult for us to drink than the one we've been given."

"True, but then I've seen a few others with 'cups' that I wish I'd been given," Carolyn countered.

"Ah, but appearance can be deceiving," I contended. "One example in particular comes to mind. This occurred back when I was attending graduate school, struggling with a tight budget and envying those who were already successful and prosperous. Each morning I drove by a big house with a big ski boat parked next to the garage. The owner of this house would leave about the same time driving a silver Mercedes sedan, and each morning I would think, 'Man, would I like to trade places with that guy.' Until, one morning I came by later than usual. I had to stop for a small school bus parked in front of the grand house. Its hydraulic ramp was being lowered, and a woman was pushing a child in a wheelchair toward the bus. The child appeared to have cerebral palsy. I immediately began to think of my five children: healthy, unimpaired, and vibrant. I felt grateful for not having been given such a 'cup' to drink. But then, the parents that lived in the grand house would probably be glad that they had not been given the 'cup' that I'd been given."

"Especially if they had to go through what we went through when we were living in Reno," Carolyn interjected.

I echoed her sentiment. "Especially when we were in Reno."

***

Fall 1948

Reno, Nevada

Mom desperately tried to hold things together, but our existence remained tenuous. Thanks to the black eye Dad had given her, she lost her job. When she finally looked presentable again, she found another waitress job.

Since we now lived quite a ways out from town, she had to leave before dawn to get to work on time. She would leave a light on in the trailer, casting just enough light outside to allow her to get her bearings, and she'd head up the gravel road to the highway, about a mile away.

Mom tried not to wake us in the morning, but it was so cold that I was usually already awake when she got up. Some mornings, after she quietly closed the trailer door, I'd climb out of bed and look out the window. I'd rub a large peephole in the frost and watch her trudge through the snow, gradually disappearing into the darkness. For a few lonely minutes, I'd just stare at her footprints.

Her path was always the same, angling away from the trailer to a wire fence that ran along the far side of the road. There were no streetlights, and few cars passed by that early in the morning, so the fence posts had to serve as her guide to the highway, where she'd catch the bus into town.

Mom wanted to celebrate her first payday, so after school, Carolyn and I caught a bus into town, planning to meet her when she got off work. We waited outside the café, talking about how we might celebrate. Just as she stepped outside, two rough-looking men started walking toward her.

The men explained that Dad had a gambling debt of one hundred and forty dollars that was supposed to have been paid by last Friday. Gambling debts are taken seriously in Nevada, so since they had not been able to find Bernie, they were going to collect from his wife. They included the customary threats of what would happen if she did not give them at least some of what was owed and how they would be back for the rest.

Reluctantly, Mom handed over fifty dollars, and the two men walked away. Mom just stood there, tears running down her face.

The three of us waited for the bus in silence. When it arrived, Mom merely motioned Carolyn and me on and then plopped down in an empty seat. As the bus followed its route, she stared blankly out the window.

"Isn't this your stop, lady?" the bus driver asked after a while, glancing back in the rearview mirror.

Mom pulled her eyes away from the window and stood up, looking confused. She moved us toward the door but still she said nothing.

"You all right, ma'am?" the driver asked as we stepped off the bus.

Mom gave him a feeble smile.

Carolyn turned to her after the bus pulled away. "It's been a rough day, huh?" she said softly.

"Rough doesn't begin to describe it," Mom sighed.

As we walked through the snow, Mom explained that the men at the café would keep coming back until Dad's debt was paid.

"But what are we going to do without money?" I asked.

"I'm afraid I'll have to go talk to someone at St. Thomas's tomorrow," she replied. "I don't know where else to turn, and the church has come to our rescue before."

Instantly, my concern turned to fear, remembering the help we'd received from the Catholic Church in Phoenix. "They won't put us in another foster home, will they?"

"No, Buddy," Mom smiled reassuringly. "We'll just be asking for a little food to tide us over."

The next day Mom went to St. Thomas's and talked to a priest, Father Sullivan. He assigned a couple by the name of Lamont to work with us, explaining that they were retired and kept themselves busy by helping out with church projects. But by the time Mom got home that night, she was so tired that she forgot to tell us the about the Lamonts.

While she was at work the next day, I heard a car pull up and looked out the window. An elderly man and woman were walking toward the trailer with their arms full of grocery bags. They were slightly overweight, with white hair and wrinkles.

"That's not too heavy for you, is it?" I heard the man ask as they knocked on the door.

"I'm fine. It's just bulky," the woman replied.

I opened the door a crack and peered out at the strangers.

"Is this the Poduskas'?" the man said.

"Yes," I answered cautiously.

The man smiled. "My name is Mr. Lamont, and this is my wife."

"What do you want?" I asked suspiciously.

"What do we want?" he chuckled. "Why, we want to give you these groceries."

Carolyn squeezed past me. "Are you sure those are for us?"

"They sure are," Mrs. Lamont grinned.

"We're from St. Thomas's," Mr. Lamont continued. "Father Sullivan asked us to bring you these groceries. Had a little trouble finding you, but we made it."

Carolyn opened the door all the way and invited them in. "You can put the bags over there," she said, pointing at the foldout table.

They'd barely set them down when I started pulling cans and boxes out as fast as I could grab them. "Wow! Look at all this food! There's peas and green beans. Here's some corn and a can of tuna fish." Then I paused, wrinkling my nose. "And a can of spinach."

"My little brother gets excited over just about anything," Carolyn explained, acting like the embarrassed adult.

Mrs. Lamont patted me on the head. "That's all right. Let him have his fun. He seems to be enjoying himself."

"Can we help you put some of this away?" Mr. Lamont offered, looking around the interior.

"No, thanks," Carolyn reassured.

"You're sure now?" Mrs. Lamont persisted. "We'd be more than glad to help."

"That's okay, we'll manage," Carolyn insisted.

"Then is there anything else you need? Heating oil? Toys?"

At the mention of toys, I looked up hopefully from the fort of pork-and-bean cans I was building.

Carolyn gave me a stern look, as if to say, "Don't you dare," then turned and smiled at the Lamonts. "No, we're okay for now. We were just a little short on food."

I stared at her in amazement. *Okay, except for food? Are you out of your gourd?*

If the Lamonts noticed the nonverbal exchange, they didn't let on. "Well, I guess we've done all we can for now," Mr. Lamont concluded. "It's time we got back to town. Looks like it might start snowing again."

Following her husband's lead, Mrs. Lamont opened the door. As they stepped out, she offered some parting instructions. "If you do think of anything else, please have your mother get in touch with Father Sullivan. We'd love to help."

"Just let us know," Mr. Lamont added. "Anything at all."

"Thanks," Carolyn replied, waving good-bye.

"Can you believe all this food?" I exclaimed as soon as she closed the door behind them.

"Yeah, I can believe it. What I can't believe is that you were about to ask them for toys."

"They brought it up," I replied indignantly.

***

Even after Dad's gambling debt was paid off, the Lamonts continued to bring us groceries, throughout the rest of that winter and into the summer. My fear of starving to death gradually subsided. When fall arrived, we once again had our "shopping spree" at the Goodwill store before school started.

Because we lived in the country, the school we attended was an old, two-room schoolhouse. The east room held grades one through three, and the room on the west had grades four through six, so since her trial in the sixth grade last year had failed, Carolyn and I were in the same classroom. Carolyn wasn't too thrilled about it, but I thought it was pretty neat.

I was the new kid again, but I soon began to feel like one of the old-timers. For the first time ever, I was actually enjoying school. That is, until the day the principal, old Mrs. Pettinguil, walked in to the classroom without knocking, interrupting our lesson in multiplication tables.

"I apologize for the intrusion," she announced, "but we have an unusual situation."

I'm not sure any of us heard a word she was saying because we were all staring at the disheveled tramp standing in the doorway. The dark figure epitomized the proverbial candy-toting stranger that parents warn their children about.

"Is either Carolyn or Buddy Poduska present?" the principal asked, scanning the room.

At first it was only my eyes I couldn't believe, but now I couldn't believe my ears either. *Why me*, I thought, shame-faced. *How could he come here looking like that?*

"Carolyn or Buddy Poduska?" the principal repeated, and then her eyes followed the gazes of the other students, whose curious stares had now shifted to us.

Carolyn looked at me helplessly. Seeing no way out, I slowly raised my hand. "Yes, ma'am," I said quietly.

"Do you know this man?" the principal asked sternly.

"Yes, ma'am."

"Is he your father?"

"Yes, ma'am." I said again, my voice dropping lower with each repetition. Several children began to snicker.

"Then would you please tell your father where you live?"

The snickers gave way to a roar of laughter. "Yeah! He really looks lost," one of the students remarked. The laughter grew even louder.

"Now, children," the principal scolded, "there's no cause for such an outburst." She came down the aisle and put her hand on my shoulder. As she was guiding me up the aisle, she motioned for Carolyn to follow.

"Why don't the two of you step out in the hall with your father? There you can talk in private," she suggested, coaxing us through the doorway.

Even after the door closed behind us, I could still hear the laughter. But Mrs. Pettinguil ignored the commotion. "Carolyn and Buddy, this should only take a few minutes, and then I want you to return to class." She turned to Dad, adding, "I'd like you to leave as soon as possible. I think you've disrupted your children's educations enough for one day."

As she was walking away, Dad mumbled, "What makes her think she's so high and mighty?"

I looked up at him, still unwilling to believe this was happening. "What are you doing here?"

"What do you think I'm doing here?" Dad replied irritably. "I'm trying to find out where you guys live."

"I don't know the address," I answered defiantly.

"Look, I tracked down your Mom in town, and she gave me the same cock-n-bull story. How 'bout you, Carolyn?" he asked menacingly. "Do *you* know where you live?"

"You back to stay?" she said hesitantly.

"Right now, all I want is to get cleaned up."

Carolyn caved. "We're living in an old trailer on Dry Creek Road."

"How far's that from here?"

"About a mile and a half," I admitted.

"Well, is one of you going to tell me how to get there?"

Carolyn rolled her eyes, surrendering to the inevitable and gave him directions to the trailer.

"How do I get in?"

"There's no key, so the door's never locked," Carolyn told him. "There's nothing inside worth stealing."

"What time do you get home?"

"Around three thirty, if we come straight home," I replied.

"Well, come straight home today," he said. "Your mother might be getting off early."

With that, he was gone as quickly as he'd appeared. Now we had to go back into the classroom and face further humiliation.

The rest of the afternoon crawled by. When the last bell finally rang, Carolyn and I leaped up from our desks and ran for home—not because we were anxious to get there, but because we wanted to get as far away from school as possible.

As we were walking up to the trailer, Dad came to the door and threw out a pan of water. Mom appeared in the doorway behind him. I was a little surprised, but then Dad had said that she might get off early.

The four of us were crowded around the foldout table in the kitchen area. Even before we got settled, I blurted out the question that had been nagging all afternoon. "How'd you find us?" If it came off sounding as if we'd been hiding, Dad didn't seem to notice.

"I left town right after the fight at the hotel," he began. "I rode the rails for a while but eventually drifted back to Reno. That's when I found out that you'd been evicted. Your friend, Doyle, said he didn't know where you lived but that you kids were going to school in an old, two-room schoolhouse."

"Buddy and I met Doyle at the movies one day," Carolyn interjected. "That's when we told him about the schoolhouse."

"So how'd you find us?" I pressed.

"I went to the cafe where your mother used to work and found out she didn't work there anymore. But I knew that if you were still in Reno, she'd have to find another job, so I began checking some of the other cafés. That's how I found her."

Mom interrupted. "I saw this tramp waving at me through the front window. I keep telling myself that nothing can surprise me anymore, but a tramp waving at me was something new."

Dad held up a hand. "Bet you can't guess what the first thing your mother said to me was." He didn't wait for her to respond. "No, 'Long time no see.' No, 'How ya doin', honey.' Just, 'Where in the world have you been?'"

"Well, maybe you think it's okay to just run off and leave us stranded, but I don't," Mom shot back, wounded. "You left us with nothing. No money and only three days to find somewhere else to live."

"I know it's been rough on you and the kids, but I had no choice," Dad said defensively. "Those guys can play rough."

"Well, I can play rough too."

Dad tried to put an arm around Mom, but she pulled away. "Don't touch me. You're filthy, and you smell like an outhouse."

"Look, can we talk about this later? I just want to clean up and get some rest."

"You can bathe in the Truckee River, for all I care!" Mom shouted, as she jumped up and stormed out of the trailer.

A few minutes of awkward silence passed.

I finally spoke, frustrated that he'd never answered my question. "So, did Mom tell you where we lived?"

"Your mother wouldn't tell me the time of day. But I remembered what Doyle said about you kids going to school in an old schoolhouse, so I asked around. Seems like the only schoolhouse that fit Doyle's description was one that was out on the east side of town." Dad paused, chuckling. "Boy, you should've seen your principal's face when I walked in."

"Old Mrs. Pettinguil," Carolyn laughed.

"Yeah, old Mrs. Pettinguil," Dad echoed. "Thought she was going to have a heart attack."

"She wasn't the only one," I muttered, just as the trailer door flew open.

Mom was standing in the opening with her hands on her hips, her head cocked to the side, and looking directly at Dad.

"Exactly where did you go after you left us?" she demanded,

"Like I told you before," Dad countered. "I went to California, trying to find some work."

"What part of California?" Mom asked, suspiciously.

"What do ya mean, what part?" Dad retorted. "I went to California."

"You went to Fresno, didn't you?" Mom shouted, as she reached out and slapped Dad across the face. "You went to see her! You dirty, good-for-nothing . . ."

Mom continued screaming obscenities and slapping at Dad with both hands.

Crossing his arms protectively in front of him, Dad pleaded, "Now, Gladys, just calm down."

As I stood there watching the familiar scene, the yelling seemed to fade and the hitting seemed to take place in slow motion. I knew that much of the struggle we endured was due to Dad's disappearing, but although Carolyn and I missed Dad, we didn't seem to feel the loss nearly as intensely as Mom. Curious as to why she was in such torment, I finally asked, "Why are you hitting Dad?" I was woefully unprepared for her answer.

Mom stepped back, wiped at her eyes, and replied, "You might as well know now; you're bound to find out sooner or later. Your father has another wife and family in Fresno. When your father's not with us, he's with his other family."

This news was shocking enough, but I was in for an even bigger surprise. "There's more," she continued, glancing menacingly at Dad. "There's a son and daughter in the other family. The son is ten years older than you, but your names are identical."

"We're both called Buddy?" I blurted.

"No," Mom corrected me. "You're both named Bernard Edmund Poduska Jr."

I felt a mixture of jealousy and humiliation, but the full implication of this news would not fully manifest itself until many years later. At the time, I was more concerned about whether or not my own family would be able to stay together than I was about the existence of another family of Poduskas.

Carolyn nudged me out the door and declared, "Dad's back."

I rolled my eyes and sighed, "Yeah, but for how long?"

Chapter 13

CAROLYN TRIED REPOSITIONING HERSELF IN the waiting room chair, her movements accompanied by a groan and then a grunt. Her eyes began to flutter and then stare blankly at the tile floor.

"Sleep well?" I offered in jest.

"I don't think anyone could call being twisted up like a pretzel sleeping well," she complained. "How about you?"

"I dozed off occasionally, but just for minutes at a time. Nothing I could call a deep sleep," I replied, stifling a yawn.

"Well, I may not have slept very well, but I'm still going to need a cup of coffee before I'll be able to get my eyes all the way open," Carolyn declared. Then turning to me, she added, "Mormons don't drink coffee, do they?"

"Nope. We try to live what is called the Word of Wisdom. When I joined the Church, I gave up coffee, alcohol, and tobacco."

"Sounds like you had to give up a lot when you joined this church," Carolyn observed.

"Not really. I only gave up things that were harmful," I contended. "I didn't have to give up anything that was healthy."

The furrows on Carolyn's forehead reappeared. "What in the world made you switch from a full-fledged atheist to a practicing Mormon?"

"Nothing less than a miracle could have accomplished such a change," I admitted, "and only a God who is personally involved in each of our lives could explain what really happened."

"So from a mortal's standpoint, tell me what happened."

"It all started with dreams—vague, persistent dreams. I would awake with the strong impression that there was *something* I was supposed to be doing. I'd check my appointment book and search for some forgotten note, never finding a clue to what might be generating such a strong impression, but I knew that there was *something* I was supposed to be doing."

"Did the dreams come and go?" Carolyn asked.

"No. The dreams and the impression persisted along with an underlying sense of urgency. I spent endless hours talking with Barbara about what soon became an obsession. I even attempted to write another textbook, thinking that by being creative I might discover what it was that I was supposed to be doing. But to no avail. It felt as if I had made a promise to someone and then failed to keep it. But I had no idea what it was I might have promised or to whom such a promise might have been made."

"How was Barbara taking all of this?"

"Not very well," I acknowledged. "My obsession began to interfere with our daily routine. On one occasion, Barbara and I were at a restaurant when I suddenly asked, 'Was I supposed to meet someone tonight?' Concerned that I might be in the early stages of a nervous breakdown, Barbara declared, 'No, you're *not* supposed to meet someone or be somewhere else, so cool it.'

"I tried to reassure her that I wasn't going crazy, but I don't think I was very convincing. After we left the restaurant, we drove for a while. Talking seemed to come more easily in the privacy of the car. However, the uneasy feelings continued unabated. That is, until I began talking about Dad. I have no idea how Dad became the subject of our conversation, but the intensity of this strange feeling began to subside. The persistent urging by no means went away completely, but talking about Dad at least seemed to be a step in the right direction."

"So what you were supposed to be doing had something to do with Dad?" Carolyn interjected.

"I thought so at the time," I admitted. "In retrospect, I know that it wasn't my earthly father that I was being prompted to seek, but rather my Heavenly Father. However, lacking any such insight at the time, I began searching for Dad. I was feeling more on track than I had in weeks."

"How long had it been since you'd seen Dad?"

"At least four years. He'd been on a 'Brinks robbery pick-up.' Apparently, he'd robbed a Brinks truck years before and then stashed the money until things cooled off."

"Do you think he was telling the truth?" Carolyn asked.

"Knowing Dad," I replied with a smile, "anything's possible."

"Where would you even begin to look for him?"

"Dad had said something about taking the money to some people in Elko. So, I began my search with a phone call to the police department in Elko. They had no record of him so I called some of the county jails, but it soon became obvious that this method was not going to work; finding Dad wasn't going to be easy. While I was considering my options, I remembered my encounter with the army intelligence officer when I was trying to get a top secret clearance."

Carolyn interrupted my story with a thought. "You know, you've never told me what you actually did in the army."

"There's really not much to tell. After I completed basic training, I was sent to radar maintenance school and then to a missile range near White Sands, New Mexico. However, because of the sensitive nature of the activities conducted at the missile range, I needed a top secret security clearance. As part of the process, I was fingerprinted. A few weeks later, I was ordered to report to intelligence headquarters in order to clear up some irregularities. During a routine investigation of my background, no less than *three* Bernard Edmund Poduskas had been identified. All from California: one from Stockton, another from Fresno, and a third from Eureka. Each name had a different Social Security number, and one was connected with a number of arrests."

"Hmmm, I wonder which one had the criminal record," Carolyn teased.

I acknowledged her insinuation with a broad grin and then continued. "I explained that the Bernard Edmund Poduska with the criminal background was Dad. The Bernard from Fresno was most likely my half-brother, and I was the third Bernard Poduska. Eventually, I did obtain my security clearance. But the most important thing I remembered from that encounter was that the other Bernard lived in Fresno," I continued, "so I decided to call him, hoping he might know of Dad's whereabouts."

"That's all you had to go on?"

"That's all I had . . . a name and a town, so I called directory assistance in Fresno," I said. Then, with a big grin, I added, "How many Bernard Edmund Poduskas could there be?"

Carolyn chuckled while rolling her eyes.

"Fortunately, there was only one in Fresno," I continued. "I was nervous when I dialed the number, but as soon as Bernard answered the phone in that deep, cheerful voice of his, I began to relax. He asked who was calling, and I told him it was Bernard Edmund Poduska Jr."

"I'll bet he was surprised," Carolyn commented.

"Dumbfounded was more like it!" I exclaimed. "Bernard declared that it was about time we got together and invited me and the family to drive over that weekend. Eventually, we got around to the reason I had called in the first place, and I asked if he knew where I could find our dad. '*Our* dad' sounded strange, but it was something I needed to get used to. He said that he'd heard Dad had had a heart attack and was in a hospital in Independence, Missouri. After a few phone calls, I located the hospital where Dad had been admitted. They told me he had died two days earlier."

"That's when you called me to tell me that Dad had died," Carolyn acknowledged, "and since Dad was still a vagrant, the hospital had planned on burying him in a pauper's grave."

"Fortunately," I confided, "Bernard volunteered to send some money to give Dad a proper burial."

"Pauper's grave," Carolyn said thoughtfully. "You don't hear the term *pauper* very often, but I suppose that's what we were when we were homeless . . . paupers."

"That's certainly what we were that winter in Reno," I admitted.

***

Early winter 1948

Reno, Nevada

For the life of me, I couldn't figure out why Mom and Dad stayed together. They fought almost constantly. One time, Dad started ranting and raving about how unfair life was, smashed his fist through a cabinet door, and then tore the cabinets off the wall. After that, we had to stack our dishes on the floor.

Another time, he started swearing about that dump that we were living in and kicked out some of the boards in the back wall of the lean-to. Carolyn and I would usually run outside during these rampages, but if it was too cold outside, we just sat in the middle of the mattress and held each other.

By December, things had gone from bad to worse. Dad was getting drunk almost every day, and he no longer bothered to ask Mom for money; he just grabbed her purse out of her hands and took whatever he could find. In order to have bus money to get to work, Mom had to hide dimes in the crevices of the fence posts that she followed to the highway.

Dad even tried to get money out of the Lamonts. They had been showing up regularly with groceries about every other week, until he tried to finagle money out of them. After that, they waited a ways down the road till they saw him leave before making their deliveries.

Mom was always careful to order only what we really needed from Father Sullivan, but the Lamonts always added a few extras, like a bag of cookies or a can of fruit cocktail. On one of our visits to the church, Father Sullivan started asking questions about our plans for the upcoming holidays.

"It's getting pretty close to Christmas," he said. "Would you like me to include a small canned ham, or maybe a turkey?"

"Thank you, Father," Mom replied gratefully, "but the manager of the restaurant where I work invited us to eat there on Christmas Eve. Every Christmas, he opens his restaurant to anyone who's in need."

"He sounds like a very generous man," Father Sullivan said with a smile. "And speaking of Christmas . . . would you mind if some of us helped out with a few gifts for the children? The Lamonts would especially like to give you and the children a few things."

My ears immediately perked up, but I knew better than to say anything.

"That's very thoughtful," Mom said. "I don't really need anything, but I suppose the children could use a few things, mostly clothes."

"I'll certainly take that into consideration, but why don't you leave the details to me. Several merchants donate clothing and toys to the church this time of the year, and we distribute them according to the needs of individual families," Father Sullivan said, patting me on the head as we turned to leave.

Mom reached for the door, hesitated, and turned back to the priest. "I feel I need to explain our situation a little more thoroughly," she said quietly. "I really appreciate everything you've done for us, Father, and I don't want you to think that I'm ungrateful, but we've always had to leave things behind when it comes time to move on. So I wouldn't want you to . . ."

"To what?"

"To . . . go overboard. Carolyn and Buddy have learned not to expect too much for Christmas. They're very good about whatever they get. They seem to understand our situation." She turned to me and smiled. "At least, I think they do."

I nodded.

"I understand perfectly, Mrs. Poduska. Now, don't you give it another thought. I'll take care of everything. After all, I rather enjoy playing Santa Claus. Drop by Christmas Eve, and I'll have everything ready."

"That's very kind of you, Father. I'm going to Midnight Mass with the Lamonts. We could stop by after the service."

"That would be just fine," the priest smiled. "I'll have the gifts wrapped and waiting."

Mom tied her scarf under her chin and started down the steps. "Thanks again for everything, Father. Merry Christmas."

"Merry Christmas to you, Mrs. Poduska. And to you, Buddy."

After Mom fed us that night, she asked Carolyn and me to go to bed early so she and Dad could have some privacy. Since we all slept in the same bed, the only way for them to have any privacy was for us to go to bed early. At least, they thought that gave them some privacy. In reality, the clapboards forming the trailer's missing wall provided no real barrier to sound.

This particular night, after the customary waiting period had passed, Mom came to the doorway and peeked in. "They must've been tired," she said softly. "They're already asleep."

"What was it you wanted to talk about?" Dad asked.

"Buddy and I stopped by to see Father Sullivan today, and he asked me what we needed for Christmas."

"Did you tell him we needed everything?"

"No," Mom said irritably. "I merely told him how much I . . . *we* appreciated everything he'd done for us already and that he shouldn't go overboard because we wouldn't be able to take any gifts with us when we moved."

"I've only met that priest once, but he didn't impress me as the kind who's likely to take your advice. I'll bet you anything it'll take a pickup truck to haul all the presents."

At that, I nudged Carolyn under the blankets.

"Did you hear what he just said?" she whispered.

I nodded, unable to stop grinning.

"I just hope he doesn't get too carried away," Mom continued. "He said the local merchants donate new clothes and toys during the holidays, and I'd hate to have to leave a lot of nice things behind."

There was more nudging under the blankets. I covered my head with my pillow, trying to muffle a giggle.

"At any rate," Mom went on, "I told Father Sullivan I'd drop by to pick up the presents on Christmas Eve, after Midnight Mass was over. Do you want to come with me?"

"To pick up the presents or go to church?"

"Either."

"Nah. I've got a few errands to run tomorrow night," Dad said distantly, as if lost in thought.

He was lying, of course, but I didn't really care. I'd heard everything I needed to hear.

***

Mom didn't have to work Christmas Eve morning, so we all stayed in bed with the oil stove turned up high. When we finally did get up, Dad made everyone his special pancake recipe, which called for beer in the batter and gave him an excuse to start drinking earlier than usual.

Shortly after we finished breakfast, someone knocked on the front door. I jumped up on the couch to look out the window and saw the Lamonts standing there. Mr. Lamont was carrying a small Christmas tree with a little red stand. The whole thing couldn't have been more than two or three feet tall. As soon as Mom opened the door, a broad smile came to her face.

"Merry Christmas!" Mrs. Lamont said cheerfully.

Mr. Lamont held the tree up high so we could all get a good look. "Merry Christmas! We apologize for coming out so early, but the missus and I thought you could use this little tree. It should fit nicely on top of the table."

"That was very thoughtful of you." Mom smiled.

Stepping up to the door, Dad interjected, "We'd be glad to pay you for it."

Mrs. Lamont's eyes momentarily narrowed when she saw Dad, but she quickly recovered, and if Dad noticed, he didn't let on.

"Oh, that won't be necessary," Mr. Lamont replied, handing the tree to Mom.

"Won't you please come in?" Mom asked, graciously.

Mr. Lamont shook his head, and they both began backing away. "Thanks anyway, but we really should be getting along," he said. "We still have to stop by our daughter's house . . . grandkids and all that. But thanks anyway."

"Thank you for the tree and for coming all the way out here," Mom called after them.

I watched the Lamonts drive off and then followed Mom as she carried the little tree over to the table and carefully set it down in the middle.

"Now doesn't that look nice?" she said with a sigh of satisfaction. "I suppose the next thing we should do is make some decorations for it.

Maybe some paper chains. And if my memory serves me, the last bag of groceries we got had a jar of popping corn in it."

I rested my chin on the edge of the table and looked up at the tree. "It's not very big, is it?"

"What do you mean, it's not very big? It's as big as we can manage in this little place."

"I mean, there isn't much room to put presents under it."

"Don't you worry about room for the presents. For what you're getting this Christmas, this tree is plenty big."

We all rode the bus into town that evening and then walked over to Mom's restaurant for our free Christmas dinner. We were served turkey with all the trimmings, with the manager's family and friends acting as the waiters, dishwashers, and cooks.

As we were leaving, the manager handed each of us a large candy cane. "Thanks for coming, and Merry Christmas," he said.

"Thank you for having us," Mom said in return. "That was a wonderful dinner. And Merry Christmas to you and your family."

It was still relatively early when we left the café. "What are we gonna do now?" I asked as we were walking.

"Well," Mom began, with a twinkle in her eye, "we could look at the Christmas displays in the store windows . . ." The twinkle in Mom's eye seemed to get brighter. "Or I suppose we could go to the movies. *Bambi* is playing over at the Rialto."

"Where'd we get enough money for a movie?" I asked, looking up in surprise.

"The manager gave each of us a little Christmas bonus, and he said we were to spend it on Christmas."

"You didn't bother to mention any bonus to me," Dad huffed.

"For obvious reasons," Mom shot back then quickly changed the subject back to the idea of going to the movies.

Movies were few and far between for us, so this really was a special treat. Carolyn and I ran ahead to save a place in the ticket line. It was long, but it moved quickly, and I was soon being transported into Disney's magical world of animation.

About the time Thumper and Bambi were meeting each other on the screen, Dad whispered to Mom, "Let me have some of that bonus money, Gladys. I've got a few things to take care of."

"That money is for Christmas gifts," Mom said firmly.

"Well, that's what I need to take care of. I want to buy some Christmas gifts for the kids."

Mom hesitated, and I knew that she didn't believe him.

"Well?" he pressed. "Am I going to be able to get some Christmas gifts or not?"

Mom sighed in defeat. "It's against my better judgment . . . but here's five dollars. Promise me you'll really use it for presents and not head for the nearest bar."

"Hey, come on. What kind of Scrooge do you take me for?" Dad said defensively as he took the money and left.

He hadn't returned by the time the movie ended. We waited outside the theater for about ten minutes, and when he still didn't show up, I concluded that he was sitting in a bar somewhere, drinking up Mom's bonus money.

Mom looked down at us anxiously. "Your dad had some errands to run, so he'll probably meet you back at the trailer." Then her eyes settled on Carolyn. "How quickly you've had to grow up," she sighed. "You're twelve going on twenty-one." Turning to me, she added, "You haven't had much of a childhood, either."

She pulled up the collar of my coat to shield the back of my neck and gave me a weak smile. "I'd really like to have you go to Christmas services with me, but Midnight Mass gets out so late. It's probably best if you two go straight home."

"That's okay, Mom," Carolyn said, speaking for both of us. "We'd just fall asleep in the middle of it."

"Besides, the incense stinks," I added comfortingly.

"I'd hoped that your father would take you home," Mom went on, "but I don't know when he's liable to show up. I guess you'd better head back without him."

"We'll be all right, Mom. We've ridden the bus by ourselves lots of times," Carolyn reassured.

Mom made sure we were safely on the bus, asked the driver to watch after us, and then told him where to let us off, even though we both knew the route by heart. Mom worried a lot.

Once we got back to the trailer, we lit the oil stove, huddled together, and waited for Mom and the presents to arrive.

Soon, car headlights indicated they'd turned off the snow-packed road. "They're here!" Carolyn cried out. "Get ready to run for bed."

"I'm ready. I just want to see how many presents they brought."

The two of us peered out. "I don't think Dad's with them," Carolyn observed.

"Who cares? He'd probably be drunk anyway and spoil everything for the rest of us," I whispered.

"I think it's just Mom and the Lamonts," Carolyn continued. "And Father Sullivan."

I was already off the couch and headed for bed, so there was no time to confirm what she had said. We hurried into the lean-to and climbed under the covers. A moment later, the door opened and someone turned on the light.

"He didn't bring the presents out here," Mom said, sighing heavily.

"Are you sure?" Mr. Lamont asked.

I crawled closer to the small crack in the boards to see what was happening.

"See for yourself," Mom declared, pointing at the empty space around the tree.

Mrs. Lamont had squeezed her way into the small space inside the door. "I just can't believe it!"

Carolyn and I were up on our elbows now. Carolyn frowned. "What's going on?" she whispered.

I shrugged and peeked through one of the slits.

Mrs. Lamont looked particularly upset. Then Mom excused herself, telling the others that she wanted to check on the children. Carolyn and I scrambled into our "sleeping angels" positions, long enough for Mom to look in on us. As soon as it was safe, we returned to our eavesdropping.

"I still can't understand how something like this could happen," Mrs. Lamont lamented as she sat down at the table.

Father Sullivan slowly shook his head. "Like I said, I was surprised when I came into the parlor and found Mr. Poduska there." The priest paused, turning to Mom. "I told him that you were planning to stop by after services."

Mom nodded. "That was the plan."

"But he said there'd been a change in plans. He said that since the kids no longer believed in Santa Claus, the two of you had decided they might as well open their presents on Christmas Eve. I didn't have any reason to suspect anything, so I showed him the pile of presents . . . it was quite a stack, so I suggested that he let the Lamonts drive him out here."

"I bet he didn't jump at that," Mom said sarcastically.

"No, he didn't. He said it would be too late to surprise the kids if he waited, and he started scooping up presents."

"But where'd he take them?" Mr. Lamont asked.

"He'll probably return them for refunds so he can buy booze," Mom said quietly.

"And on Christmas Eve," the priest muttered. "What kind of a man would do such a thing?"

Mr. Lamont slapped his knees and stood up. "Well, there's nothing more we can do tonight," he said, zipping his coat. "We might as well let Mrs. Poduska get some rest."

"I'm sorry for the way tonight turned out," Father Sullivan said, apologetically. "It hasn't been much of a Christmas."

"We're survivors," Mom replied, softly. "We'll manage."

They were halfway out the door when Mrs. Lamont stopped and grabbed her husband by the elbow. "Wait a minute. I just remembered something." She turned back to Mom with a triumphant smile. "Your husband didn't take all the presents, after all."

"What are you talking about?"

"Before we met you tonight, Mr. Lamont and I were out doing some last-minute Christmas shopping for your family. Those gifts are still out in the trunk!"

"By golly, you're right!" her husband laughed. "Your kids are going to have Christmas after all."

Carolyn and I watched the trio of Samaritans open the trunk and hand packages over to Mom. "That's not exactly what I'd call a pick-up load," I noted.

"Yeah," Carolyn agreed. "I count only six."

"Maybe Dad's bringing the rest," I joked, but my heart wasn't in it.

"Ha, and maybe pigs'll fly," Carolyn said with contempt.

Mom was heading our way, so we ran back to bed. I heard her come in and set the packages on the table. When I peeked through the slit, I saw her slumped over the table with her head in her arms, and I realized she was crying.

Carolyn saw it too. "We've got to promise that no matter what kind of presents we get, we'll act like we really love them," she said. "No matter what it is. Okay?"

"Okay."

"Promise?"

"I promise."

"Cross your heart?"

"Cross my heart and hope to die." I traced an *X* across my chest with my finger to prove my sincerity.

Mom sat in the dark and cried for a long time before she finally gave in and quietly climbed into bed with us.

Carolyn and I woke up early the next morning and peeked through the doorway to see if the presents were still there. "You know, six means only three apiece," I whispered then added thoughtfully, "How many of something do we have to have before it's a lot?"

"For this year, a lot will have to be three."

We were whispering but apparently not quietly enough. "You kids already awake?" Mom asked sleepily. "What time is it?"

"It's Christmas morning," I said excitedly.

"Already?" she said in mock surprise.

"Can we open our presents now?" I asked breathlessly.

"It's still cold in here. Carolyn, could you light the stove and then bring the presents. We'll open them in bed."

"I'll get the presents!" I cried out happily.

"Don't open any till I get there!" Carolyn called after me.

As soon as she returned, we got back in bed and sat with our backs against the wall and the blankets up to our chests.

"Who gets to go first?" I asked.

"Let Mom go first," Carolyn suggested.

"No, Christmas is for children," Mom said. "Buddy, why don't you start with that red package? It's got your name on it. And Carolyn, your name is on the one with the white ribbon."

I tore into the wrapping. Then my mouth fell open.

"A Roy Rogers cap pistol!" I shouted. "Just what I've always wanted!" I grabbed it out of the box and held it up in the air. "And there's two boxes of caps, too," I added, with increased excitement. I started loading a roll of caps then noticed Carolyn smiling at me approvingly. "I'm not acting, Carolyn," I said emphatically. "I really do like it."

Mom was watching Carolyn open her gift and didn't seem to notice my last comment. Carolyn carefully untied the bow, systematically loosened the scotch tape, and unfolded the paper. "*Black Beauty*," she said reverently, lifting the book to her chest as her eyes filled with tears. "Oh, Mom. Thank you!"

"Don't thank me," Mom said innocently. "I wasn't the one who bought it."

"But *Black Beauty* . . . you must've told someone."

"Never you mind about that. You like it, and that's what counts." Then Mom looked at me. "Buddy, why don't you open another one?"

I handed Mom a red-and-green package with no name on it and said, "It's your turn to open something."

"Yeah, Mom. It's your turn," Carolyn agreed.

"Oh, all right. If it'll make you two happy," Mom said, with a pixie-like smile on her face.

Mom's gift was a five hundred-piece puzzle of Lake Tahoe. In addition to the cap pistol, I got a pair of gloves. Carolyn got a new set of jacks and a scarf. The sixth package was a glass ball with a small village inside. When it was shaken, snow drifted down. Regardless of how few presents there were, we had gotten a lot this Christmas.

Chapter 14

THE HOSPITAL WAITING ROOM HAD obviously been designed for those who had shorter waits than Carolyn and I were experiencing. There were six chairs but no couch. A couch would have allowed us to take turns stretching out. At one point, I even considered stretching out on the floor.

The two of us were not only uncomfortable, we were bored. Having thumbed through every magazine on the table several times, Carolyn tossed a *Better Homes & Gardens* back on the pile.

"Do you want me to see if they have some cards at the nurse's desk?" I asked. "It might help pass the time."

"No. I'm not in the mood for cards. Besides, the time seems to pass more quickly when we're talking."

I shrugged and asked, "What do you want to talk about?"

"Tell me about when you and the other Bernard actually met."

"The weekend after I called, Barbara, the kids, and I drove from Santa Cruz to Fresno following the directions Bernard had given me over the phone. We eventually turned into a long driveway between an assortment of buildings, trucks, and a barn."

"Sounds a little like the Lundquist's farm that we stayed at in Utah," Carolyn interjected.

"There were a lot of similarities, but Bernard was a beekeeper, and the Lundquist farm had more orchards," I explained. "Anyway, once the introductions were finished, we followed them into the barn, where he had been working when we arrived. And that's when things started to get a little weird."

"What do you mean weird?" Carolyn asked, leaning forward.

"You'll see," I assured her. "I asked Bernard if he was working on his honey business, and he told me, no, he was working on their food storage.

So, I asked him why he was storing so much food, and you'll never guess what he said."

"That he had been hungry as a child and never wanted to be hungry again," Carolyn teased.

"No, actually Bernard and his sister had been raised in a middle-income family and lived most of their lives in one place. But I'm sure his answer will surprise you as much as it did me. Bernard told me that the prophet had told him to store a year's supply of food. So that's what he was doing."

"The prophet told him to store food!?" Carolyn echoed.

"At the time, my response was the same as yours: What in the Sam Hill had I gotten myself into, and how soon could I get out of there? Bernard must have picked up on my bewilderment because he immediately tried to explain. He told me that he was a Mormon and that the head of the Mormon Church had counseled the members to store a year's supply of food. I asked him if he knew something the rest of us didn't. Bernard said that they were not told when, or even if, they would ever have to use it, but it would be wise to have it on hand."

"So Bernard was a Mormon," Carolyn conceded.

"That's right, and as we were walking toward the house, Bernard asked me what religion I belonged to. So I told him that I didn't belong to any religion. I was an atheist."

"I somehow thought he'd be a Catholic," Carolyn contended. "Dad was Catholic when he married Mom."

"That's what I thought, too, but he was raised Presbyterian," I explained. "Then, more out of politeness than real curiosity, I asked him how he ended up becoming a Mormon."

"That seems to be the $64,000 question," Carolyn commented, shaking her head. "I still don't know how you became a Mormon."

"It will all make sense in a minute."

"That's what you said before."

"Wait till you hear what he said when I asked him how he had become a Mormon."

"I'm waiting."

"Bernard told me, 'A few months ago I began having these strange dreams . . .'"

"You've got to be kidding!" Carolyn exclaimed.

"Scout's honor," I vowed. "As soon as I heard those familiar words, you better believe he had my attention."

"What kind of dreams?" she asked.

"Actually, in Bernard's situation, there was only one dream, but he kept having the same one over and over." I glanced at Carolyn, and she appeared totally engrossed with what I was saying, so I elaborated. "In this dream, he was walking down a long tunnel with a bright light at the end. He felt drawn to the light, and although he'd quicken his pace, he could never get any closer to it. In this dream, he was carrying two books—one in each hand. When he held the books up to the light, he could see that one of them was the Bible, but he couldn't make out the identity of the second book. Then the dream ended and he woke up."

"That's one strange dream, alright," Carolyn acknowledged.

"Bernard said that his dreams were very vivid," I continued, "and that he had no difficulty recalling them. I asked him if he ever figured out what the dream meant. He said he tried but didn't have a clue until one day he shared the dream with a friend. As soon as he finished telling him the dream, this friend told him that he knew what it meant."

"This friend of his didn't happen to be a psychiatrist?" Carolyn asked playfully.

I chuckled, shaking my head. "No, his friend wasn't a psychiatrist. He was a Mormon, and he told Bernard that since the one book in the dream was the Bible, the second book in the dream could be the Book of Mormon. Bernard didn't know very much about the Mormon religion, let alone the Book of Mormon, so when his friend asked Bernard if he could invite two young men to come to his home to explain the Book of Mormon to him, Bernard said yes. The moment he and his wife, Joan, heard what the missionaries had to say, they knew that what they were being told was true. The rest, as they say, is history."

"There could have been some other explanation," Carolyn proposed. "The second book could have been a Sears catalog."

"That's more or less what I said when Bernard was telling me this story," I acknowledged. "But then, in a calm, serious tone, Bernard responded, 'Except for the feeling.'"

"The feeling?" Carolyn echoed.

"Yes. He said that while being taught by the missionaries, a feeling came over him. He said it was hard to describe, but it was a feeling that confirmed the truthfulness of what he was being taught. He went on to say that if I ever felt such a sensation, I'd have no doubt about its meaning."

"Mom used to rely a lot on what she called a 'special feeling'," Carolyn interjected. "She said that sometimes it was all that kept her going."

"If it hadn't been for Mom," I added, "I'm not sure any of us would have made it. My heart goes out to her for the sacrifices she made for us."

***

Winter 1949

Reno, Nevada

Christmas had passed, and there was still no sign of Dad. Reno was experiencing an exceptionally hard winter, and the schools closed a few times because of the deep snow. Of course, Carolyn and I never complained about not having to go to school. But they didn't close the café, which meant that Mom had to trudge through that deep snow to get to and from work. She would wear a pair of short rubber boots over her work shoes, but the snow was so deep that it caved in over the tops, so she had to work all day in wet shoes. These "inconveniences," as she called them, gradually began to take their toll. The shoes went first and then her health.

Mom found another pair of shoes at the Goodwill store, but they didn't fit well and made her feet hurt. She began wearing just the rubber boots, carrying her work shoes in her hands, but the boots provided little protection from the cold.

When she came home from work, Carolyn would heat a pan of water to warm her feet. Sometimes Mom would shake so much that the water would splash over the side of the pan. Eventually, the shakes became severe enough to tip over the pan.

Once that began to happen, we started a new ritual. We would take off Mom's shoes, dry her feet, and help her to bed. Then we would lie down by her feet and hold them to us until she stopped shaking. I would take a deep breath before pulling her feet to my chest, since the shock of how cold they were, even through my undershirt, made it hard for me to breathe.

Most of the time, Mom would fall asleep by the time the shaking stopped. On those nights she wouldn't get anything to eat. I would try to wake her and get her to at least drink some soup, but she would usually just thank me and tell me she was too tired to eat. Mom told us she was eating at the café, but she was losing weight and getting progressively weaker.

Late one afternoon, the manager of the café drove up with Mom slumped over in the front seat. Carolyn and I hurried outside to meet them.

"She just collapsed," he explained, looking bewildered. "She was picking up an order and just collapsed. She didn't hit her head, but she was out like a light."

Carolyn and I slowly approached the car and peered through the window. Mom rolled her head and stared back at us. She smiled weakly but didn't try to talk.

The three of us lifted her out of the car, carried her into the trailer, and put her on the mattress. I finally got up the courage to ask, "How sick is she?"

"I can't really say just yet," the manager said, "but she looks pretty bad. She may have to go to a hospital." I sensed that he was trying not to alarm us, while making sure we knew that it was serious.

"How much would a hospital cost?" Carolyn asked.

"Don't worry about that. If she has to go to the hospital, the county will take care of her for free."

He helped us settle Mom in before he left. Once he'd gone, Carolyn made Mom some hot tea and gave her three aspirins.

"Try to get some rest," she said quietly and then turned off the light and motioned me to follow her into the trailer. "Mom looks awful sick, Buddy," she whispered. "If she doesn't get better real soon, we'll have to take her to the hospital."

I nodded, too scared to speak.

Mom coughed all night. We took turns getting up with her. The next morning, Carolyn felt Mom's head. "She feels hot."

"And her cough sounds like it's getting worse," I added.

"It doesn't look too good, does it, little brother?"

Mom spent the day in bed, with one of us by her side at all times, taking turns to go to the outhouse. Carolyn walked to the little store near the bus stop to get some Smith Brothers' cough drops, but the cough kept getting worse.

Sometime during the night, Carolyn nudged me awake. "Buddy?" she whispered.

"Yeah?"

"It sounds like Mom's having a tough time breathing."

I sat there in the dark, listening. Mom's breath was coming in short gasps, followed by weak coughing. I was scared again—scared of being left behind.

In the morning, we decided that we had to take Mom to the hospital. She was so weak that we had to lift her off the mattress. The three of us slowly made our way down the road to the bus stop, resting against every other fence post, searching the crevices for any dimes Mom may have hidden.

Once we reached the bus stop, we only had to wait a few minutes before the bus pulled up. As soon as the doors opened, Carolyn pointed at Mom. "Our mom's real sick, and we need to take her to the hospital."

A look of concern immediately came over the bus driver's face.

Carolyn held out some coins. "I've got five nickels."

"I'm afraid I can't accept any nickels today," the bus driver said seriously. Then, when Carolyn's face fell, he quickly added, "So I guess I'll have to let you ride for free."

Carolyn let out a sigh of relief. "Thanks, mister," she said, turning to help Mom onto the bus. The three of us sat down on the bench seat directly across from the driver. "We have to take her to the county hospital," she continued. "We've never been there before, so could you tell us when to get off?"

The driver looked at Mom. "Your mama don't look too good."

"She can't breathe," I volunteered.

About twenty minutes later, the bus slowed, and the driver turned to us. "The bus stop on the next corner is the closest I come to the county hospital on this route. The hospital's just a few blocks down on your right." He hesitated, glanced at Mom again, and looked up in his overhead mirror, and addressed the passengers. "Folks, we've got an emergency up here. Got a couple of kids with a sick mama. I'm going to be taking a little detour from my regular route so we can get them over to the county hospital." He looked back at Carolyn and me. "I could lose my job for this, but your mama looks real sick."

A few blocks later, the bus pulled up at the hospital's emergency entrance. Once inside, we settled Mom into a chair, and Carolyn hurried over to the nurse's station. "Excuse me," she said to a nurse behind the desk. "My mom's real sick. She needs to see a doctor."

The nurse looked sternly over the top of her glasses. "Where's your mother now?"

"Right over there," Carolyn replied, pointing at Mom.

The nurse stood up, took one look at Mom, and called for a doctor. An orderly appeared with a gurney, followed by a flurry of white uniforms and stethoscopes. One of the nurses began asking questions.

"Your name, ma'am?"

"Gladys Poduska," Carolyn volunteered.

Then they quickly wheeled the gurney through a set of swinging doors.

"You two wait here until I come back," the nurse ordered before disappearing through the doors behind them.

About thirty minutes later, a doctor came into the waiting room. He asked us to sit down as soon as we stood up. "You must be Carolyn and Buddy," he began.

We both nodded.

"How's Mom?" Carolyn asked

"Well, your mother's a very sick woman. I'm afraid she's going to have to stay in the hospital for a while."

"What's wrong with her?" I asked.

"Right now, it looks like pneumonia."

Pneumonia! I panicked. *People die from pneumonia!*

"When can we see her?" Carolyn asked.

"Only children twelve or older are allowed to visit the patients," a nurse at the desk interjected. "How old are you?"

Since she'd just recently celebrated a birthday, Carolyn replied without hesitation, "Thirteen."

"Then you can go back, but the boy will have to wait here."

Seeing my disappointment, Carolyn put her hand on my arm. "I won't be long. Maybe you'll get to see her tomorrow."

"Your mother's in room 214. You'll only be allowed to stay a few minutes. She needs her rest."

As Carolyn started down the hallway, the doctor fished a coin out of his pocket and handed it to me. "Here's a nickel for the pop machine." Then he, too, headed down the hall.

As he'd suggested, I headed for the pop machine standing near the waiting room. I was studying the choices when the desk nurse told her aide that she was going to a meeting on the third floor. As soon as the elevator door closed behind her, I ran down the hall and caught up with Carolyn.

We slowly pushed open the door of Mom's room. The room was dimly lit, which added a sense of foreboding. Three of the four beds in the room were occupied.

"Who are you looking for?" one of the patients asked.

"Our mom," I replied. "She came in a little while ago."

The patient pointed to the other side of the room. "That must be her over there, under the oxygen tent."

Carolyn and I moved hesitantly to the frail-looking figure lying under the transparent tent. Mom looked pale, except for under her eyes, where it was dark. Her eyes opened slightly when Carolyn started to speak.

"Hi, Mom. How're you doin'?"

Mom slowly turned her head toward us, her voice weak and raspy. "Oh, I've been better, but I'm doing all right."

"What are they doing to you?" I asked, pointing at the plastic tent.

"I'm having a little trouble breathing, so they put me under this tent to make it easier."

"How long are you going have to stay?" I asked.

"Probably only a couple of days. As soon as I get my strength back, I'll be able to leave."

"Do you want anything from home?" Carolyn asked softly.

Mom smiled reassuringly. "No, I'm fine," she said, but then she started to gasp for air. She rested silently for a few seconds, breathing in short shallow breaths. Finally, she motioned Carolyn closer. "I want you to call Father Sullivan and have him arrange for someone to take care of the two of you." She pointed weakly at the nightstand next to the bed. "My little brown address book is in that top drawer. Take it . . . his phone number is in . . ." Another gasping episode stopped her in mid-sentence.

A nurse came into the room and quickly began adjusting the valves on the large green cylinder next to her bed.

"Are you all right, Mrs. Poduska?" she asked as she tucked in the edges of the tent.

"I'm okay, I just had to catch my breath."

The nurse turned to Carolyn and me. "I'm afraid you'll have to go now. Your mother needs her rest." She ushered us out of the room, following right behind.

"Is my mom going to be all right?" Carolyn pleaded.

"Of course she will," the nurse replied.

"When can we see her again?" I asked.

The nurse pointed at Carolyn and stipulated, "*You* will be able to see her in a couple of days."

The nurse walked with us as far as the desk. "What about you two? Is there someone you need to call?"

"Mom had me call Father Sullivan at St. Thomas's," Carolyn replied matter-of-factly. "He's already on his way over."

I looked up at her, stunned.

"We'll probably be staying with the Lamonts," she went on, giving me a sly wink. "They've been helping us out a lot."

I still had no idea what her plan was, but I decided to play along. "Yeah, they're nice people."

Hesitantly, the nurse turned to leave. "Do you want me to wait with you until someone arrives?"

"Father Sullivan will be here in just a few minutes," Carolyn added. "We'll be just fine."

As soon as the nurse was out of hearing, Carolyn related her plan. "We'll wait till we're sure the coast is clear then catch a bus back to our place."

"Then you're not really going to call Father Sullivan?" I asked, somewhat relieved.

"Are you crazy? They'd just put us in another foster home. We Poduskas can take care of ourselves."

***

Mom was in the hospital for about a week before the Lamonts became suspicious. "Is your mom needing to work late?" Mrs. Lamont asked one evening while dropping off some groceries.

"Yeah," Carolyn lied. "They're shorthanded down at the café, so she's had to work a lot of overtime."

The Lamonts seemed to buy the story, but we knew it was only a matter of time before they discovered the truth.

Sure enough, during our next visit to the hospital, the Lamonts opened the door and stuck their heads in. "Thank the good Lord, we've found you!" Mrs. Lamount cried.

"What do you mean, you've found me?" Mom asked in surprise. "Haven't Carolyn and Buddy been staying with you?"

Carolyn and I looked at each other.

Mom turned her eyes on us, her expression hardening. "I think you two have some explaining to do."

"We were afraid we'd be taken to a foster home," I mumbled.

Mrs. Lamont started waving a finger. "I *thought* there was something fishy going on. I couldn't quite put my finger on it." She paused and then added triumphantly, "We stopped by where you work and found out you were in the hospital."

To put it mildly, Mom was really upset with us, but the doctor had told her that she would be able to leave the hospital in time for my tenth birthday; our deception didn't seem to matter anymore.

Mom was released from the hospital, and the Lamonts opened their home to us in much the same way as the Lundquists had; once again, the strays had been taken in. But no matter how loving and generous they were, there was a certain dignity that came from being able to make it on our own. So the letter from Dad was more than welcome.

In the letter, Dad wrote that he was sorry he had taken the Christmas gifts and that the best gift he could give us was a sober father and a nice place to live in Eureka, California. He enclosed some money, and the next day we packed the black suitcase. The cardboard box was left behind, along with a part of me. We said our good-byes and climbed onto a Greyhound bus.

"Do you think we'll live in a house when we get to Eureka?" I asked Mom once we were underway. "A place of our own that no one can kick us out of?"

"Your dad said he'd found a nice place for us to live," Mom replied noncommittally.

"And we'll be a real family?" I went on, looking over at Carolyn. I wanted to make sure she was aware of how wrong she'd been about my dream of being a real family never coming true.

Mom squeezed my hand. "I sure hope so."

At that, I leaned back in my seat and fell silent.

"Carolyn?" I finally said, while staring out at the snow-covered Sierras.

"What?"

"Do you ever wonder?"

"Wonder about what?"

"What's on down the road?"

She shook her head. "Not anymore. I'm just going to take it as it comes."

"Not me," I said, as much to myself as to her. "I'm going to make my own road someday."

Chapter 15

A PREDAWN GLOW WAS FINALLY beginning to appear through the windows. The night seemed to have passed with agonizing slowness. However, the long hours were offset by the satisfaction of having had by far the most intimate conversations that Carolyn and I had ever shared.

Carolyn had gone to the restroom located near the nursing station. We had decided to take turns being away from the waiting room in case Mom's condition changed and someone came looking for us. When she returned, she sat down and placed a finger at the corner of her mouth and slowly announced, "I've been thinking . . ."

"About what?" I prodded.

"I've been thinking about those weird dreams you and Bernard were having," she continued. "What did you think of Bernard's conversion story?"

"At the time, I found his story fascinating, but I remained firm in my conviction to *never again* believe in God. The conversation eventually shifted to sharing stories about our childhoods, which continued late into the night. The next morning, Bernard and I began telling stories again, but time was limited. We had a long trip ahead of us, and Bernard's family had their church services to attend. In parting, we mutually agreed that we liked each other, said our farewells, and agreed not to allow thirty-five years to pass without contacting each other."

"And I thought you and I were bad when we let five or ten years pass without seeing each other," Carolyn observed.

"The best is yet to come," I assured her. "Once we were back on the road and the children had settled into their travel games, Barbara and I began critiquing the visit. However, the monotonous drive across the San Joaquin Valley soon stifled any desire to talk, and my thoughts gradually turned inward to memories of childhood hitchhiking, being abandoned, and my futile search for my—our—dad. While I was thinking about the ramifications of Dad's death, a new thought gradually emerged along with the familiar there's-something-I'm-supposed-to-be-doing feeling. The strength of the impression grew stronger until an incomprehensible realization burst into consciousness.

"'So that's what I'm supposed to be doing!' I cried out, startling both Barbara and the children. Barbara, completely taken aback by the unexpected outburst, asked me what the heck that was all about. I told her that I finally knew what I was supposed to be doing. 'I'm supposed to join the Mormon Church!'

"By this time, Barbara was totally confused and asked me if I'd just said that I wanted to become a Mormon. I hesitated for a moment, and then I knew the answer. The *feeling* Bernard had told me about. He said that if I ever had a feeling that seemed to confirm the truth, I would know what it meant."

"I don't know what feeling, but wanting to join a church . . . the Mormon Church!?" Carolyn repeated in disbelief.

"Only another atheist could fully comprehended the tremendous impact this sudden revelation had had on me," I confided. "But I *knew* I was supposed to join the Mormon Church."

Carolyn furrowed her brow but didn't say anything.

"I asked Barbara if she knew anything about the Mormon Church. She said, 'A little. I was baptized a Mormon when I was eight.' Can you believe that?"

"Barbara was a Mormon when you married her!" Carolyn gasped in disbelief.

"Technically, but she hadn't been active for years," I explained. "Her whole family was inactive, except for her brother Wilf. When she was growing up, her parents would send the kids to church but never went with them. She said that most the time, she'd just pretend she was going and then hang out with her friends."

"How come she never told you any of this before?"

"Knowing the way I felt about religion, she didn't see any point. Besides, she hadn't been interested in becoming active."

"What do you mean becoming active?"

"Being active means going to church on Sunday, attending Relief Society—that's the women's organization in the church—and having home teachers visit."

"Home teachers?" Carolyn asked, furrowing her brow again.

"I didn't know it at the time, but home teachers are men who hold the priesthood that are assigned families to watch over. However, my first run in with them was not a good one."

"How so?"

"Sometime after Barbara and I were married, I came home from work and found two men standing on our front porch. I asked them who they were, and one started to answer, 'We're from the Church of . . .' but that's as far as he got before I started throwing rocks and sticks at them until I chased them off our property. I called them 'blasted block wardens.' I wanted to make sure they never came back."

"So what you called block wardens," Carolyn clarified, "the Mormons refer to as home teachers."

"I'm afraid so," I said with a shrug. "Anyway, I asked Barbara what she knew about the Mormon Church. She told me that she hadn't paid much attention in Sunday School, but that her brother Wilf could probably answer most of my questions.

"As soon as we arrived home, I called Barbara's brother. I could tell that he was surprised to get a call from his wayward brother-in-law, and at first he was worried something might have happened to Barbara or the kids. I assured him that everyone was well and that I'd called because I wanted to ask him a few questions about the Mormon Church. He thought I was kidding. I had a heck of a time convincing him that this wasn't another one of those let's-make-fun-of-the-Mormons discussions."

"So far, it sounds like you surprised just about everyone," Carolyn acknowledged.

"Understandable, since everyone was used to me being an atheist," I agreed. "But I wanted answers to some questions I had about what the Mormons believed, and Wilf seemed like the logical one to ask. So I hit him with one of my unanswerable questions: 'Does God care about us as individuals and about what happens to us?' Wilf paused for a moment, apparently giving this question some serious thought. Then he answered by telling me a story from the Gospel of Luke. He said that when Jesus was passing through Jericho, a sinner named Zacchaeus wanted to see Jesus, but since Zacchaeus was a short man, he couldn't see over the crowd—so he climbed up a tree. When Jesus saw him, he called Zacchaeus by name, even though they had never met, and offered to be his guest. Some who observed this criticized Jesus for associating with a sinner, but after the sinful man repented and vowed to make amends,

Jesus announced that 'the Son of man is come to seek and to save that which was lost.' As with Zacchaeus, Jesus knows each of us by name, and He has come to spiritually save each of us and offer us the gift of eternal life . . . if we will only accept His gifts."

"Well, if anyone was ever lost," Carolyn pointed out, "you would most certainly fit the bill."

"I don't want to overload you with scriptures, Carolyn, but I've found that they explain so much, so clearly. I'd like to read something from Matthew. 'How think ye? if a man have an hundred sheep, and one of them be gone astray, doth he not leave the ninety and nine, and goeth into the mountains, and seeketh that which is gone astray? And if so be that he find it, verily I say unto you, he rejoiceth more of that sheep, than of the ninety and nine which went not astray. Even so it is not the will of your Father which is in heaven, that one of these little ones should perish.'"

Carolyn nodded and said, "I can certainly see how that scripture would apply to your life."

"And it applies to your life, as well," I insisted. "You told me that because your husband was being sent back to prison for the third time, you had your third child adopted."

"So?" Carolyn questioned.

"So, Mom told me that even though you still had your other son and daughter, you searched for years trying to find the son who was adopted, vowing never to give up until you found him."

"Mom was never very good at keeping secrets," Carolyn declared, rolling her eyes again.

"But the great thing is that you finally found him!" I declared. "And do you remember the joy and love you felt when you once again held him in your arms?"

A tear trickled down her cheek and she smiled knowingly. "I guess we've both been lost in our own way," she conceded.

"That's why the scriptures can apply to everybody," I counseled, before continuing. "My next question was based on what Barbara had mentioned about the importance the Mormons place on families, so I asked her brother if that was true. He didn't hesitate in answering this question. He explained that the family is eternal and that much of the work Mormons do in the temples is associated with that concept. He said that after I got baptized and became a worthy member of the Church, Barbara and I could be sealed to each other in the temple. To be sealed to each other means we can be with each other for eternity and not merely until one of us dies. That goes for our children, as well. Having been sealed, our family will be together forever."

I paused for a moment, letting the implications of what I had just shared with her sink in; once again I was experiencing the feeling of peace that I had felt before.

"You always wanted to have a family that would be able to stay together," Carolyn said in a serious tone. "It looks like you found a way to stay together after all."

"I most certainly have," I agreed.

"Did you get baptized right away?"

"Not right away. Once I was through talking to Barbara's brother, I began looking in the phone book for a listing of the Mormon Church. Much to my surprise, I couldn't find a listing."

"That seems rather strange," Carolyn noted. "They've got churches just about everywhere."

"Barbara solved the mystery when she told me that they'd be listed under The Church of Jesus Christ of Latter-day Saints."

"No wonder people call them Mormons," Carolyn muttered.

"Needless to say, I found the address of a church in Santa Cruz, and the following Sunday, we appeared on the church's doorstep, ready to join. The what-am-I-supposed-to-be-doing feeling was completely gone. We were cordially received, and the members of the congregation were genuinely friendly. I wanted to get baptized right away, but they said that I would first have to be given lessons by the missionaries. Since Barbara had retained little from her earlier connection with the church, she agreed to take the lessons with me. In a very real sense, we went through the conversion process together."

"Two for the price of one," Carolyn quipped.

"Actually, there were three of us. Since our eldest daughter, Keisha, was eight, she was old enough to be baptized, too," I corrected before continuing with the story. "Anyway, the missionaries came to our home each week, taught us one of the lessons, and then challenged us to pray about the truthfulness of what they had taught us. On Sundays, we'd put on our best clothes and head down the crooked Soquel Highway to attend church."

"What time did their services begin?" Carolyn inquired.

"In those days, the church meetings were still divided: Sunday School and Sacrament meetings in the morning and Priesthood and Relief Society meetings in the afternoon. Since it was a thirty-mile round trip from our home to the church, this would mean having to drive sixty miles each Sunday. To save time and gas, we decided to stay down for the afternoon meetings rather than driving up and down the mountain a second time. To help pass the time between meetings, after attending the morning session, I'd buy a six-pack of beer and we'd go to the beach until it was time for the afternoon meetings."

"I thought you said Mormons don't drink alcohol," Carolyn interjected.

"They don't, but I hadn't found out about that, yet," I confessed, feeling embarrassed all over again. "I followed this Sacrament/six-pack/ Priesthood routine faithfully until the missionaries introduced me to the Word of Wisdom; as I recall, it was around the fourth lesson. I had tried to stop smoking and drinking several times in the past with no success. The thought of quitting both at the same time was daunting. But the missionaries said that they would pray for me, and quitting cold turkey turned out to be a minor miracle. Much to my amazement, I experienced absolutely no cravings after quitting. I truly believe this was possible only through the power of the Holy Ghost."

Carolyn shook her head and confided, "I don't know how many times I've tried to quit smoking."

"Well, don't give up trying," I encouraged. "There are lots of benefits that come from quitting. For instance, one of the missionary lessons introduced the need for me to pay a tithe, which is ten percent of my income. At first, I was absolutely convinced that there was no way I could pay it; we were living paycheck to paycheck as it was. But I soon discovered that since I was no longer spending money on alcohol and tobacco, I had more than enough to pay tithing."

"I try not to think about how much I spend on cigarettes and booze," Carolyn lamented before adding, "So you eventually got baptized?"

"I sure did. A few weeks after having given up alcohol, smoking, and all the other unhealthy habits of an atheistic lifestyle, I was ready to be baptized. This was a big occasion. Wilf and his family came out from Utah, and the other Bernard and his family drove over from Fresno. At the time, Santa Cruz and Fresno were in the same mission district, and word had spread that two brothers with exactly the same name but raised separately—one as a Catholic-turned-atheist and the other as a Presbyterian—had both been called to join The Church of Jesus Christ of Latter-day Saints within a few months of each other. So when

December 31, 1979, arrived, the day of my baptism, there were several missionaries there as well."

Becoming more excited as I remembered that great event, I enthusiastically continued, "And if that wasn't strange enough, as we all gathered at the baptismal font, someone realized that Bernard Edmund Poduska Jr. was baptizing Bernard Edmund Poduska Jr.—each a son of Bernard Edmund Poduska. In order to avoid unnecessary confusion or unintentionally giving the impression that I had baptized myself, a note of explanation was written on the bottom of the baptismal form."

"Just how do you avoid confusion with three people having the same name?"

"We agreed to call Dad, Bernie," I explained. "The Bernard from Fresno is called Bernard. And I'm referred to as Bud."

"So you finally got baptized," Carolyn sighed.

"Being baptized was one of the most gratifying, liberating experiences I have ever had. Up until my baptism, my life was becoming a replica of my childhood—wandering aimlessly with no particular destination or purpose. After I was baptized, I felt completely renewed, filled with a love of life and a deeper love for my wife and children. I had a sense of identity and a great thirst for spiritual knowledge."

"I can understand that you might have felt like that right after the baptism," Carolyn conceded, "but did the magic of the moment eventually slip away?"

"Not at all," I declared. "Shortly after I was baptized, the 'meaningful dreams' began—prophetic dreams. Along with an embedded religious lesson, the dreams revealed what was going to happen in my future. These dreams were easily distinguished from normal dreams. They were similar to the dreams Bernard had described: vivid, rich in detail, and easily recalled. These dreams occurred on a regular basis and became an integral part of our lives."

"Did you have the same dream over and over?" Carolyn asked.

"No. Although each of the prophetic dreams was unique, they always followed the same format. In each dream I was taken someplace, a place I had never been to before. As soon as I arrived, a man dressed in Biblical-style clothing would show me around, giving me an opportunity to familiarize myself with my new surroundings. The man I refer to as the 'teacher' would then give me a short lesson from the scriptures. As soon as the lesson was finished, the dream would end, and I would wake up."

"But you said that these dreams were prophetic."

"Strange as it may seem, within a few days or weeks, I would physically find myself at the place where I had been taken in one of the dreams. Whenever this occurred, I would announce, 'This is one of the places from the dreams.' Then, with as much detail as I could recall, I would describe what we were about to see. Without fail, my descriptions proved to be flawless. I soon came to realize that if what I had been *shown* in the dreams turned out to be true, then what I had been *taught* in the dreams must also be true."

"For example . . ." Carolyn prompted.

"In one of my earlier dreams, I was walking past the LDS chapel in Santa Cruz; the teacher walked beside me, pointing to something in the distance. I looked in the direction he was pointing, and I saw a large lake, with an odd assortment of sailing vessels moving across the water. Suddenly, my point of view changed, and I found myself high in the mountains, standing beside a rushing river, looking down on the large number of ships sailing toward the mouth of the river. The teacher began to speak and much of what he said was from Isaiah."

I once again pulled out my Palm Pilot and found Isaiah 2:2, "And it shall come to pass in the last days, that the mountain of the Lord's house shall be established in the top of the mountains, and shall be exalted above the hills; and all nations shall flow unto it."

"I'm not very familiar with Isaiah," Carolyn confessed.

"That's okay," I reassured. "The important thing is that a few weeks after I had had this dream, Barbara and I visited her family in Salt Lake City. I took Barbara to see some of the landmarks from my first encounter with the Mormons—back when we were hitchhiking and homeless. Then she showed me points of interest from her childhood, including Bear Lake. The moment I saw the lake, I exclaimed, 'This is the place in the dream!'

"However, this experience was only the beginning. On another occasion, I dreamt that I was flying over a large body of water toward a wooded peninsula with a steel bridge connecting it to a distant shore. When I reached the shore, I passed over a cluster of houseboats docked under the bridge. A highway passed through a long tree-tunnel on its way to the top of a hill. I met the teacher at the top of the hill. The two of us walked a short distance and then stopped in a large, open field, a field filled with little animals. This lesson was also from Isaiah: 'The wolf and the lamb shall feed together, and the lion shall eat straw like the bullock: and dust shall be the serpent's meat. They shall not hurt nor destroy in all my holy mountain, saith the Lord.'

"A few weeks later, our family drove up the coast to British Columbia. While crossing a bridge in Vancouver, the landscape began to look familiar; it suddenly dawned on me, and I cried out, 'This is a place from my dreams!' Barbara immediately asked, 'What are we going to see?' I told her that we would go around the hill ahead of us and through a long tree-tunnel that will take us to the top of the hill. At the top of the hill, there will be a large field on the left, filled with little animals."

"So what happened?" Carolyn interjected.

"We drove around the hill, up through the long tree-tunnel to a small parking lot at the top of the hill. On our left was a large field filled with hundreds of little rabbits. Once again the thought passed through my head, *If what I was shown is true, then what I was taught is also true.*"

"How long did you have these dreams?"

"For the next year and a half, I was to have numerous such experiences. In one dream, I was shown Utah Valley and Brigham Young University, but this time I was told, 'Get thee hence!' In this dream I was told to enroll as a graduate student and that as soon as I received my PhD, I would be hired as a member of the BYU faculty . . . *but not in the field in which I graduated.* During the interim years, I often wondered how Brigham Young University's five-year moratorium on hiring its own graduates would be circumvented and in what field I would ultimately be hired."

"So what happened?" Carolyn prodded once again.

"Believe me, the directive in this dream was to become a real test of my faith. I had to quit my tenured teaching position at De Anza College, sell our home, and move my family to Utah. I also had to get accepted into Brigham Young University's PhD program for marriage and family therapy, which meant I would have to be a student for the next three years. I was forty years old, with a wife and five children to support; the magnitude of what lay ahead was overwhelming. Nevertheless, we packed our belongings in a large U-haul truck and trailer, and we headed for Utah."

"That must have been some trip," Carolyn interjected.

"It was indeed. Traveling across the Nevada desert reminded me of the time we came across it in the army caravan."

"Ah, those were the days," Carolyn said kiddingly.

"A year earlier, Barbara, the kids, and I had been sealed in the Salt Lake Temple. Of course, being married for eternity didn't preclude the hardships of everyday life and trying to live on the paltry earnings of a student's part-time job. The cost of getting settled in our home in 'Happy Valley' had been far greater than expected and quickly exhausted our meager savings. Eventually, we had to rely on food from the bishop's storehouse and buy clothes from Deseret Industries, the Mormon equivalent of a Goodwill store. Our situation became even worse when we received notification that the people who had bought our house in California could no longer make their house payments. Since we were carrying a large second mortgage, we couldn't afford to allow it to go into foreclosure. But to do this, we would have to raise tens of thousands of dollars."

"What did you do?"

"I prayed first and then approached friends, relatives, and my brother Bernard. None of them could really afford to loan us the amount of money we needed, but in spite of the risk, several of them obtained short-term, signature loans. These loans allowed us to regain possession of the house in Santa Cruz, but unless we were able to resell quickly, we'd have to sell our home in Utah in order to repay these loans. Facing the possibility of once again being homeless filled me with dread."

Carolyn nodded her head empathetically.

"The financial stress became overwhelming. I wasn't able to sleep or concentrate on my studies. In desperation, I went to the temple to pray. As soon as I entered the celestial room, I sat down and began pleading for a solution to our struggle, begging for an end to the hardship. I had been praying for only a few minutes when I heard a voice in my mind. *'If you knew me, you would know that I would do nothing that was not an act of love in your behalf.'* As soon as I 'heard' these words, I began to weep. What peace these words imparted—a soothing balm to my troubled soul. But then, I realized that I didn't really know Him. After I regained my composure, I returned home and began reading the book *Jesus the Christ.*"

"What were the words you thought you heard?" Carolyn asked.

"If you knew me, you would know that I would do nothing that was not an act of love in your behalf," I repeated solemnly. "Fortunately, the house in Santa Cruz was finally resold and the borrowed money repaid. I knew there would still be hardships ahead; I also knew I would never again feel abandoned. From that day forward, I enjoyed a deeper understanding of the true love of Jesus Christ and a truer knowledge of the nature of His relationship with each of us."

A nurse came down the hall and went into Mom's room. I sighed and pushed myself up out of my chair. Carolyn stood up beside me, and the two of us slowly walked over to the windows next to the elevators. Carolyn turned toward me and asked, "Did things get any better after that?"

"Financially, only a little, but my attitude toward life got a whole lot better. With renewed confidence, I returned to my studies and eventually graduated with a PhD in marriage and family therapy. I was immediately hired as a member of the Brigham Young University faculty, and as foretold in the dream, I was not hired in the field from which I had graduated; instead, I was hired into a newly organized program called Family Financial Planning and Counseling."

Carolyn sat down again just as a doctor came out of the elevator and hurried down the hall toward Mom's room. Carolyn noticed the doctor as well and alternately tried to divide her attention between me and the door to Mom's room. When she looked back at me, she said, "You've experienced a long spiritual journey, Buddy, but it seems like it has been worth it. Is there any doubt left in your mind that there is indeed a God?"

I was about to reply when I saw a doctor coming toward us.

The doctor stopped in front of us and asked in a solemn tone, "Are you Mrs. Poduska's children?"

Carolyn and I nodded our heads but said nothing.

"I'm sorry to inform you that your mother has passed away."

I slowly lowered my head and quietly began to sob. It was hard to believe that Mom was gone; her earthly struggles had finally ended, while a life devoid of care was just beginning. With both Mom and Dad gone, Carolyn and I were now the last of the hitchhikers.

"The two of you may have a few minutes alone with your mother," the doctor continued, "and when you feel up to it, there are papers at the nurses' station that need to be signed."

I looked up at him and nodded again.

Reluctantly, Carolyn and I got up and began walking down the long hall to Mom's room. I didn't know what to expect, so I took a deep breath as I slowly pushed the door open.

"Mom looks just like she did when we left her," Carolyn whispered.

The lump in my throat prevented any attempt to reply . . . I hated good-byes.

***

You will never know what's on down the road until after you've made the journey; be grateful for any rides others may give you along the way, and whatever your destination, the journey is everything—make the most of it.

—Buddy

Epilogue

GLADYS PASSED AWAY IN 1997, just two months short of her ninety-first birthday. However, from the time she had decided not to go back on the road, her life had begun to improve. She stayed in Eureka and found a steady job as a nurse at St. Joseph's Hospital. Eventually, she was able to buy an old car so she wouldn't have to ride the bus. When she heard they were tearing down World War II dependent housing in Vallejo, she bought one of the prefabricated houses for eight hundred dollars.

The completely disassembled house arrived stacked on the back of a flatbed truck. Once it was reassembled, it was a twenty-four-foot square box with a flat-roof, no porch, and was ugly as sin. But it was a house, our first real home.

Although I left home when I was nineteen, Mom lived peacefully in that little house for the rest of her life; that is until, at the age of ninety, she decided that she shouldn't be living alone and moved to Bakersfield to be near Carolyn.

Carolyn's "trip through life" was not so simple. After enduring the hardships of her first marriage, which included a husband that went to prison, she married a second time and gave birth to another girl, which was followed by a second divorce. Her third marriage was to a truly good man. Unfortunately, he died of cancer twelve years later. Carolyn made her living by working as a security guard at some of the casinos in Nevada and as a cook at a rest home. She died of lung cancer in 2004. Fortunately, I was able to visit her while she was in the hospital, and I attended her funeral. She was buried next to Mom in Carson City, Nevada.

I, too, struggled to escape the past, but compared to the journey through life that Carolyn experienced, the road I traveled in the later part of my life was one of relative ease.

My first marriage included the birth of two wonderful daughters, but it ended in divorce after seven years. Their mother became involved in psychedelic drugs and subsequently died in a small village in Guatemala.

Fortunately, by the time I had met, and married, Barbara, I had managed to rid myself of most of my baggage, and we've been able to enjoy forty wonderful years together. Barbara had no children from her previous marriage, and she adopted my two girls, Keisha and Tasha, shortly after we were married. In addition, she gave birth to our three boys, Brandon, Clinton, and Ryan.

In contrast to the vagabond existence of my childhood, all five of our children grew up in just two homes and obtained college educations; four have been married in the temple, and our three sons have served church missions in Switzerland, the Ukraine, and Russia. To date, we have fifteen grandchildren. I finally have the "real" family that I had always wanted. All in all, I'd say that life has turned out rather well.

About the Author

IT HAS BEEN A LONG journey; however, along with opposition in all things, God also gave us agency and the spiritual love and support we need to enable us to prevail. In my case, although I was declared "functionally illiterate" in high school, I managed to go on to earn a BS and an MS in psychology and a PhD in marriage and family therapy. I taught at colleges and universities for over thirty-five years, twenty-one of which were spent at Brigham Young University. I have also written a textbook on personality adjustment, a self-help book on managing stress, and two books on finances and relationships.